RESTLESS GODS

RESTLESS GODS

THE RENAISSANCE OF RELIGION IN CANADA

Reginald W. Bibby

NOVALIS

© 2004 by Reginald Bibby

Cover design: Caroline Gagnon
Cover image: Whit Slemmons
Text design: Andrew Smith/Page Wave Graphics Inc.
Page composition: Kevin Cockburn/Page Wave Graphics Inc.

Published in 2004 by Novalis/Saint Paul University
Business Office:
49 Front Street East, 2nd Floor
Toronto, Ontario, Canada
M5E 1B3

Phone: 1-877-702-7773 or (416) 363-3303
Fax: 1-877-702-7775 or (416) 363-9409
E-mail: cservice@novalis.ca
www.novalis.ca

Published in 2002 by Stoddart Publishing Co. Limited

Library and Archives Canada Cataloguing in Publication

Bibby, Reginald W. (Reginald Wayne), 1943–
Restless gods : the renaissance of religion in Canada / Reginald W. Bibby.

Reprint of the ed. published: Toronto : Stoddart, 2002.
Includes bibliographical references and index.
ISBN 2-89507-555-7

1. Canada–Religion–21st century. I. Title.

BL2530.C3B526 2004   306.6'0971   C2004-904285-8

Printed in Canada.

We acknowledge the financial support of the Government of Canada
through the Book Publishing Industry Development Program (BPIDP) for our
publishing activities.

5 4 3 2 1   08 07 06 05 04

To Mom

My cherished friend,
whose cherished faith
continues to touch
and awaken us all.

Contents

Preface

Like many of you, I have never believed that God is limited to human conceptions. From the time I was very young, I had the gnawing feeling that God readily transcended what people were saying the Divine was like, and I suspected that occasionally there was probably more than a little Heavenly embarrassment over the imagery and claims associated with God's name.

With the passage of time, it became increasingly apparent to me that the presence and activity of God were hardly restricted to the inner walls of churches, or to the lives of those who claimed to be devout. On the contrary, my own experience of what I believe to be the presence of God both inside and outside of church circles has given me a profound appreciation for the words of the Apostle of old — that God "does not live in shrines made by human hands." In addition, it seems equally clear to me that God's activity is not limited to or necessarily synonymous with the "human hands" of people who are officially religious. Rather, as Paul told the people of Athens, God is an incredibly autonomous Being who cannot be boxed up in predictable places but can be expected to show up in some unexpected places, including a good number of unsuspecting lives. In Paul's words, we're all expected to "search for God and perhaps grope for him," and eventually "find him — though," the Apostle reminds us, God "is not far from each one of us."[1]

We are living in a period when a lot of spiritual searching and groping is going on in Canada — as often as not outside the doors of religious groups. At a time when observers, including many journalists and academics, are giving most of their attention to the numerical problems of churches and the fads and fancies associated with spiritual quest, there's another story that needs to be told. It's the story of the large number of Canadians who believe they are experiencing the activity of God in their lives, people who are experiencing a spiritual restlessness that may be spilling over into the churches. This book looks at the observable part of what's going on, drawing on research that spans the years 1975 to 2000, and slightly beyond.

I suppose the dominant emotion I have as I write "these last words that come first" is gratitude to the countless people who have made it all possible. I want to emphatically thank approximately ten thousand adults and ten thousand teenagers who have expressed their thoughts about virtually all of life through our nine *Project Canada* national surveys dating back to 1975. In addition, during the winter of 2001–02, a quota sample of another two hundred people from across the country offered their personal thoughts and experiences in helping us to better understand such complex issues as life's purpose, the meaning of suffering, what happens when we die, what people have in mind when they speak of God, and what it means to experience God. My debt to all these people, who have not only given time but in many cases also shared some very deep and personal experiences and emotions, is simply enormous.

I again want to express my great appreciation to my sons, Reggie, Dave, and Russ who have provided the backbone of my "mini-infrastructure" for almost 20 years. Reggie has served as Project Manager, while Dave and Russ have carried out a variety of important tasks. I also wish to acknowledge the exceptional contributions over the years of three gifted individuals who have cared: Jim Savoy, Michèle Therrien, and Diane Erickson. The commitment and competence of these six individuals has been key to the success of the overall project.

The cost of carrying out nine national surveys has, of course, been significant. The initial contribution of $2,000 by Dave Stone and the United Church of Canada in 1974 will always be special. Funding through 1985 by the Social Sciences and Humanities Research Council was very important and appreciated. Since 1990, the Lilly Endowment has covered the costs of five of the surveys and made the research and dissemination a joy. My gratitude to Craig Dykstra, Jim Lewis, and Chris Coble is immense. I also want to thank the University of Lethbridge and my colleagues in the Department of

Sociology, who have provided me with the resources, encouragement, time, and tranquility over the years to carry out my work.

In 2001, I had the opportunity to "try out" some of my ideas and new data in a number of settings. I thank my summer class at McMaster and my fall Sociology of Religion class at Lethbridge for listening to my hunches, enduring some early and crude data, and offering their thoughts on some of life's deepest questions. I benefited very much from being invited by Rachel McCleary to come to Harvard University in October to present the research as part of Harvard's "Religion, Political Economy and Society Seminar," a pivotal event that gave me an opportunity to see how well my ideas and data were holding up. And in early November, I hosted a Lilly-sponsored weekend "Project Canada Consultation" in Vancouver that brought together some 20 diverse religious leaders from across Canada and the United States. The purpose was to reflect on implications for ministry of the main findings from the latest surveys and to give leaders an opportunity to respond to some of my central interpretations. Both of these latter events were extremely stimulating, encouraging, and helpful to the development of this book.

I again wish to thank Stoddart's managing editor, Donald G. Bastian, who has been with me now through eight of my nine books. Don's keen mind and sense of humour, combined with his ability to be appropriately critical and yet always encouraging, have made him an extremely valued friend and colleague over the years. Kathryn Dean has carried out the copyediting, and needs to be commended not only for the high quality of her work, but also for her grace in dealing with an author who insists on keeping his personality in the book, "for better or for worse."

My final expressions of gratitude are directed toward two of the people who are closest to me — Lita, who has patiently provided immeasurable support and made life easier during the demanding months that this book has required, and my 83-year-old mother, "Margaret," who, despite having to deal with the effects of life-altering health problems in recent months, has continued to be a great resource and a marvellous friend.

It will soon become apparent that I am taking a number of chances in this book. I am going to go against the stream and propose that organized religion is making something of a comeback, and suggest it is all to be expected. I will be true to my role as a sociologist, yet dare to offer the idea that the glasses of a social scientist might not be strong enough to see an important part of what is actually going on. I am going to say that we need to take people seriously when they tell us about the activity of the gods in their lives, and will further claim that I've found support for the idea that even people who don't give much credibility to the idea of God nonetheless are giving off all kinds of clues that they believe in Something beyond themselves. I'll close by showing why the wise men of old were wrong and by questioning the ability of religious groups to respond to "all this" — while arguing that they can and they must.

To take chances is to invite criticism. But so what? These days we need to take some chances, because there's a lot of confusion out there as to what is happening in religious groups and what is back of widespread spiritual stirrings. We need some sound data and some good ideas. This book is offered as a step in that direction.

REGINALD W. BIBBY
Lethbridge, Alberta
April 2002

Introduction

What a difference 40 years makes. Back in the early 1960s, experts who were trying to make sense of religious developments told us that religion in the Western world was in decline, an inevitable result of societies becoming more highly industrialized. The rest of the world would, with increasing industrial development, suffer a similar fate. Science made it difficult for people to think in supernatural terms, while institutional specialization left religion with a limited role to play. Religious organizations themselves were not only saying less and less to society, they were also becoming more and more like society. The overall result was that religion was declining in significance.

Such observations were part of what is known as the theory of secularization. Today, the theory has been largely abandoned — well in advance, incidentally, of the events of September 11, 2001, which poignantly underlined the ongoing presence and importance of religion worldwide. Among those who deserted the secularization ship were people who had helped to popularize the thesis. As a young seminary student in the 1960s, I was among the many who were taken by theologian Harvey Cox's fascinating best-selling book, *The Secular City*. As Cox recalled in 1995, "I tried to work out a theology for the 'postreligious' age that many sociologists had confidently assured us was coming. Since then, religion seems to have gained a new lease on life. Today it is secularity, not spirituality, that may be headed for extinction." And it all happened so quickly: "Before academic forecasters could even begin to draw their pensions," he notes, "a religious renaissance of sorts is under way all over the globe . . . Buddhism and Hinduism, Christianity and Judaism, Islam

1

and Shinto, and many smaller sects are once again alive and well. But why were the predictors so wrong?"[1]

Similarly, in 1999, sociologist Peter Berger acknowledged that he himself had contributed to the secularization theory in his early work, but now realized "the assumption that we live in a secularized world is false. The world today, with some exceptions . . . is as furiously religious as it ever was, and in some places more so than ever."[2] Berger says that, globally, the two most dynamic religious upsurges are currently Islamic and Evangelical — the former occurring primarily in countries that are already Muslim or among Muslim emigrants, the latter taking place throughout the world, largely as a result of American missionary efforts. He makes the important point that "on the international scene, it is conservative or orthodox or traditionalist movements that are on the rise almost everywhere," be they Evangelical, Catholic, Orthodox, Jewish, Islam, Hindu, Buddhist, Shinto, or Sikh in nature. "These developments," he says, "differ greatly in their social and political implications. What they have in common is their unambiguously *religious* inspiration. Consequently, taken together they provide a massive falsification of the idea that modernization and secularization are cognate phenomena." Berger adds, "At the very least they show that *counter*-secularization is at least as important a phenomenon in the contemporary world as secularization."[3]

Cox's question as to how the experts could be so wrong is an important query that I will come back to in the Conclusion to this book. Berger, on the other hand, is helpful in explaining why the secularization thesis continues to be propounded today, despite the evidence that fails to support it. He points out that there are two exceptions to "the desecularization thesis": (1) Western Europe and (2) a subculture of people, especially in the humanities and social sciences. "While its members are relatively thin on the ground," he says of the subculture, "they are very influential, as they control the institutions that provide the 'official' definitions of reality" — notably, education, the media, and the legal system. "What we have here is a globalized *elite* culture," Berger maintains, which can easily fall into the misconception that their views about religion reflect those of their respective populaces. This, says Berger, is "of course, . . . a big mistake."[4]

One of the correctives to misreading what is happening in any society is to ask average people what is taking place in their lives. The late Queen's University historian George Rawlyk commented shortly before his death in 1995, "I remain convinced that if you want to know what people are doing in the religious realm and why they are doing it, you *have to ask them.*" He cited Aberdeen sociologist Steve Bruce's perceptive comment: "They might not always know, or they might know and not tell you. But all other sources are inferior."[5]

Does American Episcopal Bishop John Spong, for example, speak for most Anglicans when he sees himself as a "believer in exile" who rejects the authority of scripture and creed? Do they, too, "not believe that there is a being, a supernatural deity, standing over against my world" and concur with Spong's assertion that "the deity I worship is rather part of who I am individually and corporately"?[6] Or are Anglican voices better heard through someone like University of British Columbia historian and church leader George Egerton, when he calls Canadian Anglicans to "be true to the Lord of the church in reaffirming the essentials of a scripturally revealed faith that transcends time and culture," asserting that such reaffirmation "holds the greatest promise of regaining cultural relevance in a 'post-modern world'"?[7] There's only one way to find out. We need to hear from people.

Since 1975, I have been asking Canadians about life as they are living it, through the use of a series of national surveys under the *Project Canada* banner. They've been carried out every five years — in 1975, 1980, 1985, 1990, 1995, and 2000 — monitoring Canadian social trends generally and religious trends specifically. These six adult surveys have been complemented by three national youth surveys, completed in 1984, 1992, and 2000. *Fragmented Gods* (1987), my first book looking at the results of these surveys, told the story of the widespread decline of participation in organized religion that took place in the post-1950s. This was largely because cultural conditions had turned Canadians into highly selective consumers of what religious groups had to offer. The second volume, *Unknown Gods* (1993), updated the material from the earlier book and pointed to the important role that religious organizations themselves played in the participation drop-off.

Restless Gods draws on these two previous books to varying degrees, as well as on many of my other papers — a fact that shouldn't surprise and hopefully doesn't disappoint readers. Berger wrote in the preface to one of his books a number of years ago:

> The relatively frequent references to previous writings of my own should in no way be construed as a conviction on my part that these writings are terribly important or as advice to the reader to go back to them. But every process of thinking must be a conversation with oneself and particularly one's previous thought, and one cannot at each step start all over again from the beginning.[8]

Not having to do this, he added, "should perhaps be one of the fringe benefits of having written more than one book." I share his sentiments.

This book, however, does far more than simply update the old. It makes extensive use of valuable new information from two adult surveys, one carried out in 1995, and especially the one conducted in 2000, along with the latest youth survey, also completed in 2000. The book's primary focus is descriptive rather than prescriptive. I look at the state of organized religion in Canada, while also giving considerable attention to religion and spirituality in the lives of Canadians beyond their involvement in religious groups. But I also attempt to go beyond simply providing descriptive trend data. The book makes extensive use of a theoretical framework that builds upon the work of sociologist Rodney Stark to try to make sense of what is taking place now, what happened in our recent past, and what can be expected to happen in the foreseeable future.

The findings point to a religious and spiritual renaissance in Canada — new life being added to old life, sometimes within religious groups but often outside them. Looked at through theistic eyes, there is good reason to believe that the gods are extremely restless. They are stirring in the churches and in the lives of average people across the country.

Perhaps what is happening is consistent with St. Augustine's well-known "thesis": "Our souls are restless until they find their rest in Thee, O God." But that may be only half the story. Historian

Arnold Toynbee is one of many who have maintained that the world "is not limited to that part of it which is accessible to the human senses and which can therefore be studied scientifically. The key to a full understanding of this part," according to Toynbee, may lie "in that other part which is not accessible" to the senses.[9] The primary reason why "souls are restless" may lie in the fact that Something is pursuing us. In these early years of the new millennium, the words of the writer who attempted to describe the earliest moments in all of history ring out over the centuries with haunting familiarity:

> In the beginning God created the heaven and the earth.
> And the earth was without form and void:
> And darkness was upon the face of the deep.
> And the Spirit of God moved upon the face of the waters.[10]

Restless Gods documents what is observable "on the human side." In the process, it also attempts to sensitize readers to what could be happening "on the other side." It may well be that one makes sense only in terms of the other.

CHAPTER ONE

The Old Story about What's Happening in the Churches

Chronicling religious developments in the last half of the 20th century was not a particularly popular job to take on. Things were not going all that well for the churches, and more than a few leaders were suspicious and even hostile toward someone who attempted to describe and analyze what was happening. The negative news was sometimes seen as the product of a negative sociologist, despite the fact that I personally have valued faith, have been sympathetic to the problems of organized religion, and have given a chunk of my life to trying to help religious groups respond to Canadians. Regardless, in the minds of some, I was "Bad News Bibby."

Something that might come as a surprise to such people is the fact that I wasn't exactly enthralled with the emerging picture either. I must confess that in the early 80s I seriously considered moving out of the area of sociology of religion and turning my sociological focus to other, more promising areas of human activity — like pro sports, for example, one of my loves since boyhood.

Frankly, as I looked at religious developments in Canada, they seemed predictable to the point of not being particularly interesting and, as such, certainly not worth giving one's life to chronicling. Secularization seemed rampant and relentless, the inevitable product of the country's modernization. The phenomenon had already levelled organized religion in Europe and was said to be making more subtle inroads into the United States.[1]

It appeared to be just a matter of time before secularization would overwhelm Canada. The decline of religion seemed irreversible. How long does one want to describe the agonizing details of an old family business gradually going bankrupt or a close friend slowly dying? Maybe, I thought, it was time to make a living by studying more viable and uplifting activities. In pro football and pro hockey, for instance, even a team with a losing season has the perennial hope that things will get better next year. Religion in Canada didn't seem to have the hope of a better next year.

Secularization Without Limits

It wasn't as if I was alone in holding such a pessimistic view of the future of religion. One of my graduate student idols, the American sociologist Peter Berger, had predicted in the *New York Times* in 1968 that by "the 21st century, religious believers are likely to be found only in small sects, huddled together to resist a worldwide secular culture" — a claim he would later recant.[2] Adding to the gloom was the fact that, in the course of minoring in history, I had encountered no historian who spoke of so much as a single nationwide religious reversal in either Europe or North America in the 19th and 20th centuries. Once things started going downward, they seemed to keep going downward. What's more, in feeling that dominant days were essentially over for organized religion, I was in the company of respected social analysts whose work had spanned a hundred years — from France's Emile Durkheim in the late 19th century to Oxford's Bryan Wilson in the late 20th. As many readers know, these proponents of the secularization thesis had maintained that religion was destined to decline in importance as societies developed.[3] In the last decades of the 20th century, it appeared that they had Canada pegged pretty accurately.

By way of a brief refresher, the secularization thesis can be summed up as follows: with industrialization comes institutional specialization and changes in personal consciousness. Simply put, religion loses control over areas such as politics, economics, health care, and education, as happened to the Roman Catholic Church in Quebec in the 1960s. Religion's role becomes increasingly specialized and is relegated to matters of meaning, morality, and mortality, as well as to performing rites of passage. So it was that respected historian John Webster Grant wrote that by the end of the 1960s, "the nation had come to carry on its business as if the church were not there."[4] And *National Post* columnist John Fraser wrote in June 2000: "Religion, as a source of excellent stories of all sorts, is one of two great no-go areas in the contemporary media (universities being the other)." He noted that there are exceptions, "but as a general rule over the past few decades, stories on religion will break into the media only if they are (a) sensational, (b) bizarre, (c) goofy, (d) gee-whiz, or (e) contemptuous."[5] Such lack of media attention hardly suggests that Canada's churches have been seen in recent times as institutional heavyweights.

At a personal level, individuals are not as inclined as their predecessors to participate in organized religion. They live highly compartmentalized lives that are not significantly informed by the gods. How one works and how one plays increasingly become matters of personal discretion. Business ethics and sexual morality, for example, are not based on what the gods have to say, but on what people think and feel. Asked about their basis for determining what is right and wrong, 35% of Canadians told us in late 2000 that their criteria are primarily internal — based on personal judgement, personal morality, and how they feel at the time; just 17% cited religious factors. Among teenagers, 49% emphasized personal ideas and feelings, while only 16% said that religion is foundational.[6] It's not that religion ceases to have a place in the life of a secularized society or individual, it's just that religion's place is very specific and very limited.

But secularization does not merely stop with institutions and individuals. Religious groups themselves are increasingly influenced by secular culture. They consciously and unconsciously take their cues from sources such as media, education, business, and government, rather than from something that transcends culture, so their structures, ideas, and programs begin to closely resemble those of other organizations. Their measures of success sound like those of business, their priorities are frequently dictated by what the culture says is important, and their activities often look much like secular imitations

— perhaps well illustrated by a focus on efforts to update forms of worship and music. An extreme but telling example is a U.S. congregation featured in a CTV News item in the early 1990s that built an evening service around a World Wrestling Federation format as a means of attracting youth. The result of such organizational secularization is that most religious groups run the risk of saying little to their cultures that those cultures are not already saying to themselves.[7]

By the 1980s and 1990s, such characteristics of secularization appeared to be highly pervasive in Canada. But it hadn't always been that way.

Pre-1960s Prosperity

Golden ages are difficult to pinpoint with precision, including those of a religious variety. Peter Beyer of the University of Ottawa notes, for example, that things were looking pretty good for organized religion as Canada entered the 20th century. He says that in 1901, religious groups had enough seating capacity to accommodate more than the total Canadian population — to be precise, "3,842,332 seats for a population of 5,371,315," working out to some eight million places assuming churches had an average of two services a week. A survey carried out by Toronto newspapers in 1896 showed that 57% of the available seats in the Toronto area were occupied during any given service.[8]

If things were good then, they got even better a few decades later. The post–World War II years of the 1940s and 1950s seem to have been a time of unparalleled church attendance and influence in Canada. John Webster Grant summed things up this way:

> What happened in Canada, as in North America generally, was so different that it remains to this day a source of wonder. Men and women who had shown no more than a perfunctory interest in the church before going off to war demonstrated on their return an enthusiasm that confounded all prognosticators. From soon after 1945 until about 1960 there was a general boom in things religious.[9]

According to the first known national poll of attendance on record, conducted by the Gallup organization in 1945, some 60% of

Canadians reported that they were attending religious services on nearly a weekly basis. In Quebec, where Roman Catholics constituted about 95% of the population, an astounding nine in ten people claimed to be in services at least once a week.

Such high levels of religious participation continued through the 1950s and 1960s. Catholic attendance appears to have held steady at about 85% both in Quebec and in the rest of the country, while weekly Protestant attendance remained strong, at about 45%. This was a time when Cardinal Léger would say of Montreal, "At seven every night, Montreal would be kneeling, saying the Rosary with me."[10] Similarly, membership in the United and Anglican churches peaked at over one million each in 1965. During these heady days of the mid-40s to mid-60s, the United Church alone built some 1,500 new churches and church halls.[11] Other faith groups were growing as

TABLE 1.1 **Membership of Select Denominations in Canada, 1871–1966**

In 1,000s

YEAR	UNITED	ANGLICAN*	BAPTIST	PENTECOSTAL	LUTHERAN	PRESBYTERIAN	ROMAN CATHOLIC*	
1871	n/a	n/a	n/a	n/a	n/a	n/a	43%	1,586
1881	170★	n/a	n/a	n/a	n/a	117	41	1,773
1901	289★	368	n/a	n/a	n/a	214	42	2,256
1921	401	690	n/a	n/a	n/a	351	39	3,427
1931	671	794	132	n/a	n/a	181	39	4,047
1941	717	836	134	n/a	n/a	174	42	4,806
1951	834	1,096	135	45	121	177	43	6,069
1961	1,037	1,358	138	60	172	201	46	8,343
1966	1,062	1,293	137	65	189	200	46	9,160

Anglican figures = inclusive membership; in 1967, full Anglican membership = 657,000 vs. 1,060,000 for the United Church. RC figures = % of Canadian population and approximate numbers, respectively. United figures for 1881 and 1901 = Methodist.

Baptist = Canadian Baptist Federation. Pentecostal = Pentecostal Assemblies of Canada. Lutheran = Evangelical Church of Canada, Lutheran Church in America, and Lutheran Church-Canada (Missouri Synod).

Sources: Yearbook of American and Canadian Churches, 1916–1966; United, Anglican, Baptist, Pentecostal, Lutheran, and Presbyterian yearbooks. Also McLeod, 1982.

well. Between 1941 and the end of the 1960s, the number of Jews increased from 169,000 to 275,000. During the same period, Jehovah's Witnesses experienced explosive growth, jumping from 7,000 to 170,000. The religion business seemed to be booming.

Post-1960s Decline

As I pointed out in 1987 in my first book on religion in Canada, *Fragmented Gods*, things were good, but not quite as good as most people thought.[12] Sheer numbers were up in this alleged peak period, but the proportion of people who were participating was actually declining. The Canadian religious roof had developed a noticeable leak. One reason the formation of the ominous hole went unnoticed was confusion over numbers versus proportions. In the mid-1950s, 43% of Canadians were attending services every week, representing a total of some 3.4 million people, based on a national population of about 8 million. By 1960, there were 3.8 million regular churchgoers, but the proportion had fallen to 38% because Canada's population had increased to about 10 million. No wonder it was easy for people to misread the times. In reality, even during this period of apparent expansion, not a single major religious group in the country increased its proportional share of the population.[13] Historian Grant has pointed out that by the end of the 1960s, membership was not keeping pace with population growth; attendance at churches and Sunday schools was declining; money was becoming harder to raise; and ministers, priests, and nuns were deserting their posts in alarming numbers. "Those who remained in the church were constantly reminded of their failings by critics both within and without," Grant wrote, adding, "The religious boom was definitely over."[14]

By the mid-1970s, the slowdown in Canada's burgeoning "religious economy" was widely evident. People telling Gallup they had been to a service in the previous week dropped from 61% in 1956 to 41% by 1975. Those claiming to attend services on a weekly basis (a more general summary report of one's behaviour than attendance in "the past seven days") slipped to 27% for Protestants and 45% for Roman Catholics. Among Mainline Protestants — the United, Anglican, Lutheran, and Presbyterian churches — membership was falling for perhaps the first time in Canadian history.

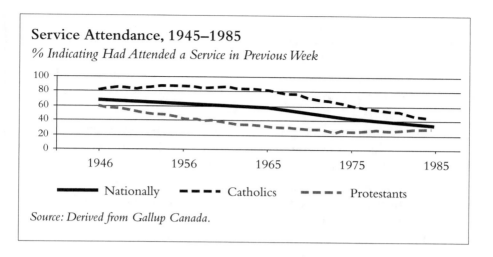

Service Attendance, 1945–1985

% Indicating Had Attended a Service in Previous Week

Nationally   Catholics   Protestants

Source: Derived from Gallup Canada.

In large measure, the declines appeared to reflect the classic features of secularization: advancing industrialization was leading to increasing specialization that reflected itself at both the social and the personal levels. Churches were losing authority and influence in areas such as education, politics, entertainment, and social services. Growing numbers of people were not seeing life through religious eyes. Individualism and relativism, combined with a growing number of choices in products, services, and lifestyles, were contributing to an accelerated level of selective consumption, including selective involvement in religious groups.

Religion à la Carte

Simply put, Canadians were becoming increasingly fussy customers in all areas of life. And they weren't giving religion an exemption. More and more were developing a pick-and-choose approach. *Religion à la carte* was becoming highly pervasive, characterized by a belief here and a practice there, rites of passage, and irregular appearances at church. The late Archbishop of the Toronto Anglican Diocese, Lewis Garnsworthy, who was always adept at summing things up in a poignant and colourful way, offered this observation about the place of the churches in his 1984 Charge to Synod: "We survive — great at Coronations, charming at weddings and impressive at funerals as long as we don't eulogize. We are welcome mascots at family do's and offer respectability to the Christmas cocktail circuit. We grace any community as long as we stay out of social issues and do not change a jot or tittle of well-worn liturgy."[15]

In summing up the situation, I described things this way in *Fragmented Gods* in 1987:

> For some time now, a highly specialized, consumer-oriented society has been remoulding the gods. Canadians are drawing very selectively on religion, and the dominant religious groups are responding with highly specialized items — isolated beliefs, practices, programs, and professional services, notably weddings and funerals. A religion that speaks to all of personal and social life, pronouncing and, when necessary, denouncing, is largely dead in Canada. Ironically, in trying to get in step with the modern age, organized religion — by dismantling the gods and serving them up piecemeal — is running the risk of becoming increasingly trivial.[16]

Yet the research through the 1980s was pointing to another important finding: people were not "dropping out." Some nine in ten were continuing to identify with the predominantly Roman Catholic and Protestant ties of their parents. The answer to the question "Where have all the people gone?" was not "to the Conservative Protestant churches, New Religious Movements, the electronic church, or the inclination to have no religion."[17] In fact, this last option didn't particularly make sense because it wasn't and isn't functional to be nothing. Just as a person needs a good doctor, lawyer, or plumber, so there are times in life when it is handy to have access to a good minister, priest, or rabbi. No, people had not dropped out; they were still at home. I noted back then that a student of mine, now my colleague Mary Thompson, summed up the situation well when she wrote on an exam that people were not "dropping out; they were dropping in." Or as Archbishop Lewis Garnsworthy said in his much-cited line, it was not that they were leaving — it was just that they were not coming.

Fragments of religion, I suggested, were being adopted for a simple reason: because they "work." Historically, religion has been seen as an overarching meaning system that ideally informs all of life.

Christianity, for example, calls followers to live out the faith in every facet of their existence. The problem here for many people is that commitment complicates things by calling for a level of role consistency that is very difficult to achieve. Business ethics, for instance, are frequently incompatible with religious ethics, and sexual inclinations are commonly in conflict with religious expectations. The adoption of religious fragments reduces this role conflict because it allows a person to retain some central belief and practice elements without demanding a high level of role consistency. Believing in God means one can still have recourse to prayer; believing in life after death gives one a measure of hope in the face of bereavement. But such beliefs do not necessarily require ethical correlates. Such selective consumption is not an accident. People choose fragments not because there are no complete systematic options available but because fragments are more conducive to life in our present age.[18]

Religious Family Patterns
In Quebec during the 1970s, the religious market was beginning to experience nothing less than a severe crash. Developments provided something of a classic contemporary illustration of institutional secularization.[19] Because of the magnitude of the Quebec attendance drop-off and the subsequent implications for the national levels of participation, that province's situation warrants a closer look.

Dating back as far as the British conquest and the *Quebec Act* of 1774, the Catholic Church had played a central role in the life of the province. Education, health, and social welfare, for example, were under the control of the Church. In a recent *New York Times* article, Quebec playwright Jacques Godbout recalls that even though considerable social change had taken place after World War II, the Roman Catholic Church still maintained "its stranglehold on Quebec society, controlled social life from birth to death, ran schools and hospitals, censored the press and kept a tight lid on the intellectual and artistic pot." As one of many examples, he writes that in 1959, film buffs "who wanted to see the complete version of one of the films of the French New Wave had to drive from Montreal to New York, eight hours on the road, to outwit the censors."[20]

I noted in *Fragmented Gods* that even Canada's current prime minister attested to the reality that writers like Godbout describe. In his 1985 memoir, *Straight from the Heart*, Jean Chrétien wrote that the Church and the Quebec government were closely fused through to the era of Premier Maurice Duplessis's government in the late 1950s and that the Roman Catholic Church benefited from the fact that Quebeckers continued to be poor, rural, and uneducated. This instilled a mentality of grim resolution, obedience, and gratitude, which Chrétien opposed:

> Even as late as 1960 I had a fight with my parish priest, who suggested in his weekly newsletter that we owed our allegiance to the Union Nationale because it had given us a tennis court. It was as scandalous then as in my grandfather's day for a feisty young lawyer to tell a priest to mind his own damn business during an election.[21]

But with the election of the Liberal party in 1960 and its emphasis on modernizing Quebec, the alliance of Church and State came to an end. The emergence of trade unionism, the revision of labour, health, and welfare laws, and the nationalization of electricity characterized what came to be known as the Quiet Revolution. The province took control of institutions that previously had been under the control of the Church — notably education, social welfare, and health. However, the transfer of power was stealthy, typically involving a transfer from Catholic clerics to Catholic laity, with religion continuing to have a presence in places like schools and hospitals. Jean-Paul Rouleau, who was teaching at Laval University in Quebec City at the time, has made the important observation that the Catholic Church had become increasingly aware that the nature of the modern era and the aspirations of the people called for physical and human resources beyond its own.[22] The result, as a CBC documentary expressed it in the early 1970s, was that "there was no confrontation between Church and state during those years in the 60s — no holy war."[23]

Summing up the situation, author Ron Graham has said that with the Quiet Revolution, "The state replaced the hierarchy, language replaced faith, and nationalism replaced religion."[24] Godbout

Some Random Thoughts about Organized Religion from 1975

From the West

"The church is saying the same things now as when I was a child, and I am bored."
— *A 55-year-old from Prince George; he attends a United Church two to three times a month.*

"Formal religion seems useless, boring, and petty to me. Church beliefs for the most part seem to derive from dogma, not reality."
— *A never attender from Edmonton, 28, with no religious ties; she went to her Protestant church weekly as a child.*

"The Church didn't seem abreast of the times, and couldn't hold the interest of young people."
— *A Regina 30-year-old with two preschoolers; she attends a United Church less than once a year.*

"Since living in a church-oriented farm community, my interest in the church as a positive social force has greatly increased."
— *A Lutheran, 31, who lives in rural Manitoba; she seldom attends after being active growing up.*

From Ontario and Quebec

"I am a warden in my church. I go there to give thanks and don't care a damn about the hypocrites I meet."
— *An Anglican father of four from Cornwall who attends his church just about every week.*

"My main reason for not being more involved is my lack of time."
— *A Toronto father of two teens who attends a Lutheran church several times a year.*

"A number of things bothered me: the church's tendency to interpret things literally, the members' tendency to view church as social organization for their own benefit, and the failure of the church to keep abreast of relevant social issues."
— *A never-attending Montrealer, 37, with no ties; he was raised Protestant and used to go often.*

"The Church did not adjust to contemporary world."
— *A Catholic, 31, who lives in Drummondville, PQ; he attended regularly as a child, now once a year.*

"When I was growing up, I had no choice but to go. I still regard myself as religious."
— *A 36-year-old from Champlain, PQ; he was raised RC but now has no ties and never attends.*

From the East

"Religion has changed so much that we do not gain an awful lot from it."
— *A 27-year-old Halifax-area father of a preschooler; he attended services weekly as a child, but now goes only a few times a year.*

"Religions are being run like big businesses, with as much power and money."
— *A single woman, 21, from Saint John, who seldom attends after having gone as a child; she is exploring other possibilities.*

"I've taught Sunday school for 27 years and served on committees. Now it's someone else's turn."
— *A 61-year-old who lives in Summerside, P.E.I.; she attends her United Church just about every week.*

"I've been bothered by the financial emphasis of the church and leaders."
— *An Anglican, 25, from Cupids, Nfld.; he was active as a child, but now seldom attends.*

Source: Bibby, Project Can75 National Survey.

writes that "secular discourse replaced Sunday sermons, church pews emptied, and Rome's dictates began to look dated." Although "Pope John XXIII summoned a council to modernize the rites, . . . [in] Quebec it was already too late."[25] As I suggested in *Fragmented Gods*, modern industrialization and post-industrialization have tended to lead to a loss of religion's authority in Canada and other Western nations. In the case of Quebec, secularization was only as belated as its modernization. The factors were virtually the same as elsewhere; only the timing was different.[26]

With the Quiet Revolution came a sense that there was no need to attend mass regularly anymore — a phenomenon that spread rapidly. It is also apparent that there was a certain amount of disillusionment with the Catholic Church. The 1975 *Project Canada* national survey found that more than 50% of Quebec Catholics who described themselves as "no longer active" cited disenchantment with what the Church was doing as contributing to their inactivity. More than 40% cited concern about hypocrisy. Some 34% complained about the fact that religion had been forced on them as children. The decline in regular weekly service attendance in Quebec from the mid-1950s onward was nothing less than spectacular, dropping from 88% to 42% by 1975 and falling further, to 28%, by 1990.

Among Catholics in the rest of the country, a measure of disenchantment with the Church was also evident. The drop in attendance was dramatic between the mid-50s and mid-70s, sliding from 75% in 1957 to 48% in 1975. However, the decline was far less severe over the ensuing 15 years, slipping to 37% by 1990. Heavy immigration from Catholic European countries — notably, some 300,000 people who came from Italy between 1951 and 1971 — served to stimulate attendance, particularly in Ontario. Ron Graham has noted that during the 1960s and 1970s, Catholicism was on the ascent in Toronto: "While religions throughout North America were selling some of their buildings to developers and discotheques because of the decline in attendance, the Archdiocese of Toronto was constructing seven or eight churches a year to accommodate the doubling of the Catholic population in two decades, much of it still sincerely committed to the faith."[27] Without such an infusion of immigrants,

TABLE 1.2 **Why People in the Mid-1970s Said They Were No Longer Active in a Religious Group**

"Which of the following would you say have contributed to your no longer being involved?"

% Indicating Factors "Very Important"

	NAT (818)	RCOQ (107)	RCQ (149)	MLPROT (329)	CPROT (38)	OTHER (39)	NONE (102)
Disenchantment with what relig. orgs. are doing	41	57	54	31	10	33	47
Increasing awareness of hypocrisy	40	43	44	39	45	28	36
Religion was forced on me as a child	21	34	25	11	11	6	38
Existence of cliques among members	21	27	33	18	16	6	6
Increasing disbelief	20	14	21	14	<1	28	42
The restrictions religion places on life	18	31	27	5	25	12	24
Conflict between religion and science	18	22	13	13	12	21	36
Decreasing interest in questions of meaning and purpose	16	24	23	10	12	<1	22
Lack of interest of a husband or wife	12	28	10	12	23	12	2
The absence of God in time of need	12	27	14	9	12	<1	6
Conflict between religion and psychology	12	<1	14	5	6	6	41
Lack of close friends in church/synagogue	8	4	7	12	12	17	<1

Nat = Nationally; RCOQ = Roman Catholics outside Quebec; RCQ = Roman Catholics in Quebec; MLPROT = Mainline Protestants; CPROT = Conservative Protestants.

Source: Bibby, Project Can75.

the percentage drops in Catholic attendance may have been even more severe. In the Atlantic region and western Canada, secularizing factors were also obviously at work. Still, in those parts of the country, Catholic attendance levels remained higher than those of their Mainline Protestant and Other Faith counterparts.

The decline in Protestant attendance nationally over this period was far less severe than that experienced by Catholics, primarily because the attendance level had been lower to begin with and had less distance to fall. Still, between the 1950s and 1970s, Protestant attendance dropped by more than ten percentage points, from 38% to 27%, and by 1990 it had declined another five points, to 22%. Here again, disillusionment with what churches were doing, along with their perceived lack of integrity, stood out as reasons people cited for their inactivity.

Significantly, levels of involvement were far from uniform across denominations.

- After slipping to about 40% in the 1970s, weekly attendance for people identifying with *Conservative Protestant* (evangelical) groups rebounded to its 1950 level of some 50% by 1990.
- In sharp contrast, weekly churchgoing for individuals aligned with the four *Mainline Protestant* groups dropped from 35% to 23% between the 1950s and the 1970s and fell to a mere 14% by 1990.

TABLE 1.3 **Weekly Service Attenders in Canada, 1957–1990**

	1957	1975	1990
NATIONALLY	53%	31	24
Roman Catholic	83	45	33
Outside Quebec	75	48	37
Quebec	88	42	28
Protestant	38	27	22
Mainline	35	23	14
Conservative	51	41	49
Other Faiths	35	17	12

Sources: 1957: March Gallup poll; 1975 and 1990: Bibby, Project Canada surveys.

There was much speculation as to the reasons for these divergent patterns. Some observers maintained that the Conservatives were growing primarily because of the demands they made of their followers, as well as their ability to address life's ultimate questions.[28] Others, including me, saw their superior growth as resulting not so much from their ability to reach outsiders, as from their relative success in retaining both their children and their geographically mobile members.[29]

The Mainliners, particularly the United Church, were frequently criticized for emphasizing justice issues at the expense of addressing spiritual needs.[30] Their extended debate in the mid-1980s over the issue of the ordination of gays and lesbians was also seen as having a negative impact on participation.[31] One important factor that I think has been very much underplayed, however, was suggested to me a few years back by the United Church moderator at the time, Marion Best. To the extent that Mainliners did not give high priority in the 1970s and 1980s to aggressively establishing new congregations, particularly in new suburbs, they missed out on the opportunity and the need to minister to young families who already identified with them. The number of United Church congregations, for example, dropped from 4,355 in 1973 to 4,112 by 1990; during that same time, Sunday school enrolments declined from about 274,000 to 196,000.[32] Because adequate numbers of new Mainline churches had not been created, the flow of younger active affiliates was reduced and dying members were not replaced with younger ones.

In contrast, for many evangelical denominations, "church planting" in new areas was a high priority. The Pentecostal Assemblies of Canada, for example, had about 850 churches in 1975, compared to 1,050 in 1990, while the Christian and Missionary Alliance expanded from some 195 churches in 1975 to 350 by 1990. Planting churches was also a priority for a group like the Mormons, whose congregational numbers grew from about 260 to 380 during the same 15-year period.[33] Significantly, a major emphasis of all three groups was family ministry generally and child/youth ministry specifically.

Between 1970 and 1990, an unprecedented number of immigrants came to Canada from Third World countries, resulting in growing numbers of people aligning themselves with Other Faiths. However, despite having greater numbers, leaders of faith groups such as Hinduism, Buddhism, and Islam were encountering the same trends that Catholic and Protestant groups had previously discovered: it was extremely difficult to sustain the religious commitment of immigrants through the first and second generations. Intermarriage typically resulted in Other Faith offspring "defecting" to the numerically dominant Christian tradition, not so much reflecting conscious conversion as the cultural adoption of a Catholic or Protestant religious group preference.[34]

TABLE 1.4 **Membership of Select Denominations, 1966–1991**
In 1,000s

YEAR	UNITED	ANGLICAN*	BAPTIST	PENTECOSTAL	LUTHERAN	PRESBYTERIAN
1966	1,062	1,293/667	137	65	189	200
1971	1,017	1,088/616	132	100	200	183
1976	940	1,009/604	128	117	209	169
1981	900	916/579	128	125	218	165
1986	881	851/558	130	179	208	163
1991	786	848/530	130	203	208	157

*Anglican: inclusive membership/active membership.

Baptist = Canadian Baptist Federation. Pentecostal = Pentecostal Assemblies of Canada. Lutheran = Evangelical Church of Canada, Lutheran Church-Canada and Lutheran Church in America–Canada; 1991ff = Evangelical Lutheran Church in Canada and Lutheran Church-Canada.

Sources: Yearbook of American and Canadian Churches, 1916–2000; United, Anglican, Baptist, Pentecostal, Lutheran, and Presbyterian yearbooks. Also McLeod, 1982. Where data for exact years are not available, estimates have been made from closest years.

So it was that as of the 1991 census, only about 4% of Canadians were identifying with a faith other than Christianity — scarcely higher than the 3% figures for both 1931 and even 1871. Such findings suggested that the Canadian religious mosaic heralded by so many was largely a myth.[35] Beyond their relatively small numbers, people identifying with Other Faiths could hardly be expected to transcend the cultural factors in Canada that promote secularization to a greater degree than other Canadians. Attendance patterns suggest that they did not: participation levels for individuals identifying with Other Faiths closely mirrored the levels of Mainline Protestants, dropping from 35% in the late 1950s to 12% by 1990. It is important to remember, however, that some groups, including Jews and Hindus, may not emphasize weekly attendance, so an attendance cut-off point of "at least once a month," for example, may be a better reflection of their attendance expectations. But such a recalculation brought the figure up to only 19% as of 1990, still appreciably below comparable monthly-plus figures for the four other major "religious families."

Census findings show that other, smaller religious groups, such as Jehovah's Witnesses and Unitarians, also had difficulty sustaining growth in the post-1970s, levelling off at about 170,000 and 15,000, respectively. Mormon growth was steady, but very modest. In 1941, 25,000 Canadians said they were Mormon (Church of Jesus Christ of Latter-Day Saints); 50 years later, in 1991, the figure had risen to just over 100,000, still representing only 0.4% of the population.

Of course, the general attendance and involvement drop-off during the post-1960s had serious resource implications for religious groups. Fewer people meant reduced workforces and less money. In the early 1990s, two dominant features of the Canadian religious scene were widespread financial concern and organizational downsizing. Groups were struggling to adjust to the reality of diminishing resources. My sense at that point was that closures and mergers, shared facilities and shared ministries, hiring freezes and layoffs, program reviews and revisions would only become more common.[36] These were days when — in the words of one Lutheran leader — many groups were being challenged just to keep their boats afloat, let alone embark on creative ministry initiatives, including new church starts. Religion in the 1980s and 1990s was not a growth industry.

Adding to the bleakness of the situation was the increasing realization that some key potential "lifelines" were turning out to be precarious. Contrary to much media hype, primarily American in nature, *Baby Boomers* were not returning to churches in the numbers needed to replace aging Boomer parents and grandparents. The dominant pattern was recently summed up this way by one 52-year-old Boomer survey participant from Red Deer, Alberta:

> From age 7–12 my mother took us to church each Sunday; dad stayed at home. From age 13–17 I went once a month; mother stayed home with dad. After age 18 we all stayed home or went out visiting and driving together.[37]

For all the talk about *evangelism*, groups of all kinds were failing to demonstrate much success in recruiting people outside their own boundaries. Most were growing by adding people who were primarily their own — children and geographically mobile members. Even new *ethnic churches* that were sometimes seen as examples of new organizational vitality typically consisted of people who were already Catholics or Protestants when they had arrived in Canada. And, as noted, they faced the same problem as all congregations, Christian and otherwise — holding onto their increasingly acculturated and assimilated children.[38]

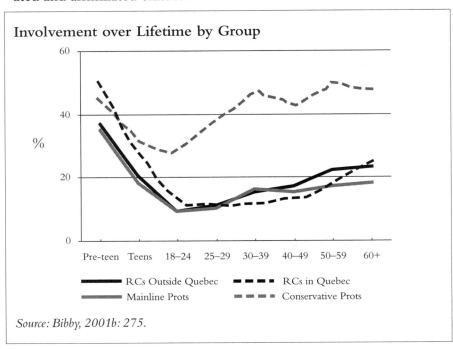

Involvement over Lifetime by Group

Source: Bibby, 2001b: 275.

A Grim Prognosis

By the mid-90s, the collective picture was not a good one for Canada's religious groups. In most instances, their participants were disproportionately old. This meant that, unless their sizeable elderly age cohorts were replaced with aging Baby Boomers in the next decade or so, most groups were going to be looking at a considerable reduction in the number of active participants. Demographic snapshots in the 1990s of the age structures of religious groups indicated that the replacements weren't there. Comparisons between 1990 and 1975 illustrated the predicament:

- 51% of adults in 1975 said they had attended services weekly when they were growing up, compared to 39% in 1990;
- 31% of these adults in the 1970s reported that they were weekly attenders, versus 23% who said they attended that often in 1990;
- 35% of parents with school-age children in 1975 said their offspring were attending Sunday schools or receiving comparable religious instruction that was not part of their regular school days; by 1990, that figure had fallen to 28%.[39]

This downward spiral of intergenerational religious socialization meant that fewer and fewer young people were coming from so-called "religious homes." Our national youth surveys corroborated such a reality. In 1984, 23% of the country's 15-to-19-year-olds said they were attending services on a weekly basis; just eight years later, in 1992, the figure had fallen to 18%.[40]

An examination of involvement by age around 1990 suggested something of the magnitude of the possible coming crisis facing

TABLE 1.5 **Weekly Service Attendance and Age for Select Groups, 1991**

AGE GROUPS	NAT	RC	PROT	ANGLICAN	UNITED	CONSERVATIVE
18–34	14%	15%	22%	7%	8%	54%
35–54	23	30	23	13	12	56
55+	37	51	31	21	25	62

Source: Statistics Canada, 1991 General Social Survey.

organized religion in Canada. The most involved people in the country were 55 and over. Almost 40% of these older Canadians were weekly attenders, compared to some 25% of people in their mid-30s to mid-50s, and only about 15% of adults under the age of 35. What's more, this pattern of higher involvement among older people was consistent within almost every major religious group in the country. It didn't take a brilliant demographer to deduce the obvious. The disappearance of people aged 55 and over throughout the next three decades would have very dramatic negative consequences for organized religion in Canada.

TABLE 1.6 **Projected Weekly Service Attendance, 2015**
In 1,000s

	1991	2015
NATIONALLY	4,600	3,500
Roman Catholic		
Outside Quebec	1,500	1,200
Quebec	1,200	550
Mainline Protestant		
Anglican	220	100
Lutheran	80	50
Presbyterian	80	75
United Church	400	200
Conservative Protestant		
Baptist	200	225
Other	740	900
Other Faiths	200	175

Source: Bibby, Unknown Gods, *1993: 106.*

Simple demographic projections based on Statistics Canada data that I published in 1993 in *Unknown Gods* suggested that by the year 2015, the number of weekly attenders would decline from:

- 1.2 million to about 600,000 among Quebec Catholics,
- 400,000 to 200,000 in the case of the United Church,
- 220,000 to 100,000 among Anglicans,

- 80,000 to 50,000 for Lutherans,
- 80,000 to 75,000 among Presbyterians, and
- 200,000 to 175,00 for Other Faith groups.

Conservative Protestants were the only religious grouping where age structure pointed to increases in attendance by 2015, and even here, the projected gains were fairly modest.

Such changes, if in fact they occurred, were seen as producing a drastically revised Canadian religious landscape by 2015, with the following characteristics:

- *Mainliners* would be on the sidelines and the formerly marginalized *Conservative Protestants* would constitute the new Protestant majority;
- *Roman Catholics* would remain prominent nationally but would experience a severe loss of active people in Quebec;
- *Other Faith* groups, faced with the debilitating realities of acculturation generally and intermarriage specifically, would continue to find it difficult to sustain numbers, let alone grow.[41]

It hardly added up to a pretty picture. But then again, that was the old story of what was happening in the churches.

The Critical Asterisk

In spite of these stark projections, an important part of this "old story" was that, for all the problems of the churches, a considerable market continued to exist for the themes that religious groups have emphasized historically. As a transition from "the grim prognosis" I had laid out in *Unknown Gods* in 1993, I offered these thoughts:

> If that were all that there is to the Canadian religion story, those who value faith and are in touch with reality would be in a state of despair. There's little doubt that organized religion is in very serious shape, with its golden years apparently relegated to history. But as one looks out on the cultural landscape and watches

the dust settle on the grey ruins of much of organized religion, an interesting spectacle can be seen. In the midst of the debris and desolation, a large number of green patches of spirituality can be detected. The temples may be disintegrating, but the grass is far from dead.[42]

I suggested that to look beyond organized religion to Canadian culture is to observe at least three important indicators of latent spirituality — fascination with mystery, the search for meaning, and religious memory.

Mystery
Through the early 1990s, Canadians were continuing to express intrigue with mystery, including experiences that do not have readily apparent explanations — strange coincidences, vivid dreams that reflect subsequent real-life events, deep-felt impressions about people that turn out to be accurate, puzzling sensations in some physical settings that point to Something Else.

I offered a number of illustrations. There was a young Canadian in Sweden who, while gathering wood from a shed, was overcome with feelings so intense that he dropped the wood and ran out of the shed. He learned later that three people had committed suicide there. A friend travelling in Europe had a dream that her brother back in Alberta had lost his arm in an accident; when she called home the next day, she learned he had been in an accident and had broken his arm. After a former student lost her husband in a plane crash, her sister-in-law had a vivid dream in which he appeared, discussing the pros and cons of heaven and telling her to tell his wife not to worry about him. He also gave his sister a word that would convince his wife that they had spoken — a word the couple had learned and used playfully with each other during a stay in Australia and had not shared with anyone since returning to Canada — including his sister.

The commonality of such experiences was suggested by the finding that close to one in two Canadians in the 1980s and 1990s acknowledged that they themselves had experienced precognition ("anticipation of a coming event"), while the same proportion indicated they had experienced mental telepathy ("awareness of others' thoughts"). Further, as of 1990, some 59% said they believed in ESP, and 59% indicated they believed that "some people have psychic powers, enabling them to predict events."

Canadians also continued to address the great mystery of death. Nine in ten said that during their lifetimes they had raised the question of what happens after death. About seven in ten claimed to believe in life after death, 70% in heaven, and 46% in hell. Moreover, close to 40% maintained that we can have contact with the spirit world, and 23% believed that we can communicate with the dead.

In addition, more general supernatural beliefs continued to be widespread. In 1990, more than 80% of people across the country said they believed in God; what's more, more than half of these (44%) said they had personally experienced God's presence. Significantly, young people were no less likely than adults to endorse beliefs about the paranormal and supernatural. In fact, our *Project Teen Canada* surveys showed that young people tended to exhibit belief levels that were as high as or higher than those of adults.

Meaning

With respect to meaning, some 90% of Canadians indicated that they raise questions about life's purpose. As of 1990, one in three — led by people under 55 — reported that they were troubled by the sense that they "should be getting more out of life." One in two said they were concerned about the purpose of life.

Large numbers still wanted to bring the gods in on major life events. Most Canadians not only had participated in rites of passage but also expected that additional rites would be carried out for them in the future. For example, a national study Don Posterski and I carried out for the Canadian Youth Foundation in late 1987 found that 82% of 15-to-24-year-olds expected to turn to religious groups in the future for marriages, 75% for baptisms and christenings, and 85% for funerals.[43] In many cases, such a pursuit of religious rites would reflect the pressures of relatives and friends. But in other cases, it would be "more than just for mom" — driven by a sense that somehow "God needed to be brought in" on what was happening.

Memory

The survey snapshots of what was happening in the culture through the early 1990s also revealed the pervasive existence of religious memory. Psychologically, some 88% of Canadian adults and 80% of teens were still identifying with religious groups. When they were asked point-blank, about 90% of the inactive participants said they were not abandoning the groups with which they identified and anticipated turning to them, albeit selectively, for their religious needs, including rites of passage. Culturally, the groups they identified with were the ones to which they had been introduced by family and childhood friends, as most Canadians had had some exposure to a religious setting when they were growing up. Those were the groups with which they had familiarity and in which they felt comfortable. Religious memory was everywhere.

These three realities — mystery, meaning, and memory — added up to a significant opportunity for religious groups. There is good reason to believe that opportunity continues to exist in the early years of the 21st century.

TABLE 1.7 **Mystery, Meaning, and Memory: Some Illustrative Findings, 1990**

Mystery	
Believe in ESP	59%
Believe in life after death	68
Believe in heaven	70
Meaning	
Have raised the question of life's purpose	87
Are troubled by the question of life's purpose	50
Are concerned they should be getting more out of life	34
Memory	
Identify with a religious group	88
Attend at least sometimes	82
Identify, attend less often than monthly, but not open to involvement with another group	91

Source: Bibby, Unknown Gods, *1993: 120–48.*

What If the Churches Fail?

Looking at things in the early 1990s, one could hardly be confident that the established churches would come through. But one influential American observer predicted that if they didn't, other groups would.

Since about 1980, Rodney Stark, a sociologist who spent most of his career at the University of Washington in Seattle, has offered a provocative theory about the future of organized religion. By now, his argument is well known and is variously described as a market model or as rational choice theory. Some religious leaders in the United States and Canada have reacted very negatively to the application of marketing language to religion. Recently, however, Stark has pointed out that his use of an economic model in studying religion is not meant to be offensive, nor is it mere metaphor. Rather, he uses it because of "the immense explanatory power that can be gained by applying elementary principles of economics to religious phenomena at the group or social level."[44]

Writing with William Bainbridge (1985) and Roger Finke (1992 and 2000), Stark has maintained that secularization has never spelled the end of religion.[45] Regardless of whatever happens to religious groups, people continue to have some needs "that only the gods can provide."[46] The demand for religion is constant; what varies is the supply side. In societies where the religious economy has been deregulated, groups or "firms" that have difficulties will lose "market share" to groups that typically are more vigorous and less worldly.

In short, secularization does not lead to the demise of religion. On the contrary, it stimulates religious innovation in the form of (1) breakaway groups that seek to revive faith and (2) new religious traditions — "sects" and "cults," respectively.[47] Stark and his associates claim extensive historical and contemporary support for their thesis, including research in Canada. As Stark and Bainbridge put it, "In an endless cycle, faith is revived and new faiths born to take the places of those withered denominations that lost their sense of the supernatural."[48]

Stark emphasized that people tend to value religion on the basis of how costly it is to belong. The reason is that the higher the costs of membership, the greater the material, social, and religious benefits of membership. In the words of Stark and Finke, "People tend to value religion according to how much it costs — and because 'reasonable' and 'sociable' religion costs little, it is not valued greatly."[49] Individuals consequently make "a rational choice" to belong and participate.[50] Conversely, as religious bodies ask less of their members, their ability to reward them declines. So it is that the more mainline a denomination, the lower the value of belonging to it. The eventual result is widespread defection.

Applied to Canada, the problems of groups like the United Church nationally and the Roman Catholic Church in Quebec should result in sects and cults moving in to pick up the slack. Because the demand for religion has remained fairly constant and the religion market has been deregulated, new groups can now compete with the old. The only question would seem to be, Which groups will take advantage of the opportunity to increase their market share?

Fortunately for Canada's well-established religious groups, Stark has overestimated the openness of the Canadian market. For reasons known only to the gods, Canadians have shown little inclination to abandon the dominant groups — even when those groups have frequently given up on them. Psychologically and emotionally, people across the country continue to cling, sometimes perilously, to the religious traditions of their youth. On the surface at least, their tenacity represents a great window of opportunity for religious bodies. It may turn out to be a critically important part of "the new story about what's happening in the churches." To a clearer understanding of that tenacity we will now turn.

CHAPTER TWO

Some Very Good News via Some Very Bad Myths

I grew up as a Baptist. Funny thing when you're a Baptist: you don't think of yourself as particularly strange. In fact, you look out at people in other Protestant denominations — friends and neighbours who are United, Anglican, Lutheran, Presbyterian — and see *them* as the ones who are different. And, to be honest, to a ten-year-old Baptist, groups like Catholics, not to mention Mormons or Buddhists, seem *especially* different. Their services are not ones into which Baptists readily wander.

It therefore comes as something of a surprise to Baptists when I tell them about my study of the Toronto Anglican Diocese in the mid-80s — where an Anglican woman who was concerned about changes in liturgy, commented, "We need to be careful, or one day we will end up like the Baptists"! What the Anglican woman probably didn't realize, of course, is that a Baptist in *her* worship service would also feel like the proverbial duck badly in need of some water.

To have conversations with people who are part of other religious groups is to receive a mini-revelation: *everyone thinks that their traditions are the norm* — their beliefs, their kind of worship, their music, their type of ministry. Consequently, to grow up anything is to feel a measure of comfort with one's own group and a measure of discomfort with other "different" groups. What's true of Baptists and

Anglicans can just as readily be seen when a Catholic and a Pentecostal who are dating attempt to alternate pews, or when two United and Jewish friends agree to attend their respective services together on a back-to-back Saturday and Sunday. Sometimes the ecclesiastical trip may be short, such as Anglican to Catholic or Baptist to Alliance; the occasion may also be brief — a wedding, a funeral, or a Christmas service. Regardless, confusion and uneasiness are common. People don't know what they are supposed to do when. The music and prayers and rituals and gestures are foreign. What's happening somehow doesn't resonate with the kinds of things that may have moved one in the past, or moves one in the present.

All of this is to say that faith, however personal, invariably has a pronounced social and cultural dimension. To be raised Baptist or United or Catholic or Mormon is to acquire a religious identity, which is accompanied by ideas and ways of expressing faith that one sees as normative. As basic as such a reality is, it is not one that Canadian religious leaders readily grasped, to the detriment of both their groups and millions of inactive religious people across the country.

A common impression about the attendance drop-off in the post-1960s is that it was associated with millions of Canadians jettisoning their respective religious groups. To borrow some sports jargon, to the extent that people were not involved in the groups of their childhoods, they were seen as having become religious free agents who were shopping their services to new teams. Or, to use the language of the market model, those who wanted to have their religious and spiritual needs met were said to be spending time browsing in an array of "meaning malls" and "spiritual marketplaces." Allegedly, their consumer choices were determined primarily by their personal tastes and whims. In such an environment, people were seen as having little or no regard for the religions of their parents and grandparents. Those, after all, were the "old-time religions." This was a new day — a day of individualism, freedom, and post-denominationalism. Bring on the competition, New Movements, New Age, and all.

It was a poorly informed and extremely naive reading of the times. If all we had been looking at was religion as a set of ideas, then people could have said goodbye to religious groups just as readily as they had reluctantly said goodbye to beliefs about Santa and the

Easter Bunny and tooth fairies. If the churches had been no more than religious department stores that had become outdated and no longer competitive, people could have said goodbye to them just as readily as they waved goodbye to Eaton's and headed for Wal-Mart.

But religious groups carry with them cultures and poignant memories. Some two in three Canadians say they attended Sunday schools and services when they were growing up, frequently accompanied by parents, and sometimes by relatives. These were the places where millions of people heard stories, sang choruses, participated in youth groups, were introduced to faith, and made commitments. These were settings in which many of their grandparents and parents, brothers and sisters, aunts and uncles, and closest friends were involved. These places bring back memories of poignant, moving times when they and people they loved were baptized and married, and when they said final farewells to cherished family members and friends.

As we will see, for those who look at the world through theistic eyes, there are signs that the gods are shaking up Canadians from coast to coast, leading them to ask vital questions about life and death, communicating with them directly, and giving them hints of transcendence. In the midst of it all, large numbers of Canadians seem to continue to think that at least some of the answers to what they are experiencing lie in the religious traditions of their parents and grandparents. Most are reluctant to wander very far from their religious homes and many are open to greater involvement — if they can be shown that it is worth their while.

These realities have not been well understood by the country's churches. It's time to clear up the confusion once and for all.

A Monopoly Versus a Mosaic

A key to understanding the nature of organized religion in Canada is recognizing that the country's long-established religious groups have had and continue to have a considerable advantage over newer and smaller counterparts in ministering to Canadians. Their longevity has meant that they have sizeable pools of people who have been socialized in their traditions. Their numerical strength has meant, in turn, that they typically gain far more people than they lose through religious intermarriage. This is not to disparage the presence and expansion efforts of newer and smaller religious organizations; it's simply to recognize the competitive facts of Canadian religious life.

However, during much of the second half of the 20th century, Canada's most established religious bodies were floundering instead of flourishing. They failed to capitalize on their advantage, in large part because they failed to realize they had it. Most religious leaders and active laity had probably never heard of Rodney Stark. Nonetheless they, along with him, assumed they were working in a "deregulated" religious environment where people not actively involved in a group were essentially "up for grabs." Established religious organizations sailed blindly into the marketplace and competed with each other for "customers" who had already made their "product choices." But contrary to what Stark had anticipated, even though the religious needs of Canadians ("the demand side") remained fairly constant, new rival religious groups ("the supply side") did not move in and seize the apparent opportunity. The real losers in this whole display of ineptitude were Canadians, who frequently failed to have their needs met.

There were three key reasons why Canada's religious market broke down. First, contrary to what Stark and many religious leaders had assumed, the country's well-established churches continued to have a considerable competitive advantage because of the latent loyalty of the people who identified with them — those I refer to as "affiliates." People were very reluctant to switch. The market was not as open as everyone had thought. Second, there was a widespread assumption that affiliates who attended sporadically or not at all had dropped out of their groups and had become part of a growing pool of "unchurched" people. Their affiliate religious bodies essentially gave up on them, a fact graphically illustrated by the strange delight many congregations took in cleaning the alleged "deadwood" off their rolls. Because religious groups, and just about everyone else for that matter, were working from these two false assumptions about switching and dropping out, large numbers of people failed to be touched by their churches' ministries and huge amounts of potential resources went untapped. Third, it was widely believed that people who had ceased to be active were not receptive to greater involvement. And if they weren't, neither were their off-spring. A prevalent stereotype was that people no longer involved were typically hostile — "poisoned" by bad experiences. Better to turn elsewhere in pursuing recruitment leads.

Ironically, few congregations appear to have carried out systematic studies of their marginal and inactive affiliates. If they had, they would have found that (a) many were, in fact, receptive to greater involvement and (b) especially in urban areas, many were among the Canadians who had moved once in the past five years and simply had not reconnected with churches after having been involved somewhere else.[1] They needed to be contacted; often no one called. It all added up to a bad misreading of what was happening.

TABLE 2.1 **Canada's "Religious Families," 2002**
Approximate % of the Canadian Population★

Roman Catholics outside Quebec	23
Roman Catholics in Quebec	19
Mainline Protestants *United (9), Anglican (6), Lutheran (2), Presbyterian (2)*	19
Conservative Protestants *including Baptists, Pentecostals, Mennonites, Alliance, Nazarenes*	8
Other Faith Groups *including Jews, Muslims, Buddhists, Hindus, Sikhs*	6
Religious Nones	20

★*A residual 5% or so, mostly Protestants, identify with varied groups that neither fall into any of these six categories nor collectively represent a family with compatible characteristics.*

Source: Projection based on Project Canada and Statistics Canada data.

Religious organizations should have known better. For some time they and academics who make a living from studying them had known well how they grow: the primary source of new additions is biological, in the form of family members. An example is a 52-year-old evangelical from Fredericton who playfully told us recently, "I started attending church nine months before I was born, have been carried to church, pushed to church, towed to church, and shoved to church. Now going to church is one of my favourite things."[2] The research is definitive: religious groups grow by growing their own. On national and international scales, growth also takes place through the recruitment of geographically mobile members, whether they arrive from Ontario or Saskatchewan, England or Asia. To the extent that groups recruit people outside their boundaries, the key factors are friendship and marriage — people on the inside befriend them or marry them. Frankly, for all the talk about outreach and evangelism, the research shows that "people from the outside" represent a very limited, bonus source of growth.[3]

This apparent "bad news" about the difficulty Canadian groups have experienced in recruiting outsiders had and continues to have a "good news" flip side with enormously important implications: well-established religious organizations do not lose many people to their competitors. Maybe the Canadian situation is unique, and maybe it's not. But the proverbial bottom line here is that, on the "demand side," Canadians are reluctant to try just any supplier. Most tenaciously stick with the choices of their parents and grand-parents' traditions. In the last part of the 20th century, no new or old religious "company" made significant headway in moving in and recruiting Catholics and Protestants who, ostensibly, were no longer involved in their respective groups.[4] What's more, there is little indication that such a preference for the groups of their parents and grandparents is about to change.

Consequently, for well-established religious organizations that want to grow, the starting point should be obvious: they need to relate to those uninvolved Canadians with whom they have the greatest affinity — those millions of people who identify with their traditions, people who "think" they are Roman Catholic, United, Baptist, Lutheran, Jewish, and so on.

As obvious as such a point should have been, it was almost oblit-erated in recent decades by the debilitating myths of switching, drop-out, and non-receptivity. If these were merely issues to be debated at professional meetings by academics, it wouldn't matter. Unfortunately, however, these have been "very bad myths" because of the practical implications they have had for how leaders have car-ried out ministry — who, for example, they have targeted and what they have brought to them. To the extent that leaders have accepted the three myths, explicit strategies for finding affiliates and ministering to them have seldom been formulated and put into place. In the process, they have blown their competitive advantage. The myths that have led to this debacle are so distracting and unproductive that it's worth looking at them more closely.[5]

Myth No. 1: People Are Switching

In recent years, some congregational experts and academics in North America — notably, Lyle Schaller and Robert Wuthnow — have led the way in propagating the idea that there has been a sharp decline in the importance being given to religious group loyalties. People are said to be abandoning allegiances to individual Protestant denominations and even to broader religious families such as Protestantism and Catholicism.[6] Congregational gurus tell us that North Americans who continue to want to participate in religious groups are commonly gravitating toward churches that are in touch with their needs, and they are showing little concern for denominational and religious family labels.[7] Such an alleged decline in religious group loyalties is seen as consistent with a more general decline in loyalty to institutions of all types over the last half of this century.[8] Themes such as freedom, inclusiveness, and the dismantling of boundaries are widespread. The saints are said to be circulating freely.

The unquestioning eagerness with which religious leaders have bought into such masochistic thinking is quite bewildering. Their experiences should have told them that something was seriously wrong with such claims. Consistent with what I have been saying, basic learning theory in sociology suggests there is little reason to expect that large amounts of pronounced religious switching will take place. In view of the pervasive tendency of children to identify with the religion of their parents, switching almost amounts to a form of deviant behaviour. Catholics do not expect their children to marry Jehovah's Witnesses — maybe not even Protestants. Lutheran parents may not be enthralled with their daughters or sons marrying born-again Christians, sentiments that are reciprocal for the evangelical parents involved. And Jews, Hindus, and Muslims do not typically embrace the idea of their children marrying Catholics or Protestants; on the contrary, intermarriage is seen by many Jewish observers, for example, as a major threat to Judaism and Jewishness.[9] We all know that the prospect of such kinds of intermarital "defection" is frequently greeted with a wide range of social controls, ranging from stigma to ostracism, particularly when the potential partner is a fair distance removed from one's religious "home."

The inclination to switch is also limited by the reality of cultural commonality. Most people attended services with some regularity when they were growing up. The majority turn to their identification groups when they require rites of passage, want to attend a seasonal service, or feel the need to expose their children to religious activities. That's why people see the religious cultures of their groups as normative. That's why they feel comfortable or uncomfortable in certain worship settings . . . prefer hymns and pipe organ to songs and a band, appreciate or feel disdain for a written prayer, feel reverence as they look at candles versus laser lights, kneel rather than stand, bow their heads versus raise their arms, pray silently or pray loudly. Culturally, it's a substantial stretch to move from a Jewish to a Pentecostal world — or even from a United to a Baptist world — and vice versa.

Our current emphases on inclusiveness and acceptance of religious diversity should not blind us to another ongoing reality: there are some people who are not interested in turning elsewhere for the simple reason that they favour their groups' versions of truth. So it is that an 82-year-old Catholic from rural Nova Scotia — who, incidentally, has participated in all of our *Project Canada* surveys dating back to 1975 when he was in his late 50s — told us that he was not comfortable going to a Protestant church, not because of bigotry but because "I cannot in good conscience take part in a non-Catholic service. I can go to a funeral of a friend, but I cannot participate in the service." His age notwithstanding, this candid individual is not alone.

As a result of such social and personal factors, there is little reason to believe that Canadians are open to being recruited by other groups, especially those with whom they have few common theological and cultural ties. To the extent that switching occurs at all, it would be expected both to be limited and to follow fairly predictable lines of affinity. People would be expected to circulate primarily among "the religious families" of their parents.

But don't take my word for it. Let's listen to what Canadians have been saying.

Intergroup Switching
For all the rhetoric about evangelism, outreach, and seeker-sensitive ministries, Canadians who are not actively involved in churches (a) are seldom recruited by such aggressive "outside" groups and (b) if they do become involved, tend to become involved with groups with which they already identify.[10]

Our *Project Canada* surveys show that in the course of acquiring a religious identification, most people continue to more or less "inherit" the religion of their parents, with relatively few switching to other religious families.

- Approximately nine in ten *Catholics in Quebec* and eight in ten *Catholics in the rest of the country* identify with the religion of their parents. To the extent that they don't, the tendency is to say they have no religion.
- The same pattern characterizes some 80% of people from *Mainline Protestant* homes, as well as roughly 70% of Canadians whose parents identified with *Conservative Protestant* or *Other Faith* groups.
- To the extent that people with Conservative Protestant backgrounds switch, they tend to move into Mainline Protestant denominations.
- The *Religious None* category is characterized by a very high level of switching in and switching out. This category is more like a hotel than a home for many people.

This is not to say that religious switching never takes place. Obviously, some people cross family lines. But proportionately speaking, switching is the exception rather than the norm, particularly among the largest religious families, Catholics and Mainliners.

We are also able to take a look at the prevalence of switching in recent years using some rather novel information. Our 1995 *Project Canada* National Survey included four hundred people who had participated in 1975, which generated rare and invaluable "panel

TABLE 2.2 **Extent and Nature of Intergenerational Switching, 2000**

	RESPONDENT'S RELIGION				
	RC	MLPROT	CPROT	OTHER	NONE
Mother's Religion					
RCs outside Quebec	80%	4%	1%	3%	12%
RCs in Quebec	89	<1	<1	1	9
Mainline Protestants	6	78	4	3	9
Conservative Protestants	<1	18	71	<1	11
Other Faiths	7	4	<1	71	18
No Religion	11	11	5	<1	73
Father's Religion					
RCs outside Quebec	80	7	<1	2	10
RCs in Quebec	91	<1	<1	<1	8
Mainline Protestants	4	82	4	2	8
Conservative Protestants	<1	14	76	<1	10
Other Faiths	8	4	<1	80	8
No Religion	20	13	4	5	58

Source: Bibby, Project Canada 2000.

data." Here we are literally looking at the same people over time. The panel findings corroborated the cross-sectional trend findings: limited switching between religious families took place over the two decades. Some 90% of Mainline Protestants and Roman Catholics, along with close to 85% of Conservative Protestants, had the same religious identification in 1995 as they did in 1975. To the extent that switching did occur, it tended to follow Protestant-Catholic lines, versus a pathway to Other Faiths or the No Religion category.

While the panel sample sizes are small for Conservative Protestants, Other Faiths, and Nones, the tentative findings show that Conservatives are rarely drawn to either the Catholic or No Religion camps, and people identifying with Other Faiths or having No Religion seldom gravitate over time to Christian groups.

In the 2000 *Project Canada* survey, we bluntly asked Canadians two questions pertaining to religious identification: *"How important is your religious tradition to you (that is, being Catholic, United, Buddhist, etc.)?"* and *"Are you open to the possibility of switching to a different tradition?"*

TABLE 2.3 **Intergenerational Identification
by Religious Families: Panel, 1975 and 1995**

| | | | SWITCHED TO: | | | | |
1975 IDENTIFICATION	NUMBER	STAYED	MLPROT	CPROT	RC	OTHER	NONE
Mainline Protestant	196	88%		4	3	2	3
Conservative Protestant	31	83	11		<1	6	0
Roman Catholic	102	90	3	4		2	1
Other Faith	15	63	5	22	5		5
No Religion	19	39	33	<1	28	<1	
Totals*	363	85	4	4	3	2	2

Identification data for 1975 or 1995 missing for 37 respondents.
Source: Bibby, 1999:157.

- Some six in ten Canadians who identify with a religious group say that their religious tradition is "very important" or "somewhat important" to them, including 92% of *weekly attenders* and 50% of those who attend less often. Variations between religious families tend to be fairly small.
- More than eight in ten people say they are not open to the possibility of switching to a different tradition, led by 97% of *Quebec Catholics*. But here, differences by attendance are small: infrequent attenders are only moderately less likely to be closed to the idea of switching traditions — and in Quebec, there is no difference by attendance! As Ron Graham has observed about the legacy of Catholicism in Quebec, "Three centuries of mysticism do not evaporate in three decades of materialism."[11]
- Although the *Other Faith* sample is small, the preliminary evidence is that this is the category most vulnerable to "defections." Still, even here, resistance to switching characterizes the majority of people.

A Footnote for the Critics
Invariably, some people will say they know of exceptions to the rule. Of course, exceptions exist. I'm not saying that switching never occurs

TABLE 2.4 **Importance of Tradition and Openness to Switching Traditions**

	NAT	RCOQ	RCQ	MLPROT	CPROT	OF
Tradition Important						
"Very" or "Somewhat"	61%	70%	62%	54%	72%	53%
Weekly attenders	92	96	96	93	85	★
Others attending less often	50	57	52	46	55	★
Open to Switching						
"No"	83	87	97	75	81	61
Weekly attenders	92	93	98	86	87	★
Others attending less often	80	83	97	72	72	★

★ *Numbers insufficient to permit stable percentaging.*

Source: Bibby, Project Canada 2000.

— only that it is relatively rare. And switching typically involves fairly short theological and cultural trips. As American sociologists Dean Hoge, Ben Johnson, and Don Luidens have pointed out, the size of our *tolerance zones* for acceptable religious traditions appears to exceed our personal *comfort zones* with those traditions. They noted in the case of Presbyterian Baby Boomers, for example, that tolerance zones have expanded over the years, whereas personal comfort zones "are surprisingly narrow and traditional." "For the great majority," they wrote, "the comfort zone extends no farther than Mainline Protestantism, and quite a few draw the line at the Episcopal [Anglican] Church."[12] Sociologists Kirk Hadaway and Penny Marler have concluded that "when Americans do switch, they often remain within the same broad denominational family."[13] It's not that North Americans never switch groups: at least 40% of people in both Canada and the United States have switched denominations at one time or another.[14] However, as Hadaway and Marler have put it, "Americans switch more today than they did in the early 1970s, but when they switch they are more likely to remain in the same larger denominational family."[15]

But even in the United States, the extent of switching is exaggerated. Take two high-profile Americans, for example. In October 2000, former president Jimmy Carter, 76 at the time, announced that he

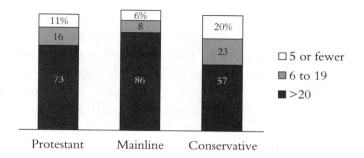

Years of Denominational Involvement
Monthly-Plus Attenders

- 5 or fewer
- 6 to 19
- >20

	Protestant	Mainline	Conservative
5 or fewer	11%	6%	20%
6 to 19	16	8	23
>20	73	86	57

Nearly 75% of Protestants, led by Mainliners, have been with their current denominations for more than 20 years. Taking age into account, Mainline Protestants on average have been involved with their current denominations for 80% of their lives, Conservatives for only 57%. Much of the Conservative switching between denominations, however, is within "the family," where choices outnumber those available to Mainliners.

Source: Bibby, Project Canada 2000.

was cutting his ties with the Southern Baptist Convention. "My grandfather, my father, and I have always been Southern Baptists," he said. But because of its growing rigidity, he had felt "increasingly uncomfortable and somewhat excluded" from the church for years.

However, Carter did not move far. He said that he and his wife Rosalyn would associate with other Baptist groups.[16] In the same year, well-known historian and author Garry Wills released his book *Papal Sin*, which has been described as a damning indictment of the Catholic Church's systemic inability to tell the truth. When he was asked in an interview why he was still a member of the Catholic Church, he responded that he doesn't believe it has the last word on Christianity, but he was born into the Church and stays because there are a lot of things about it he likes. "The church that I'm in, for instance, is better than at any time in my life," said Wills. "The people are more engaged with each other and the outside world, they do more for each other and the outside world, the women are very active in it. The priest is as co-operative as he can be." Wills maintains that despite his strong language, he's not angry at the church, and his job as an historian is to describe the problems. "Catholicism," he emphasized, "is not declining. It's just that the Vatican is out of touch with its own people. Some day," he says, "it will have to catch up."[17]

The same patterns of limited switching and switching within religious families appear to hold for Canada. The decline in active participation has not been associated with a widespread tendency for Canadians to move to other religious families, or to the No Religion category. In marketing language, the religious economy of Canada continues to be characterized by a very tight market, where the expansion of market shares through the recruitment of people from rival groups is extremely difficult. To the extent that switching does take place, it follows fairly predictable lines of affinity, frequently associated with the breaking down of family-related "social controls." But overall, the market is not particularly open; intergroup movement is very limited.

Myth No. 2: People Are Dropping Out

Closely related to the loyalty myth is the belief that if people are not attending on a regular basis, they have dropped out. Here it is assumed that identification without involvement simply doesn't count. If, for example, someone says that she or he is an "Anglican" or "Roman Catholic" or "Pentecostal" but seldom attends a service, such a self-designation is typically assumed to mean very little. In part, this is a theological assumption: if people are not involved, they have abandoned the faith. Policy-wise, such individuals are typically viewed by leaders as "unchurched" and, as such, are seen as "up for grabs" in the competitive religious marketplace. Officially, they are the prime targets of groups whose ministries are aimed at evangelism and service.

On the surface, the assumption that people have dropped out seems to be reasonable. If they aren't coming, they must have left. The assumption has led to common dichotomous classifications along the lines of "churched-unchurched," "active-inactive," and "practising-lapsed" — not to mention more pejorative dualities such as "saved-unsaved" and "saint-sinner." Even though this dropping-out myth is older, it has been reinforced by the more recent myth about loyalty decline. People are assumed to be dropping out in part because they have little group loyalty, and it is thought that where they attend next will not, in turn, be guided by group loyalty, but by a consumer-like response to the group that comes up with the most attractive and engaging offer.

Religious Identification

In contrast to radically declining attendance figures, religious identification in Canada stood at 88% in 1991 and at about 85% in 2000. But individuals who indicate that they have "no religion" tend to be disproportionately young. Research shows that such a situation is short-lived for many, who frequently re-adopt the religious group identification of their parents in the course of requesting and receiving religious rites of passage.[18] Their links to their parents' religious groups appear to be sustained not so much by religious content as by family history and these rites of passage.

What is perhaps rather remarkable is not that large numbers of North Americans *identify but are not involved*, but rather that they continue to *identify even though they are not involved*. They can be chastised, ignored, and removed from congregational lists — and they frequently are. But still, they don't really leave. Psychologically, emotionally, and culturally, they continue to identify with the traditions of their childhood.

The Meaning of Religious Identification

The *Project Canada* surveys have also asked respondents directly about their inclination to stay versus switching or dropping out, while probing the meaning of their ongoing involvement. Beginning with the 1985 national survey, respondents "not attending religious services regularly" were asked "how well" the following observation describes them:

> Some observers maintain that few people are actually abandoning their religious traditions. Rather, they draw selective beliefs and practices, even if they do not attend services frequently. They are not about to be recruited by other religious groups. Their identification with their religious tradition is fairly solidly

fixed, and it is to these groups that they will turn when con-
fronted with marriage, death, and, frequently, birth.

Through 2000, about 85% of Canadians who *identify but attend
less than monthly* have said that the statement describes them either
"very accurately" or "somewhat accurately." Nationally, there has
been little change since the mid-80s in the tendency of inactive
attenders to acknowledge the accuracy of the description.

TABLE 2.5 **Accuracy of the Religious Identification Statement:
Canadians Identifying and Attending Less Than Monthly,
1985 and 2000**
% Indicating It Describes Them "Very Accurately" or "Somewhat Accurately"

	NAT	RCOQ	RCQ	MLPROT	CPROT	OF
1985	87	84	90	88	86	74
2000	85	89	88	82	86	70

Sources: Bibby, Project Can85 and Project Canada 2000.

It adds up to a situation where, beyond the 20% or so Canadians
who attend services almost every week or more, there are another
60%-plus who continue to identify with the country's dominant
traditions. Most people in this latter category attend occasionally,
believe and practise selectively, are not about to be recruited by
alternatives, and are looking to their identification groups for rites of
passage. They most definitely have not "dropped out."

As I mentioned at the outset of this chapter, the confusion over
switchers and drop-outs involves far more than academic wran-
gling. It has critically important implications for how religious
groups relate to Canadians. If groups see the religious market as
essentially wide open, Americans and Canadians will be viewed
as religious free agents who can be recruited through effective
ministry and evangelism. The problem with such a viewpoint is
that it will result in congregations wasting much of their recruitment resources. More seriously, Canadians who might benefit from
good ministry will not be identified and pursued.

In contrast, if religious groups would concentrate less on the
switcher and drop-out exceptions and more on "the ongoing

identification rule," they would be in a position to target the very people to whom they have the best chance of ministering — the women and men who already identify with them. Identification represents a measure of affinity; as such, it is the logical place to begin in connecting with people.

Given the pervasiveness of ongoing religious identification, congregations would be wise to follow Kirk Hadaway's lead in seeing their members and others who identify with their denomination as a series of concentric rings, ranging from active members at the centre through less active individuals to an outer ring of inactive people.[19] Working with such a model, congregations need to develop creative strategies for finding people, exploring their interests and needs, and responding — doing tangible things that I discuss in detail in my 1995 book *There's Got to Be More!*

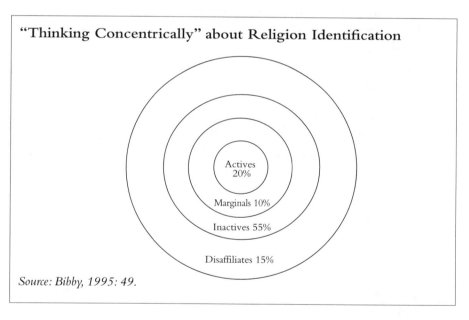

"Thinking Concentrically" about Religion Identification

Actives 20%

Marginals 10%

Inactives 55%

Disaffiliates 15%

Source: Bibby, 1995: 49.

Myth No. 3: People Are Not Receptive
One of the most common observations I have heard over the years from religious leaders and from the media is that people "just aren't interested in organized religion anymore." Such a statement is a gross overgeneralization.

As mentioned briefly earlier in the context of Catholicism in Quebec, the latest *Project Canada* national surveys of adults and teenagers have uncovered a finding that speaks volumes about the opportunity that is staring the country's religious groups in the face. In the adult survey, Canadians who attend services less than once a month were asked, *"Would you consider the possibility of being more involved in a religious group if you found it to be worthwhile for yourself or your family?"* The teen survey posed much the same question, asking young people to respond to the statement, *"I'd be open to more involvement with religious groups if I found it to be worthwhile."*[20] Keeping in mind that only 21% of adults and 22% of teens are currently weekly attenders, it's highly significant that 55% of adults and 39% of teens answered yes.

- Across adult religious families, the receptivity levels are about 55%, even among Quebec Catholics. What's more, one in three Canadians who say they have no religious affiliation maintain that they would be receptive to greater involvement in a religious group "if . . ."

TABLE 2.6 **Receptivity to Greater Involvement: People Attending Less Than Monthly, 2000**

	ADULTS	TEENS
NATIONALLY	55%	39%
Roman Catholics	56	46
Quebec	55	41
Outside Quebec	56	51
Protestants	64	47
Mainline	63	44
Conservative	73 ★	55
Other Faiths	67 ★	48
No Religion	34	21

★Numbers only 16 and 33, respectively; percentages unstable. Included here for heuristic purposes.

Sources: Bibby, Project Canada 2000 and Project Teen Canada 2000.

- Among 15-to-19-year-olds, the receptivity levels are some 40% or more across groups, with about one in five teens with no religious affiliation saying they are open to more involvement.

Rather than acting either hostile or indifferent to their identification groups, significant numbers of people are obviously receptive to greater participation. The 55% figure for adults represents almost three times the number who indicate they are currently highly involved; the teen figure is almost double the proportion of young people who presently attend weekly.

- Those 55% of adults who say they would consider being more involved in the country's religious groups include some two in three of the people who attend several times a year to yearly, and one in three who say they never attend.
- They are most frequently found in the 18-to-34 and 35-to-44 age cohorts, with receptivity particularly common among younger Protestant adults.
- Males and females are equally likely to indicate that they are open to greater involvement, although there are some variations between groups.

TABLE 2.7 **Receptivity to Greater Involvement by Select Variables, 2000**

	NAT (764)	RCOQ (133)	RCQ (143)	PROT (270)	NONE (160)
TOTALS	57%	56%	55%	64%	34%
Yearly	64	64	57	72	48
Never	36	42	33	42	27
18–34	59	58	61	79	42
35–54	57	64	56	66	27
55+	49	★	52	55	23
Female	56	62	53	71	30
Male	56	57	61	58	39

★Numbers insufficient to permit stable percentaging.

Source: Bibby, Project Canada 2000.

A parenthetical note to put things in perspective: I'm a sports fan. I'm interested in pro hockey, among other sports. But contrary to widespread perception, most people are not. For all the media hype around professional hockey, only 30% of Canadians currently say they follow the National Hockey League either "very closely" or "fairly closely." Other sports and leagues fare even worse — the interest level for Major League Baseball is 17%, the Canadian Football League 15%, the National Football League 12%; and for the National Basketball Association it's just 8%.[21] It's true that not everyone is interested in organized religion. But the numbers of those who are easily exceed the figures for those who follow any single professional sport. Pretty good news for people who are in the religion industry; other sectors of the economy should be so lucky!

These findings suggest that noteworthy numbers of Canadians are receptive to greater involvement in the country's religious groups. However, the findings also point to a critical qualifier: people have to find that such involvement is worthwhile for themselves and their families. The observation of a mother of three from Saskatchewan illustrates the hurdles that need to be overcome: "We don't attend often and when we do, it leaves much to be desired." The obvious, burning question is, "What do such people see as worthwhile?" A 66-year-old disenchanted Anglican from Vancouver provides us with a key clue: "Their role should be to minister to people who need them." We'll return to this centrally important topic in Chapter 7.

One additional piece of information that has emerged from the national adult and youth surveys speaks not only to receptivity but also to accessibility. Canadians young and old are continuing to look to religious groups for rites of passage.

- Almost nine in ten teenagers indicate they anticipate turning to religious groups for future ceremonies relating to marriages and funerals, and seven in ten say the same in the case of births — a response very similar to levels in the mid-1980s.
- In the case of adults, the levels of anticipated weddings, birth-related ceremonies, and funerals are all up, compared to the mid-80s.

TABLE 2.8 **Desire for Rites of Passage in the Future**

"In the future, do you anticipate having any of the following carried out for you by a minister, priest, rabbi, or some other religious figure?"

% Responding "Yes"

	WEDDING CEREMONY	BIRTH-RELATED CEREMONY	FUNERAL
Teenagers			
1980s★	87	76	87
2000	89	70	86
Adults			
1980s	19	14	44
2000	24	20	57

★*1980s teen data computed from Project Teen Canada 87. "Don't knows" have been included with "no's"; otherwise the respective figures increase to 93%, 85%, and 93%.*

Sources: Bibby, Project Teen Canada 2000, Project Can 85, and Project Canada 2000.

As I have emphasized over the years, these Canadians' choices will not be random. The latent religious identification we have been documenting in this chapter will come to the surface during those times when couples are reflecting on what kind of wedding they want, what should "be done" now that the baby has arrived, or what kind of arrangements should be made for a relative's funeral. And it's not necessarily a case of just bowing to family pressures. Ministers frequently encounter people who, frankly, have little understanding of theology, yet have a sometimes vaguely articulated sense that "God needs to be brought in on the event."[22] With respect to accessibility, think what the desire for rites of passage means: religious groups will not have to go out and find these people; they will be taking the initiative in contacting groups. To put it mildly, such a position would be envied by any number of businesses in the corporate sector.

To sum up, the findings so far show that the "supply side" of religion, the country's churches, have not read the "demand side" very well. At least three major myths have functioned as serious obstacles to effective ministry. The fact that affiliates have refused to switch and haven't dropped out has been bewildering and frustrating to would-be religious competitors who have misread their market opportunity. But more seriously, because misinformed established groups have failed to understand their market advantage, significant numbers of affiliates who need ministry have not been reached by Canada's dominant religious groups.

There is a possibility, however, that the situation could change. As we are about to see, there are some surprising signs of new life in the churches.

CHAPTER THREE

The New Story about What's Happening in the Churches

Historically, proponents of religion have claimed that the gods have chosen to make contact with humans by using groups. Those groups, in the form of followers, churches, congregations, and the like, have seen themselves as the bearers of revelation and the custodians of tradition. They have maintained ongoing contact with the gods, gathered people together for things like worship, education, and social support, and seen themselves as entrusted to carry out some of the work of the gods on earth.

At first it may sound like an audacious claim. But sociologically speaking, the argument for the necessity of the group makes pretty good sense. Ideas and activities do not exist in a vacuum. Social psychologists, dating back to the likes of George Herbert Mead and Charles Cooley, have reminded us that ideas are socially instilled and socially sustained. Virtually all the ideas we hold can be traced back to social sources that include family, friends, authors, media, and, very frequently, religious groups. It can also be convincingly argued that the interdependence of life means we need other people in order to have our basic emotional and physical needs met, as well as to accomplish goals of almost any kind. Not surprisingly, then, religions have not existed without explicit group components. From a theist's perspective, it could all be part of a divine plan.

Let's take this "divine hypothesis" a few steps further. To the extent that the gods have made a conscious decision to relate to humans through groups, at some times and in some places things have gone reasonably well. However, the plan has not been without its pitfalls. Groups don't always do what they are supposed to do. In the case of revelation, people have sometimes bungled the messages. When it has come to translating ideas and ideals into action, there has been a lot of slippage. Still further, like all groups — be they families or companies, universities or service clubs — religious bodies have sometimes seen their energies dissipated and their reasons for being lost amidst such problems as conflict and mismanagement, corruption and incompetence.

In the course of such reception, behavioural, and organizational mishaps, the gods have run the risk of getting a bad name — or not being taken seriously at all. History is replete with hostile critiques of religious groups by people who maintain they have done nothing less than "lousy" jobs of representing the gods, sometimes performing so badly as to make critics question and even reject the gods altogether. Lynn Johnston, the Canadian writer of the popular comic strip *For Better or for Worse*, casually told Vancouver journalist Doug Todd in an interview a few years back that she would really like to meet Jesus in another life. Involved off and on in Mainline Protestantism over the years, Johnston said, "I'd like to get his view on this religion that's been set up in his name. I'd like to ask him if he ever would have believed it could have gone so far. I'd ask him if he likes being so deified, so loved, so worshipped. I hope he'd say 'No.'"[1] In a similar vein, former Anglican priest and well-known author Tom Harpur has written: "A lifetime of observance and participation in organized religion, together with prayer and much study, has convinced me that Jesus is not only the greatest person to have lived on planet Earth; he is also the most misunderstood."[2]

There seemingly is no end to the critiques of organized religion, with insiders typically calling for reform and outsiders frequently predicting its demise. The critics never seem to lack for material. In the midst of apparent numerical prosperity, Pierre Berton wrote *The Comfortable Pew* in 1965, criticizing the churches for lagging behind culture. With the numerical problems facing many Canadian groups in the post-60s, I myself penned *Fragmented Gods* in 1987, suggesting that churches had largely sold out to culture in providing fussy customers with religion à la carte. The news of financial and sexual scandals among religious leaders in the 1980s and 1990s resulted in books such as Michael Harris's *Unholy Orders* and the award-winning 1992 CBC documentary *The Boys of St. Vincent*. And today some six thousand individual lawsuits and several class-action suits over allegations of abuse at about a hundred residential schools are threatening to drain the resources of the Anglican, United, Presbyterian, and Roman Catholic churches.[3] Ottawa has proposed splitting the liability with the churches. The issue has again left several groups open to criticism.

Any number of additional issues seem to be fodder for the critics. For example, in a July 2001 editorial, the *National Post* went after the Anglican Church, with this claim: "Long before it became enmeshed in [the lawsuits], it was deeply in the red thanks to a combination of its own management techniques, which ape the worst practices of government bureaucracies, and its skewed notion of money and assets."[4] A declaration from Rome about a year before, known as "Dominus Jesus," asserted the primacy of the Roman Catholic faith among world religions. Not surprisingly, it was greeted by many people in Canada and around the world with surprise and dismay and was seen as a serious setback to cooperative and ecumenical efforts.[5]

Canadians, for their part, have not been inclined to express particularly high levels of confidence in religious leaders, especially in recent years. In 1985, 51% indicated that they had "a great deal" or "quite a bit" of confidence in leaders of religious groups. That figure plummeted to 36% just five years later in the wake of financial and sexual scandals in the United States and sexual abuse cases in Canada; it has remained around that level ever since. By way of comparison, some 45% of the populace currently indicate that they have a high level of confidence in *school leaders* and 40% endorse leadership in the *newspaper industry*. After slipping to just below 15% in 1990, confidence in *federal government* leadership has rebounded to about 25% in recent years.

However, from the standpoint of the gods — who, according to many who value faith, are trying to have an impact on Canadians and Canada through religious organizations — when all's said and done, the important question is this: How effective are those groups — apart from how they fare on the editorial circuit and in public opinion polls? The problems of Canada's churches in the last part of the 20th century would lead one to think that they have been a source of great disappointment and consternation to Those who have been watching them. Yet, theistically speaking, faced with the option of dumping the established churches and trying something new, the gods may be defying the critics by choosing to opt for some major renovation programs.

What's happening these days may or may not have the divine backdrop of restless gods, but developments suggest that the beginnings of a resurgence of organized religion may be taking place in Canada.

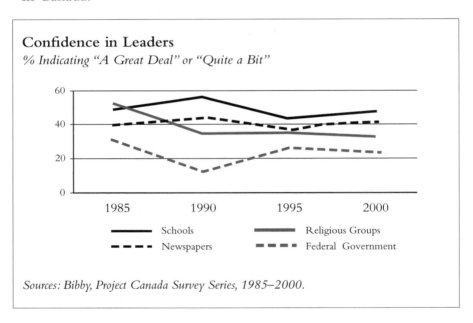

Confidence in Leaders
% Indicating "A Great Deal" or "Quite a Bit"

Sources: Bibby, Project Canada Survey Series, 1985–2000.

Secularization with Limits

There's no doubt about it. Rodney Stark is onto something. Proponents of secularization have not only been wrong in predicting the demise of religion, they also haven't even been particularly rational. In most other areas of life, we don't predict the demise of essential needs just because the social organizations are having delivery problems.

These realities are so obvious as to be embarrassingly prosaic. People keep on eating and wearing clothes, regardless of what happens to specific stores or chains. They continue to enjoy music as new means for listening to it evolve. They tolerate and, in some instances, embrace expanding versions of the family. They accept the necessity of government in the face of frequent disenchantment with politicians and political parties. You get the picture . . .

So why were the wise men of old, including such notables as Sigmund Freud and Karl Marx, so ready to write religion off, assuming that developments such as scientific advance and social-class-levelling revolutions would be the death knells of religion? The historical fact of the matter is that the problems of religious organizations have not signalled the end of religion. On the contrary, as some groups have faltered, others have moved in and prospered. For example, W.E. Mann tells us that when Alberta was being settled, evangelical groups seemed to resonate much better with the people than did Mainline Protestants.[6] With the passage of time, however, Mainliners appear to have made some short-lived headway in the same province at the expense of evangelicals.

Regardless, it seems, of location and time period, people have continued to have spiritual needs. Like those before them, they have had to deal with the realities of suffering and death; they have been perplexed by the question of life's meaning. Large numbers have continued to sense that they are experiencing the presence of God or some supernatural being. Consequently, people have no more abandoned religion because some religious groups have faltered than they have stopped shopping at department stores because Woodward's and Eaton's went into receivership. Religious needs have readily outlived the groups that meet them. For the record, such a growing realization is why I didn't abandon "the religion beat."

Stark has recently described secularization theory as being "as useless as a hotel elevator that only goes down."[7] After taking a secularization position himself in his well-known 1968 book *American Piety*, co-authored with Charles Glock, Stark began to take a very different view. In his subsequent work with William Bainbridge and Roger Finke (discussed above in Chapter 1), he postulated that secularization stimulates innovation.[8]

The essence of the argument is that people continue to have some needs that "only the gods can provide."[9] In market terms, when religious economies have been "deregulated," competition becomes intense. The demand for religion is constant; what varies is the supply side. In Stark and Finke's words, "Competition results in eager and efficient suppliers of religion, just as it does among suppliers of secular commodities, and with the same results: far higher levels of overall 'consumption.'"[10]

Typically, this means that faiths that have become too worldly are supplanted by more vigorous and less worldly ones — primarily in the form of breakaway sects and new religions ("cults") — that both demand much and provide much in the way of material, social, and religious benefits. The pattern tends to be this: the more mainline a denomination, the lower the perceived value of belonging to it, leading eventually to widespread defection. Finke and Stark viewed post-Vatican changes aimed at modernizing the Catholic Church, for example, as having the effect of lowering demands and lowering value, and inadvertently contributing to declining levels of participation.[11]

In *The Churching of America, 1776–1990*, Stark and Finke applied the thesis to American religious history. "Religious economies are like commercial economies," they wrote, "in that they consist of a market made up of a set of current and potential customers and a set of firms seeking to serve that market."[12] They argued that, historically, to the degree that denominations rejected traditional doctrines and ceased to make serious demands of their followers, they ceased to prosper and lost market share: "The churching of America was accomplished by aggressive churches committed to vivid otherworldliness."[13]

Putting their ideas to the test in the United States, Europe, and Canada, Stark and Bainbridge found a consistent positive relationship between cult activity and geographical areas where people claimed to have no religion. In Canada, they used census data and the yellow pages of telephone books to argue that cult centres around 1980 were most abundant in areas such as British Columbia, where conventional religion was weakest. They maintained that, in time, new religious movements would make inroads, recruiting people who had abandoned the established groups.[14]

Census data and our national survey results through the mid–1980s offered very little support for their thesis. Canadians who seemingly have deserted their own religious groups have shown little inclination to opt for the new religions, regardless of how plentiful or active the groups may be.[15] In a conversation I had with Stark at that time, his reaction was this: "I guess it's not showing up so far." Hardly abandoning his argument, he encouraged ongoing readings.

Lakehead University's David Nock took up the challenge in the late 1980s and claimed support for the relationship between the "No Religion" levels of provinces and the involvement of people in groups such as Jehovah's Witnesses, Spiritualists, and Baha'i.[16] Stark himself "returned" to Canada, this time with Finke. Looking at 1991 census data for 25 metropolitan areas, they concluded, "Where more people say they have no religion, new movements attract more members."[17]

Stark's creative and stimulating thesis holds much merit. However, it also has two limitations, one theoretical and one practical. First, his theory deals with only one facet of secularization. Stark and Finke are adamant that the new market model has replaced the earlier secularization model, maintaining "there is nothing illusory about a basic paradigm shift in the social scientific study of religion. A mountain of facts bars any return to the simple certitudes of the past."[18] They cite the words of Peter Berger from a 1997 interview, in their call for a burial of secularization theories: "I think what I and most other sociologists of religion wrote in the 1960s about secularization was a mistake. It wasn't a crazy theory. There was some evidence for it. But I think it's basically wrong. Most of the world today is certainly not secular."[19]

Berger may have raised the white flag too early. If secularization is conceptualized as having personal, organizational, and institutional components (as discussed in Chapter 1) then Stark's work clearly dispels the claim that *individual* religiosity dissipates. But, in arguing that churches over time tend to move away from sect-like characteristics, his theory actually co-opts, rather than dismisses, the reality of *organizational* secularization. And in no way does Stark's research negate secularization's *institutional* component, where secularization proponents maintain there is a reduction in the spheres over which religion has authority. For example, whatever he says about market vitality via sects and cults does nothing to change the reality that Quebec experienced a major transfer of authority from the Church to the State in the 1960s in the areas of education, social services, and health. In a slight modification of an old pop song, "One out of three ain't bad," but it hardly warrants the burial of a multidimensional secularization theory.

The second, practical shortcoming of Stark's theory is that it doesn't account for what has been happening in Canada.

Stark and Canada
The first of Stark's two Canadian studies claiming the existence of a relationship between the number of cult centres and the proportion of people with no religion succeeds in illustrating that personal secularization stimulates competition. However, that's all it does. To show that such a relationship exists is not the same as showing that cult centres are actually succeeding in recruiting people. It seems fairly obvious that new religious movements would set up operations in places where established religious bodies are weakest. Who wants to take on the Catholics in Quebec City or the evangelicals in Winkler, Manitoba? The important question is what kind of numerical headway the new religious businesses are making. I mentioned in *Fragmented Gods*, for example, that in 1857 a Catholic priest who turned to evangelical Protestantism started a work in Quebec City. After ten years, he had a church of 20 members![20] Second, to find along with Nock that a correlation exists between places where people have no religion and higher cult membership levels is only to observe that newer religions make their best headway in such settings. It doesn't provide evidence that the headway is particularly significant in magnitude.

- An examination of religious identification in Canada over time reveals two distinct patterns: the stable dominance of established Christian groups and the difficulty new entries have had in cracking that monopoly.
- Between 1891 and 1991 the Catholic share of the Canadian population grew from 42% to 47%. The Protestant share was 56% in 1891 and 52% in 1941, but it slipped to 36% by 1991.

The drop, however, was not because of significant proportional growth among other older and newer groups. It was rather because the percentage of "Religious Nones" grew from less than 1% through 1971 to 12% by 1991 — reflecting, in part, the methodological fact that "No Religion" had not been an acceptable option in census surveys prior to 1971.

TABLE 3.1 **Religious Composition of Canada, 1891–1991**

	1891	1941	1991
Catholic	42%	44%	47
Protestant	56	52	36
Other Faiths	2	3	5
No Religion	<1	<1	12

Source: Statistics Canada.

- The percentage-of-population growth of groups such as Jehovah's Witnesses and Latter-Day Saints between 1951 and 1991, during the period when Roman Catholic and Protestant bodies were experiencing declines, was minuscule.

TABLE 3.2 **Population %'s of Select Groups, 1951–1991**

	1951	1971	1991
Baha'i	★	★	.1
Jehovah's Witnesses	.2	.8	.6
Latter-Day Saints	.2	.3	.4
Unitarians	.1	.1	.1

★No census data available.

Source: Statistics Canada.

- Further, as of the early 1990s — at the point when the country's well-established groups had been in numerical decline for some two decades — the membership totals of would-be competitors were very, very small. For all the media hype about disenchanted and disaffiliated Canadians turning to a wide range of religious options, relatively few people were actually identifying with the available alternatives. In a nation of close to 30 million people, fewer than 6,000 individuals identified with any of such highly publicized religions as Wicca, Scientology, or New Age. To put things in perspective, the 1991 census found that Canadians describing their religion as New Age numbered 480 in B.C., 150 in Ontario, and 15 in Quebec.[21]

TABLE 3.3 **Sizes of Select Religious Groups, 1991**

Baha'i	14,730
Native Indian or Inuit	10,840
Wicca	5,530
New Thought★	4,605
Humanist★★	1,245
Scientology	1,220
New Age	1,200
Theosophy	765
Rastafarian	460
Satanism	335

★Includes Unity-Unity-Metaphysicals.   ★★Technically not a religious group.
Source: Statistics Canada.

These data suggest that what we have in Canada is an extremely tight "religious market" dominated by Catholic and Protestant "companies." New entries find the going extremely tough. In November of 2001, an evangelical organization held a conference in Montreal entitled "Igniting Our Passion for the Lost." It featured two prominent American evangelical speakers and included an emphasis on "renewed commitment to the harvest in Quebec."[22] Such organizations keep trying. They also find market gains slow in coming.

An important footnote needs to be added concerning the "No Religion" category. Claims that Religious Nones are booming need to be interpreted with caution. Apart from some important methodological issues — including the fact that the option was not a bona fide possibility until 1971 — it seems clear that being "nothing" is a temporary status for many people. Canadians who indicate that they have no religion tend to be somewhat younger than others. In fact, the 1991 census showed that just over 40% of Nones were under the age of 25 and some 80% were under 45. About one in three had not yet married, and almost half had not yet had children.

My research and that of others suggests that many of these people will turn to religious groups when they want "rites of passage" relating to marriage and the birth of children; in the process, considerable numbers will "re-acquire" the Catholic and Protestant identities of their parents.[23] In fact, since at least the mid-80s, when the Canadian census began uncovering Nones, about 20% have said they anticipate turning to religious groups for weddings, 15% for birth-related ceremonies, and 35% for funerals. In addition, as we will see shortly, marriages involving Nones and others tend to result in children more frequently being raised "something" than the reverse — where children of "somethings" are raised "nothing." In succinct terms, the people residing in the "Religious None" category often have short stays.

These findings for Canada provide little indication that the preferred suppliers are changing. Instead, the established Roman Catholic and Protestant churches continue to monopolize the religion market. In part, this ongoing monopoly may reflect "the rules" of the country's religious market.

As I have suggested in the past, especially in *Mosaic Madness*, Canadian groups operate in a cultural milieu where pluralism is highly valued to the point of legal enshrinement. Multicultural and Charter of Rights legislation has fostered a mood of suspicion and hostility toward those who claim their views are "the right" ones.[24] We don't look favourably on groups that aggressively want to "convert" other people to their way of thinking, particularly vulnerable people such as children, immigrants, and the elderly. Long-time Toronto Argonaut "Pinball" Clemons, for example, has astutely observed that "witnessing is more characteristic of American athletes than Canadian." The American-born Clemons says that, on balance, "Canadians are more noncommittal [and] more all-embracing of cultural differences and beliefs."[25] One leader even told me a few years back that he felt the day could come when evangelism would be seen as a violation of the Charter of Rights and Freedoms. The pluralistic ideal seems to translate into Canadian groups not so much competing for truth as coexisting to service the needs of their affiliates. Even religious lobbies have to be moderate. As journalist Haroon Siddiqui reminds us, "There has been no Canadian equivalent of Pat Robertson's Christian Coalition and Jerry Falwell's Moral Majority . . . The contemporary multi-faith environment demands public policies that must balance conflicting rights."[26]

Such a situation seems very different from that of the United States, for example, where a deep-seated sense of pursuing "the truth and the best" contributes to a highly open and competitive religion market, including the "witnessing" of which Clemons speaks. That market is, and has always been, a lively one, characterized by aggressive, ongoing truth claims — a style quite foreign and frankly rather repugnant to pluralistically minded Canadians. In contrast to Canada, religion in the U.S. is marketed with the flair and aggressiveness of a "hot" commercial commodity. Canadian author Pierre Berton, speaking of life in general, once wrote that, compared to Americans, "we are not good salesmen and we are not good showmen."[27]

The search for truth produces a lively market. Pluralism, on the other hand, insists on respect for diversity, and in the process both kills the ability to make market inroads and dulls the inclination to try to do so. Those of us who are attempting to understand what is happening to religious groups in such an environment would be wise to keep an eye out for possible new sects and cults that manage to defy the odds and make significant inroads. But we would be even wiser to give at least as much attention to watching the well-established religious bodies that would be expected to persist. This brings us back to Rodney Stark.

Revitalization Versus Replacement

In a paper he recently presented, Stark's associate Roger Finke offered the reminder that although "upstart sectarian groups" have been "evident throughout American history," it is "equally clear that the vast majority of sectarian groups show little potential for growth." He notes that Stark and Bainbridge's examination of 417 American-born sects two decades ago revealed that 32% had actually "reached their high-water mark on the day they began"![28] If new groups have such difficulty making inroads, there is another fairly obvious possibility that is compatible with Stark and his colleagues' argument, yet perhaps insufficiently emphasized: *secularization may not only stimulate the birth of new groups but also lead to the rejuvenation of older ones.* Throughout his work, Stark stresses that religious economies will be stimulated by religious pluralism resulting from deregulation. But having documented the decline of established organizations, he gives his primary attention to newly emerging sects and cults. He doesn't glance back much to see what kind of impact greater competition is having on the establishment.

However, in the last chapter of Stark's third major work on the topic, *Acts of Faith*, he and Roger Finke acknowledge and explore the possibility that established religious bodies may experience rejuvenation. Here they speak of the possibility of the sect-to-Church cycle reversing itself. They comment that the literature provides scarcely a hint of such a possibility — despite, as they note, something as obvious as the rise of the Counter-Reformation in the 17th century. Consistent with their argument that strictness and tension with culture are associated with greater religious rewards and church growth, they see a key component of such possible resurgence to be new, highly committed clergy, who in turn call their congregations to commitment and emphasize traditional religious content. Only people like this, they maintain, will be motivated to be involved in a profession where secular rewards are low. Growth, they theorize, will take place initially at the congregational level, and they provide preliminary data on a number of U.S. groups that are consistent with their argument.[29] Some early exploratory research that Finke has carried out with Jennifer McKinney has suggested that "the organizational decline and theological pluralism of mainline denominations has provided both the impetus and opportunity for evangelical renewal movements to arise." These "ERMs seek to restore previous teachings, renew local churches, and sway national policies. Ironically, the very theological pluralism that ERMs seek to eliminate, has provided an opportunity for their entry and a barrier for their expulsion."[30]

One doesn't need to do a literature review on major corporations and other organizations in our society to realize that many of them have been around a very long time. They have also understood that in order to survive and thrive, they have to be in an ongoing mode of change. The primary players who occupy the Canadian religious scene are no exception.

Denominations such as Anglicans, the United Church, Presbyterians, and Lutherans, along with the Roman Catholics in Quebec and elsewhere, are no fly-by-night operations. They have long histories and recuperative powers. They don't just roll over and die. Many are part of durable multinational corporations with headquarters in places like Rome and Canterbury. Such well-established religious groups don't readily perish. They retreat, retrench, revamp, and resurface.[31] Highly respected Princeton sociologist Robert Wuthnow makes a similar observation regarding U.S. groups: "Religious organizations have had the resources with which to respond to the challenges set before them," he writes. "Rather than simply being eroded, American religion has been able to play its cards with the advantage of a tremendously strong hand."[32] There may be limited literature on denominations becoming more conservative. But there is substantial precedent for religious organizations changing over time.

What's more, they have established name-brand credibility over the years and, unlike typical businesses, have thousands and thousands of people who are loyal to the point of being extremely reluctant to turn elsewhere. Such "affiliates" have relational ties to their groups through family members and friends that usually go back decades and even centuries. They typically have participated in rites of passage associated with some of the more memorable occasions in their lives — births, marriages, and deaths.

Observers, including myself, frequently use marketing language in likening religious followers to customers and make references along the lines of people being into "religion à la carte," being fussy customers, and sometimes "free-riding."[33] But it is important to keep in mind that many, if not most, people who identify with religious groups are customers with a difference. They receive psychological and emotional benefits from continuing to see themselves as being part of the Catholic or Protestant or Jewish tradition of their parents and grandparents. They may derive some similar benefits of following in parental footsteps by continuing to drive a Ford or to shop at The Bay or to take the kids to the Dairy Queen. But a long line of defunct businesses, including a couple of indigenous department store chains mentioned earlier, suggests that Canadians suspend their sentiments fairly easily when it means they can get more bang for their buck. They don't as readily say goodbye to the Roman Catholic Church and embrace Scientology, or church-shop at a synagogue or mosque when they are not happy with the preaching or music at a Baptist service. In the dialect of Stark's rational choice framework, most religious affiliates reap significant rewards for staying and incur significant costs for switching.

Steve Bruce, a sociologist at the University of Aberdeen, makes a similar point in assessing the situation in Scotland. He offers the reminder that treating religion as if it were a product can ignore too much of what we know about religion. "For most people," he writes, "religion is not a matter of choice in which opportunities to maximize or economize can be sought. Most people are born into a particular religion and so thoroughly socialized in it that alternatives are not economizing opportunities, but implausible heresies." Bruce notes that while a Ford tractor dealer with declining sales can switch to a John Deere dealership, a Presbyterian in Scotland whose faith group is declining in popularity can debate what might be done, but he hardly announces a return to Rome.[34]

Interpretations of Religion and Change

1. Secularization	Decline
	Institutional
	Organizational
	Individual
2. Secularization	Innovation
	Sects
	Cults
3. Secularization	Innovation
	Sects
	Cults
	Churches
	Reformulate
	Re-emerge

Consequently, in predicting the future of Canada's religious groups, it seems to make good sense to assume that since most of the well-established organizations are going to persist, along with large numbers of their affiliates, it will only be a matter of time before they experience rejuvenation.

It's a simple illustration, but one that perhaps helps clarify the point. Some readers are old enough to remember the old A & W drive-ins. They were popular across North America in the 50s and 60s, complete with carhops who placed trays of root beer and hamburgers and fries on rolled-down car windows. In the 1970s and 1980s, the drive-ins fell out of favour and into disrepair. Many of the old sites were sold and converted into any number of new business outlets, from restaurants to used car lots. Passers-by could easily spot their physical outlines, which served as a reminder of the life that used to be in the alleged "Happy Days" of the mid-20th century. Then, lo and behold, with the infusion of substantial amounts of new investment dollars, the brand name was brought back to life in the 90s, complete with modern new outlets.

It didn't happen by accident. The company passed through a series of new ownerships, and in the 1970s, after being purchased by the AMK Corporation, underwent a number of changes aimed at helping the enterprise become a full-fledged restaurant and food-service organization. It adopted a new trademark and revised its agreement with its franchise owners. The efforts of a number of new subsidiaries resulted in A & W root beer hitting grocery shelves, in the development of new lines such as sugar-free root beer, in the introduction of the Great Food Restaurant, and in the intensification of marketing efforts — including the 1974 creation of the Great Root Bear mascot. In 1982 the company again changed ownership, and a new era of reorganization and planning began. Franchising efforts were halted while a new prototype was being developed that would eventually see targeted expansion into high-pedestrian areas such as food courts, shopping centres, office buildings, and other "alternative site markets." Then, in 1994, A & W was sold again, so it could make the changes needed to move the corporation "into a new era of growth and prosperity." Today, it is moving forward by returning to its "Mom and Pop" roots.[35]

Fortunes are obviously being made by large numbers of individuals and large corporations who buy up promising old businesses and failing businesses and turn them around. One such highly publicized entrepreneur is Chicago-based Michael Heisley, who became well known to Canadian sports fans when he bought the Vancouver Grizzlies of the NBA in 2000 and temporarily endeared himself to the locals by singing the Canadian national anthem at the team's first home game. He is said to have made billions by buying up good but troubled companies and making them into successful operations. Unfortunately for Vancouverites, Heisley felt he couldn't turn the team around in that location, and after one season of ownership, moved the franchise to Memphis in 2001, where he presumably will continue his pattern of transforming a declining business into a profitable one. But this is more than just a sports story.

If major companies without the loyal customer advantage of large, well-established religious groups can frequently turn themselves around and be turned around, then it would be foolish to bet against the potential for revitalization among long-standing religious groups in Canada or elsewhere. Does anyone really believe that the problems of the Roman Catholic Church in Quebec mean it is about to disappear? For all their highly publicized problems, who really thinks either the Anglican or United churches in Canada will cease to have a prominent place on the Canadian religious landscape? If the Catholics in Quebec need help in resolving their problems, they have the resources of the Catholic Church worldwide. The same can be said for Anglicans, while the United Church remains a pretty powerful religious corporation, with close to four thousand franchises in Canada, considerable history, and millions of affiliates who continue to have psychological and emotional ties with the denomination.

Simply put, well-established religious groups can be expected to go down only so far before they bottom out. They may be at a low point for a while. But as new people with new ideas take on positions of influence, and as human and financial resources are put in place, these companies can be expected to stir and, to varying degrees, begin to rise again.

It's not a question of if; it's a question of when.

This revitalization argument does not assume that all well-established religious groups are going to show new signs of life at the same time or at the same pace. On the contrary, a necessary condition will be the appearance of leaders and laity who see the need for change, are able to envision what is needed to bring about change, and are capable of operationalizing and implementing ideas. We would expect to see movements arising within such resurgent bodies, perhaps stimulated by activities outside the groups. In the U.S., for example, McKinney and Finke maintain that signs of new life among Mainline denominations are frequently associated with the involvement of young clergy in evangelical organizations before and after seminary. Such associations have provided them with ideas and resources; yet these young leaders are committed to renewal from within and stress the unique identity and practices of Mainline traditions.[36]

Similarly, a wide array of para-church organizations and programs — including the Willow Creek Association, World Vision, Campus Crusade, InterVarsity, and Alpha Ministries — could potentially have a noteworthy impact on Canada's established groups. Internal movements such as the Anglican Essentials Movement, the United Church's Community of Concern, and the Roman Catholic charismatic movement may prove to be mechanisms for revitalization, drawing to varying degrees on the external resources at their disposal.[37]

At such time as organizational resurgence begins to occur, it should be evident in the numbers of people the resurgent groups are attracting. An examination of attendance trends indicates that such a turnaround may in fact be starting to take place in Canada.

Circulation-Plus among Conservatives

Dating back to the first Canadian census in 1871, the proportion of Canadians who have been identifying with Conservative Protestants has remained steady at about 8%. Research shows three important features about the Conservative Protestant numerical pool.

- First, evangelical groups have had to work extremely hard just to stay where they are. Smaller religious groups typically lose far more people to larger groups than they gain through intermarriage. The success of Conservative Protestants in remaining at about 8% of the population suggests that they have exhibited considerable vitality.[38] Further, with growth in the national population, holding at 8% translates into notable numerical growth — about 2.5 million people today, compared to 1.1 million in 1950 and 277,000 in 1867.

- Second, as mentioned in the previous chapter, their success in sustaining numbers is due primarily to their ability to retain their children, as well as their capacity to hold on to their geographically mobile members — two critically important sources of addition and attrition. Contrary to widespread belief, additions through evangelistic outreach, by comparison, have been relatively small. The currently popular Alpha courses, for example, have a primary goal of evangelism. Yet, writes Marianne Meed Ward in a recent issue of *Faith Today*, "most of the people who attend are already Christians."[39] Gains through people switching in from other groups, however, have exceeded the losses of evangelicals switching out to such groups.

- Third, people who identify with Conservative Protestant groups tend to be far more likely than other Canadians to be actively involved in their churches. Their levels of attendance have exceeded those of Mainline Protestants since at least the 1950s, as well as those of Roman Catholics since about the mid-80s. Currently, some six in ten people identifying with Conservative groups claim to be attending services almost every week or more, up from five in ten in 1990.

TABLE 3.4 **Weekly Service Attenders in Canada, 1957–2000**

	1957	1975	1990	2000
NATIONALLY	53%	31%	24%	21%
Protestant	38	27	22	25
Conservative	51	41	49	58
Mainline	35	23	14	15
Roman Catholic	83	45	33	26
Outside Quebec	75	48	37	32
Quebec	88	42	28	20

Sources: 1957: March Gallup poll; 1975, 1990, 2000: Bibby, Project Canada surveys.

The net result of these vitality, retention, switching, and participation characteristics has been numerical growth at congregational levels. In the *Project Canada 2000* national survey, six in ten Conservative Protestants who attend services at least once a month reported their churches are growing — far higher levels than those of any other religious grouping. To look at evangelical Protestants in Canada is to see considerable energy, life, and growth.

Remnant Resilience in the Mainline

From the 1960s through about 1990, Canada's four Mainline Protestant denominations seemed to be in a numerical freefall. For starters, census data show that *the proportion of Canadians identifying with each group shrank* — the United Church from 20% to 11%, the Anglicans from 13% to 8%, and the Presbyterians and Lutherans from about 4% to 2% each. Together, this meant that the Mainline Protestant "religious family" that included 41% of the Canadian population in 1961 had dropped to 23% by 1991.

- Thanks to national population growth, the actual decline in people identifying with the four groups was much less dramatic, slipping from about 7.5 million to 6.5 million over the 30-year period. It is worth noting, by way of comparison, that over the same three decades, the Conservative Protestant religious family increased in size from some 1.5 million to just over 2 million people.
- While the size of the Mainline affiliate pool consequently remained relatively large through 1990, *weekly attendance dropped significantly* in the post-1950s. After standing at 35% in the mid-1950s, the proportion of weekly churchgoers fell to just under 25% in 1975, and to 15% by 1990. In real numbers, this meant that some 2.6 million people who identified with Mainline groups were attending services "almost every week" or more in 1960, compared to only about 980,000 in 1990 — approximately the same figure reached that year by Conservatives.

This old story about Canada's Mainline Protestants is the one that many people are continuing to tell. And with the residential school lawsuits exacerbating their resource problems — to put it mildly — few observers have seen much hope for renewed vitality within the country's Mainline denominations.

However, during the 1990s, an important development occurred: the decline in the proportion of Mainliners attending services weekly stopped, remaining steady at around 15%. There are fewer people in the Mainline population pool than in the past, but those who are still there are showing signs of life. For the first time in three decades, the proportion of the "Mainline remnant" who are active in these four Protestant groups remained fairly constant between 1990 and 2000.

This is an extremely important development — so important that it needs to be checked using larger sample sizes than the 1,500 cases available in our *Project Canada* surveys.

TABLE 3.5 **A Closer Look at Weekly Attendance, 1990–2000, Statistics Canada Data**

	1990	2000
NATIONALLY	24%	19%
Protestant	24	28
Conservative	50	48
Baptist	38	38
Other	55	51
Mainline	16	18
Anglican	14	18
Lutheran	18	21
Presbyterian	24	25
United	15	14
Roman Catholic	31	23
Outside Quebec	35	29
Quebec	26	14
Other Faiths	26	27
Jewish	12	8
Other	33	36

Sources: 1990: General Social Survey; 2000: Survey of Giving, Volunteering, and Participating, analysis courtesy of Frank Jones.

- An examination of attendance patterns for 1990 and 2000 — using two Statistics Canada surveys with samples some ten times larger than ours — corroborates what we have found.
- In addition, those data sets, large enough to allow us to examine variations among the four Mainline Protestant denominations reveal that *Anglicans* and *Lutherans* have experienced increases in the proportion of their people who attend weekly, while the proportion of *Presbyterians* and *United Church* members and adherents who are actively involved has remained steady since 1990.

This finding that regular weekly attendance has remained stable overall means that, in contrast to the stereotype of most Mainline congregations declining, there is a measure of vitality and numerical growth in many settings. The fact that roughly 15% of the people identifying with these four denominations have continued to be actively involved means that younger adults have been taking the place of older adults in sufficient numbers to at least sustain their collective 15% level. Findings from the adult and youth surveys confirm that this is happening:

- In 1990, 9% of Mainline adults between the ages of 18 and 34 said they were attending weekly; that figure increased to 13% by 2000.
- Increases took place for adults under 35 in the Anglican and United Church instances. Levels remained steady for Lutherans, while the weekly attendance levels for Presbyterian young adults fell to the levels of the other three groups, after being higher than the others in 1990.
- Overall, the four Mainline Protestant denominations continue to be top-heavy with older people, yet have known an increase in adults under the age of 35.

There is also some very important news in this context about young people: the *Project Teen Canada* national surveys have found that the patterns of lower levels of identification and stable levels of attendance seen among adults have also been taking place among teenagers:

TABLE 3.6 **Weekly Attendance by Age, 1990–2000, Statistics Canada Data**

	1990			2000		
	18–34	35–54	55+	18–34	35–54	55+
NATIONALLY	15%	24%	39%	12%	16%	30%
Protestant	20	24	29	26	22	34
Conservative	46	52	53	45	44	50
Baptist	35	37	44	43	37	39
Other	52	58	58	45	47	55
Mainline	9	15	23	13	11	28
Anglican	8	14	20	13	14	26
Lutheran	14	15	24	15	16	25★
Presbyterian	21	24	28	12	14	36
United	8	14	23	12	8	23
Roman Catholic	16	30	58	12	20	38
Outside Quebec	20	39	55	18	30	41
Quebec	7	22	59	5	9	35
Other Faiths	26	26	24	26	29	23

★*Unstable; estimated using Project Canada data.*

Sources: 1990: General Social Survey; 2000: Survey of Giving, Volunteering, and Participating, analysis courtesy of Frank Jones..

- Between 1984 and 1992, the proportion of 15-to-19-year-olds who identified with Mainliners dropped from 22% to 11%, and currently stands at only 8%.
- However, among "the teenage remnant" who continue to identify themselves as Mainliners, weekly attendance rose to 23% in 2000, up from 16% in 1992 and 17% in 1984.

In light of these findings, the reports "from the pews" about what is happening in Mainline congregations is particularly interesting to examine. The results are consistent with the attendance trends: one in three people who are involved in Mainline churches say their congregations have been growing in recent years, one in three that they have stayed about the same, and the remaining one in three that they have been declining in size. These are not exactly the unified cries of people on a boat that is sinking.

There's no question that the sizes of the affiliation pools of the four Mainline denominations have been declining. Participation also continues to be highest among the older members in this religious family. Still, these findings point to considerable life among the remnants, including younger people. To paraphrase Mark Twain, rumours of the death of Mainline Protestantism in Canada appear to have been greatly exaggerated.

By way of a belated footnote, I owe United Church theologian Doug Hall an apology. For years, the highly respected professor who taught at McGill maintained that the denomination was getting down to what he referred to as "a significant remnant."[40] I, in conversation and in print,[41] frequently responded cynically, suggesting that what the United Church might be looking at was simply "all that [was] left," rather than a core that was particularly significant. I was wrong. The core, with the help of younger and committed additions, is showing signs of contributing to a measure of denominational resurgence.

Solid Stability and Latent Life among Catholics

Roman Catholicism in Quebec and outside Quebec has been buoyed up over the years by tremendous growth in its affiliate pools through birth and immigration. As a proportion of the Canadian population, Roman Catholics have succeeded in holding their own over time. Census data show they made up 43% of the population in 1871, 42% in 1941, and about 45% in 2001. With growth in the national population, such proportional stability has meant that Catholics have grown from 1.5 million in 1871 to 4.8 million in 1941 to around 14 million today, with just under half — about six million — living in Quebec.

In addition, despite the dramatic drop in weekly attendance among Roman Catholics since the 1960s, the number of active participants has remained remarkably stable, at least outside Quebec. Although attendance has declined beyond Quebec's borders from 75% in the 1950s to a current level of 32%, population growth has meant that those figures have translated into about 3 million active churchgoers in the mid-50s, as well as about 2.5 million weekly attenders today.

TABLE 3.7 **Congregational and Parish Numerical Trends**

"If you attend religious services once a month or more, in recent years, has your group been . . ."

	GROWING	STAYING THE SAME	DECLINING	TOTALS
NATIONALLY	36%	32%	32%	100%
Protestants	47	31	22	100
Conservative	59	28	13	100
Mainline	32	36	32	100
Roman Catholics	24	33	43	100
Outside Quebec	33	35	32	100
Quebec	11	32	57	100

Source: Bibby, Project Canada 2000.

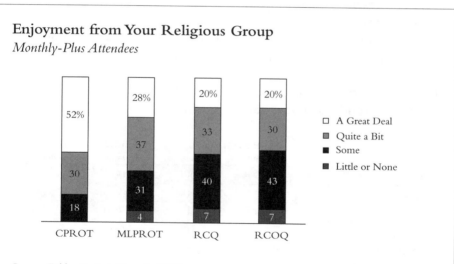

Enjoyment from Your Religious Group
Monthly-Plus Attendees

Source: Bibby, Project Canada 2000.

Clearly, some local congregations are flourishing, some are holding their own, and others are decreasing in size. Corroborating such realities, almost equal proportions of Roman Catholics outside Quebec who are involved in their parishes reported in the *Project Canada 2000* survey that their churches have been growing, staying about the same, or declining in size in recent years — almost identical proportions, incidentally, to those reported by Mainline Protestants. In short, outside Quebec, the size of the active Catholic core has continued to be significant, while the number of marginal and inactive Catholics has grown substantially.

Quebec has presented a different story. The weekly attendance drop from 88% in the mid-1950s to 20% today has represented a "people drop" from about 3.6 million to 1.2 million — a 67% loss in 50 years. However, there are some signs that the sleeping Roman Catholic giant in Quebec is beginning to stir:

- While the attendance attrition was dramatic between the 1950s and 1970s, coinciding with the Quiet Revolution and Vatican II, it has slowed down significantly, with the absolute numbers involved obviously bolstered by increases in Quebec's population. As a result, the 28% weekly attendance level of 1990 translated into about 1.6 million Catholics; today's 20%, as noted, represents about 1.2 million people.

TABLE 3.8 **Approximate Affiliate Pools and Weekly Attendees, Mid-1950s and 2000**

In 1,000s

	AFFILIATE POOL		WEEKLY ATTENDEES	
	MID-50S	**2000**	**MID-50S**	**2000**
NATIONALLY	18,000	25,000	10,000	6,300
Protestants	9,000	9,000	3,300	2,500
Conservative	1,500	2,500	700	1,500
Mainline	7,500	6,500	2,600	1,000
Roman Catholics	8,000	14,000	6,600	3,700
Outside Quebec	4,000	8,000	3,000	2,500
Quebec	4,000	6,000	3,600	1,200
Other Faiths	350	1,200	120	85

Sources: Affiliates: Statistics Canada census data. Attendance: 1957 = March Gallup poll; 2000 = Bibby, Project Canada 2000.

- Currently, about 6 million Quebeckers see themselves as Roman Catholics, compared to only 4 million in the 1950s.

What this means is that the Catholic Church in Quebec doesn't lack for Catholics; it lacks for involved Catholics.

• Consistent with dominant perception, Quebec Catholics who are involved in their parishes are inclined to see the number of their active members shrinking. Some six in ten report that their local churches have been declining in numbers in recent years. But there is a possible upside to this otherwise gloomy parishioner report, suggesting signs of vitality in some Quebec parishes. Three in ten inform-ants tell us that the numbers in their parishes have stayed about the same in recent years, while one in ten maintain their groups have actually been growing.

I am not trying to make a case for new life if the new life is not there. At minimum, these data indicate that the resurgence of the Roman Catholic Church in Quebec is lagging far behind that of both Conservative and Mainline Protestants. And as I said earlier, to postulate organizational revitalization is not to suggest that timelines will be identical for all well-established religious groups. In Quebec, the leadership and resources required may simply not yet be in place on the scale needed for the Church's re-emergence to be more widespread and visible.

TABLE 3.9 **Attendance: Canada's Major Religious Families, 2000**

	WEEKLY	MONTHLY	YEARLY	NEVER	TOTALS
NATIONALLY	20%	9%	49%	22%	100%
Conservative Protestants	58	7	27	8	100
Mainline Protestants	15	12	54	19	100
RCs outside Quebec	32	10	41	17	100
RCs in Quebec	20	8	66	6	100
Other Faiths	7	12	54	27	100
No Religion	<1	<1	37	63	100

Source: Bibby, Project Canada 2000.

What *is* clear from the latest adult and youth surveys is that Quebeckers still regard themselves as Catholics and are adamant about the fact that they have no interest in switching to another religious tradition. A nation-leading 94% maintain they attend religious services at least on occasion. Further, no fewer than five in ten of the province's Catholic adults and four in ten teenagers say that they are open to greater involvement if they find it to be worthwhile.

Quebec continues to be a Catholic stronghold. What remains to be seen is how long it will take the Roman Catholic Church to respond to the blatant "market advantage" it enjoys.

Vitality among Other Faith Groups

Other religious groups, including Muslims, Buddhists, Hindus, and Sikhs, have experienced numerical growth in the post–1960s, primarily as a result of accelerated immigration from Asia and the Middle East. These Other Faith groups, when combined with Jews and people with ties to Eastern Orthodoxy, have a pool of affiliates that has jumped in size from under 500,000 in the mid-50s to about two million as of 2000. New arrivals have typically displayed high levels of religious commitment and enthusiasm, and these most recent cohorts are no exception. They have been socially and politically active and have raised the profile of major world religions in this country while expanding Canada's religious diversity.

As we saw earlier, the hurdle for new religious groups, past and present, lies in being able to sustain and increase numbers in a Canadian religious marketplace where Catholic and Protestant groups have held a virtual monopoly. Over time, smaller religious groups have encountered considerable difficulty retaining their offspring, many of whom "defect" to Catholicism and Protestantism through acculturation and assimilation. For example, 6% of current teens between the

TABLE 3.10 **Identification of Children and Identification of Mothers and Fathers**

RELIGION OF CHILDREN

RELIGION OF: MOTHER	FATHER	NO. OF COUPLES	CATHOLIC	PROTESTANT	JEWISH	OTHER FAITHS	NO RELIGION
Catholic	Protestant	259,130	70%	11%	★	★	9%
Protestant	Catholic	254,105	42	44	★	★	14
Catholic	Jewish	3,070	38	2	25	★	35
Jewish	Catholic	2,055	29	1	45	★	25
Protestant	Jewish	3,555	2	38	26	★	34
Jewish	Protestant	2,520	1	23	52	★	24
Catholic	Other Faiths	7,600	58	1	★	21	20
Other Faiths	Catholic	3,195	58	4	★	12	26
Protestant	Other Faiths	5,735	1	45	★	26	28
Other Faiths	Protestant	3,220	2	43	★	26	29
Other Faiths	No Religion	4,415	3	5	★	22	70

*Less than 1%.

Source: Adapted from Bibby, 2000. Data source: Statistics Canada, 1991 Census.

ages of 15 and 19 who have a Buddhist, Hindu, Muslim, or Sikh parent already see themselves as Protestants or Catholics; conversely, less than 1% of teens with a Catholic or Protestant parent identify with any of those four Other Faith traditions. There is also little doubt that many young people who come from Other Faith homes will marry people outside their traditions. And Statistics Canada data through 1991 suggest that when they do, they more often than not will raise their children in the tradition of their Catholic or Protestant — or even their No Religion — partner.[42] That's the primary reason that faiths other than Christianity have had difficulty making significant proportional gains in Canada over time.

Newer groups also join older established groups in facing the secularizing effects of Canadian culture. They, too, face the problem of trying to sustain the interest, enthusiasm, and commitment of immigrant members and their first-generation offspring. So it is that 15% of current teens who have a parent who subscribes to Buddhism, Hinduism, Islam, or Sikhism say they have no religious preference — almost identical to the 14% level for teens with a Catholic or Protestant parent. Further reflecting the impact of a secular Canadian culture, findings show that levels of participation are not necessarily high among those who don't defect to Christianity. In the mid-1950s, some 35% of those individuals identifying with faiths other than Christianity maintained that they were attending religious services nearly every week. That figure dropped to 12% by 1990 and currently stands at 7%. If it is adjusted to "at least once a month" to better reflect the attendance expectations of some of these groups, the level rises to only 19% — still appreciably below the figures for the Catholic and Protestant religious families.

Despite their problems with sustaining growth, major global religions have experienced new visibility and vitality in Canada in the post-1960s. The immigrants who have helped bolster previously low numbers have brought with them new energy and new resources that have intensified religious diversity in Canada. In marketing language, the immigrants have added significant human and financial capital to Other Faith groups. As these "companies" have been strengthened, they have gained a heightened profile and had greater input into religious life and Canadian life. To the extent that some of the immigrants or their children have opted for Protestantism or Catholicism, they have added further cultural diversity to those groups.

In sum, "the rise" of Other Faiths in the post–1960s and their influence on Canadian life and the Canadian religious scene has been an important part of the new story about what's been happening to organized religion in Canada. Their vitality can be seen in our survey findings on youth — surveys that provide us with sample sizes three times that of usual adult surveys, giving us a rather unique look at the role religious groups, both newer and older, play in the lives of Canada's young people.

TABLE 3.11 **Religious Identification of Canadians, 1871–2000**

	1871	1901	1931	1961	1991	2000
Roman Catholic	42%	42%	41%	47%	46%	45%
Protestant	56	56	54	49	36	32
Eastern Orthodox	<1	<1	1	1	2	1
Jewish	<1	<1	1	1	1	1
Other Faiths	2	2	2	1	3	4
No Religion	<1	<1	<1	<1	12	20

Source: Statistics Canada; 2000 estimated.

The Emerging Generation

In 1984, 1992, and 2000, we carried out national surveys of teenagers, 15 to 19, who are still in high school and CGEP equivalents in Quebec. Each of these three *Project Teen Canada* surveys made use of highly representative samples of some 3,600 young people across the country. The results have been published in three fairly widely read books: *The Emerging Generation* (1985), *Teen Trends* (1992), and *Canada's Teens* (2001), the first two co-authored with Donald Posterski. The surveys reveal some very important trends that have been taking place since 1984.

The religious identification landscape among Canadian teenagers has been changing — significantly. There has been a large decline in the proportion of teens who identify with *Catholicism* and *Protestantism*.

- The *Catholic* drop, however, took place primarily between 1984 and 1992; there was only a slight decline in "ID" levels during the 1990s. In both Quebec and the rest of Canada, Catholic levels have just about kept up with the growth in the general youth population.

- Noteworthy increases have occurred in the proportion of teens who identify with *Other Faiths* or say they have *no religious preference*.
- On the Protestant side, the *United and Anglican churches* have been particularly hard hit: only 3% of teens currently identify with each of those denominations — a level now matched, for example, by young people who say they are Muslim. Yet, as with Catholics, proportional decreases in the United and Anglican teenage affiliate pools were fairly small in the 1990s.
- Since the 1980s, there has been a growing tendency for teenagers to identify with a greater range of religious groups, both Protestant and otherwise. This finding is consistent with

TABLE 3.12 **Religious Identification of Teens, 1984–2000**

	1984	1992	2000
Roman Catholic	51%	41%	39%
Outside Quebec	40	33	31
Quebec★	11	8	8
Protestant	35	28	22
United	10	4	3
Anglican	8	5	3
Baptist	3	2	2
Lutheran	2	1	1
Pentecostal	2	1	1
Presbyterian	2	1	1
Other/Unspecified	8	13	11
Other Faiths	3	10	14
Muslim	<1	1	3
Jewish	1	1	2
Buddhist	<1	1	2
Other/Unspecified	2	7★	7★
No Religion	12	21	25

★*Includes Hindu, Native, and Sikh, 1% each.*

Source: Bibby, Project Teen Canada survey series.

the tendency of younger people to be far more diverse in their consumption habits well beyond religion.

It is important to note that some of the smaller Protestant groups with which teens identify are evangelical in nature, resulting in a situation where — for the first time in Canadian history — the proportion of Protestant teenagers who identify with Conservative Protestant groups is greater than the proportion who identify with the four Mainline Protestant denominations.

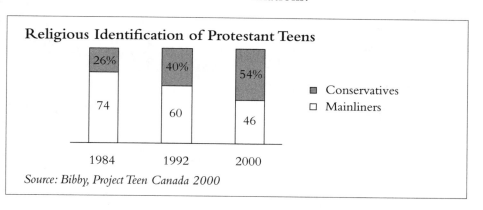

Religious Identification of Protestant Teens

■ Conservatives
□ Mainliners

Source: Bibby, Project Teen Canada 2000

Apart from group identification, there has also been an increase in service attendance among teenagers over the last decade. The current national level of 22% represents a return to the level of the early 1980s, following a slight dip in the early 1990s. As with adults, this means that although fewer young people than before are identifying with religious groups, those who do identify tend to be more involved.

- The *Protestant* attendance figures are up significantly from 1984 and 1992, not only because of a large jump in involvement among Conservatives, but also because of an increase among Mainliners.
- The attendance level for *Catholics outside Quebec* has increased slightly since the early 90s; *in Quebec*, however, attendance has continued to fall, with just 7% of teens now claiming to be weekly churchgoers.

TABLE 3.13 **Service Attendance of Teens by Group, 1984–2000**

	1984	1992	2000
NATIONALLY	23%	18	22
Protestant	26	30	48
Conservative	51	61	70
Baptist	30	55	54
Pentecostal	64	59	75
Mainline	17	16	23
Anglican	13	14	16
United	17	13	17
Lutheran	25	17	★
Presbyterian	17	34	40
Roman Catholic	28	21	21
Outside Quebec	37	27	31
Quebec	16	11	7
Other Faiths	13	15	21
Buddhist	★	10	10
Jewish	★	12	7
Muslim	★	41	26
Native	★	3	9
Hindu	★	★	44
Sikh	★	★	43
No Religion	3	2	3

★*Numbers insufficient to permit stable percentaging.*

Source: Bibby, Project Teen Canada survey series.

- The preliminary findings for young people who identify
  with *Other Faiths* point to a general increase in attendance,
  led by Hindu, Sikh, and Muslim youth. In the case of both
  Muslims and Buddhists, there are some signs of participation
  erosion, possibly due to the acculturation factors just discussed. Still, the overall involvement trend patterns for Other
  Faiths are positive.[43]

The proverbial bottom line on religion and teenagers? Fewer
identify, but those who do show signs of being more involved and
more committed. Here again, we see signs of vitality and life in almost

TABLE 3.14 **Anticipated Rites of Passage by Group, Mid-80s and 2000**

"In the future, do you anticipate having any of the following carried out for you by a minister, priest, rabbi, or some other religious figure?"

% Indicating "Yes"

	WEDDINGS		BIRTH-RELATED		FUNERALS	
	MID-80S	2000	MID-80S	2000	MID-80S	2000
TEENAGERS	87%★	89	76%★	70%	87%★	86%
ADULTS	19	24	14	20	44	57
RCs outside Quebec	18	21	12	14	44	64
RCs in Quebec	20	34	22	34	52	66
Mainline Protestants	20	24	11	20	43	58
Conservative Protestants	19	20	9	14	47	66
Other Faiths	3	26	3	23	27	54
No Religion	19	24	14	15	36	34

★*Teen "don't knows" for 1987 have been treated as "no"; otherwise the corresponding figures for weddings, births, funerals are 93%, 85%, and 93% as in Bibby,* Canada's Teens, *2001b: 197.*

Sources: 2000: teens = Bibby, Project Teen Canada 2000; *adults = Bibby,* Project Canada 2000. *Mid-80s sources: adults = Bibby,* Project Can85, *teens = Bibby,* Project Teen Canada 1987.

all groups. If there is a problem spot, where rejuvenation is still limited, it is Quebec.

And there is that final piece of good news for the churches, which I mentioned at the end of the last chapter. Over the past two decades, the anticipated demand for rites of passage has remained steady among teenagers, while it has increased significantly among adults.

- The adult increases tend to be greatest among *Roman Catholics in Quebec*, along with *Mainline Protestants*.
- Even among *Religious Nones*, the levels of anticipated rites of passage have remained steady since 1985.

This kind of "marketing research" news is still another signal that the established churches in Canada continue to have customer bases that are both sizeable and remarkably resilient. As mentioned earlier, the intriguing reality is that churches will have to do little in the way of making contact: the "customers" will be coming to them. Not a bad situation for any business or organization to be in.

These overall findings about the churches suggest that some important new developments are taking place in a variety of religious group settings and among young people — that there is something of a renaissance of organized religion in Canada. The data belong to the so-called consumer side: we have been looking at the inclination of Canadians to be involved in the churches. My assumption is that if people are responding to the churches, it's in large part because of new developments on the supply side. To varying degrees, Canada's well-established groups show signs of slowing, halting, and even beginning to reverse the downward numerical trends of the second half of the 20th century. As well-established groups in particular continue to make changes and to re-emerge, such patterns can be expected to become even more pronounced over the next few decades.

Quebec stands out as the current exception. Writing in the mid-1980s, historian Jean Hamelin expressed the belief that genuine renewal was beginning to take place within the Quebec Catholic Church, but suggested that "the noise of the things that are dying still drown out the voice of the things that are coming to birth."[44] We have seen some important indications — including ongoing identification, occasional attendance, receptivity to greater involvement, and the increase in demand for rites of passage — that suggest there will soon be much more to the Quebec story. Indeed, one of the most interesting questions concerning religion in Canada in the new century is not *will* the Roman Catholic Church in Quebec rebound, but rather *when* will clear signs of such rejuvenation begin to appear?

At the same time that there are signs of revitalization among Canada's established religious groups, there is also massive evidence that a solid majority of Canadians are feeling restless for the gods. What's intriguing about this restlessness is that its sources appear to lie not only in the pursuit of answers to important questions about life and death. The restlessness also comes from the widespread but infrequently acknowledged fact that people believe they are actually experiencing the presence of God. Speaking theologically, one might put things this way. The gods have been trying to reach Canadians

TABLE 3.15 Some Correlates of Growing, Stable, and Declining Churches: A Preliminary Snapshot

	ROMAN CATHOLIC				PROTESTANT			
	ALL	GROWING	DECLINING	SAME	ALL	GROWING	DECLINING	SAME
	(148)	(37)	(60)	(51)	(168)	(80)	(35)	(53)
Age of Church								
1–12 years	2%	9%	<1%	<1%	7%	10%	3%	5%
13–20	2	9	<1	<1	3	4	3	<1
21–50	33	24	32	40	25	35	16	15
>50	63	58	68	60	65	51	78	80
Worship Style								
Traditional	44	58	28	52	33	27	50	29
Contemporary	7	6	8	4	10	11	3	13
Blend	44	36	54	42	49	55	38	50
Separate Services	5	<1	10	2	8	7	9	8
Age of the People								
18–34	17	12	25	14	17	26	3	14
35–54	44	41	39	46	38	39	26	44
55+	39	47	36	40	45	35	71	42

*Among Roman Catholics, a disproportionate number of growing parishes are somewhat newer and characterized by traditional worship. The people most involved in growing parishes tend to be slightly older than people who are active in stable and declining churches.

**In the case of Protestants, growing churches are only slightly more likely to be newer churches. Growing and stable congregations have contemporary forms of worship more frequently than declining churches. Growing churches are also much more likely to have more actively involved younger adults.

Source: Bibby, Project Canada 2000.

through the churches. But given that the churches have had mixed success in the enterprise, there are signs that the gods have taken things into their own hands and shown up in person. Speaking sociologically, claims that people are personally experiencing God and privately communicating with God can be found all over the place.

Such realities are the subject of the next two chapters.

CHAPTER FOUR

Ongoing Questions Only the Gods Can Answer

Can a person live for any significant time on the planet without asking what it all means? Is there any purpose to life or do we simply create our own individual purposes? Have we been created by Someone or Something or have we just evolved into what we are through natural processes? Can life itself so consume us that we fail, especially at times that are intensely emotional, to ask the age-old question "If we die, will we live again?"

Seemingly not. As we will see shortly, the overwhelming majority of Canadians acknowledge that they do raise these so-called "ultimate questions" in the course of living out their lives. On at least some occasions, average people across the country feel an uneasiness, a restlessness, as they attempt to come to grips with both living and dying. As Tom Harpur has put it, "There are more and more people outside the church who are deeply searching for a center to their life beyond shopping malls."[1] Doug Todd, the highly respected *Vancouver Sun* journalist who has examined the spirituality of Canadian writers and artists in his important book *Brave Souls*, offers the following observation:

> . . . the real spiritual story today is not what particular religious group we belong to, which doctrine we profess, or which system of philosophy we follow. It is about how we cobble together

meaning in our lives. What do we really believe when we suddenly wake up at 3 a.m.?[2]

For some people, the resolution of these important questions lies with science and fate. They, along with Sigmund Freud in his classic work *The Future of an Illusion*, conclude that "it would be an illusion to suppose that we could get anywhere else . . . [than where the answers of science lead us]." [3] Many others, however, find that science falls short of being able to address "the why" of existence. In addition, the acceptance of the inevitability of death fails to confront the question of whether or not there is life after death. The fact that such questions cannot be *resolved* by science or — in the case of what lies beyond death — even be legitimately *addressed* by science, guarantees an ongoing place for religion. As Stark and Bainbridge have put it in their landmark book *The Future of Religion*, "There will always be a need for gods." So long as we exist, "we shall ache for . . . peace, immortality, and boundless joy that have never been found this side of heaven."[4]

There's no doubt that the demand for answers to ultimate questions continues to be very high in the early years of the 21st century. Sometimes the questions are triggered by life's big issues — often by deeply personal experiences. Often they take us by surprise, emerging from the fabric of everyday life in the form of unexpected experiences of joy and anguish, birth and death. But they emerge, and for all but the unthinking, impatiently call out for answers.

I will be among the hundreds of millions of people who will forever remember September 11, 2001. In my case, I will remember it for two reasons. I received two phone calls that morning. The first was from my oldest son, telling me to turn on my TV set — saying only that I wouldn't believe what was happening in New York. Who can begin to describe the magnitude of the shock, the horror, the pain, and the despair being experienced by so many as the two World Trade Center towers came toppling down and the Pentagon burned, in the process wiping out as many as four thousand lives. Such devastation and death had and continues to have a profound impact on people who have been directly affected by the tragedy, as well as on the many millions who watched it from afar. Commentator after commentator noted how it put so much of life into perspective, how it was an event that called on everyone to reflect on what matters and on whether there can be hope for the future both in this world and beyond it. What happened was so dramatic that it seemed to bring everyday life to a halt, emotionally if not practically. It was as if someone had hit life's pause button — so much so that it would take the urging of a New York mayor and a U.S. president for the start button to be pushed again.

The second phone call came about an hour after the first one, this time from one of my sisters. She was calling, not to discuss the tragic events in the U.S. as I had expected, but to inform me that our beloved "mum" of 83, whom some of you have met in my writings, had suffered a stroke and had been rushed to hospital. Readers know how such an event underscores human helplessness and mortality, how it forces us to ponder whether what was so good in this life is the end of the story, or just the beginning.

The very fact that we raise these so-called ultimate questions suggests, at minimum, that we want to know if there is more to our existence than us. If there isn't more, then so be it — we will carve out our own meanings, try to cope as best we can with suffering, and accept the inevitability and finality of death. But if there is more to life than us, a Creator who brought it into being, sustains it, and will be there at the end of history to greet it, then we need to know.[5] Such a reality has dramatic implications for how we might choose to live, as well as how we respond to death. We need some answers.

As of the early 1980s, psychiatrist Viktor Frankl's book *Man's Search for Meaning* had sold two million copies and appeared in 20 languages since first being released in 1946. In his preface to the 1984 edition, Frankl writes how the American media had often asked him how he felt about the success of the book. His frequent response was to say he did not see the sales of his book so much as an achievement on his part as "an expression of the misery of our time." In his words, "if hundreds of thousands of people reach out for a book whose very title promises to deal with the question of a meaning to life, it must be a question that burns under their fingernails."[6]

Our survey findings indicate that "ultimate" questions continue to burn under Canadians' fingernails, in the process providing a possible indicator of a populace that is restless for the gods.

Origins and Purpose

The question of where we came from continues to be raised by about nine in ten people in the course of their lifetimes. The *Project Canada 2000* survey reveals that 60% of the population ask the question of how the world came into being often or sometimes, while another 30% or so indicate that they have raised the question in the past.

TABLE 4.1 **Life's Origins, 1975 and 2000**

"To what extent do you think about the question, 'How did the world come into being?'"

	1975	2000
Often	18%	11
Sometimes	46	49
No longer	27	31
I never have	9	9

Sources: Bibby, Project Can75 and Project Canada 2000.

A comparison with 1975 shows that what has changed over the past three decades is the apparent urgency with which the question of origins is asked: fewer say they raise it often, more say they no longer ask it. But, frequency aside, the issue of how the world came into being continues to be personally posed by about the same proportion of people as raised the question in 1975.

Apart from origins, nine in ten Canadians have also felt the need, during their lifetimes, to address the question of the purpose of life. While the question of origins is no longer raised by about 30% of the population, only some 20% have put the question of life's meaning behind them. Still, that's twice the "no longer" figure for 1975. The increase may not necessarily be because more people have resolved the issue, but because they have simply dropped it — at least for the time being. We'll come back to this possibility shortly.

Besides asking about the extent to which people reflect on meaning, our surveys have also explored the extent to which "wondering about the purpose of life" is sufficiently urgent for some people that they see it as a personal concern. When we introduced the question in 1985, we found that 23% of Canadians said "wondering about the purpose of life" bothered them "a great deal" or "quite a bit." The

TABLE 4.2 **Life's Meaning, 1975 and 2000**

"To what extent do you think about the question 'What is the purpose of life?'"

	1975	2000
Often	31%	18%
Sometimes	50	52
No longer	11	21
I never have	8	9

Sources: Bibby, Project Can75 and Project Canada 2000.

Project Canada 2000 survey has found that the figure is now 28%. Relative to other concerns, it is noteworthy that the purpose issue comes in tenth, only slightly behind marriage, looks, and lack of recognition, and ahead of such highly publicized "problem areas" as sexual life, depression, and aging.

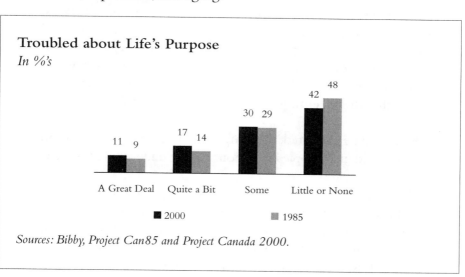

Troubled about Life's Purpose
In %'s

A Great Deal: 11, 9
Quite a Bit: 17, 14
Some: 30, 29
Little or None: 42, 48

■ 2000   ▨ 1985

Sources: Bibby, Project Can85 and Project Canada 2000.

What about answers? Asked pointedly, *"How sure are you that you have found the answer to the meaning of life?"* three in ten people say they are either "very certain" or "quite certain." Another three in ten indicate they are "rather uncertain," while the remaining four in ten say they "don't think there is an answer" to the question. The results are very similar to what we found in 1975, although uncertainty is up a bit.

TABLE 4.3 Certainty of Life's Meaning, 1975 and 2000

"How sure are you that you have found the answer to the meaning of life?"

	1975	2000
Very certain	11%	11%
Quite certain	24	22
Rather uncertain	22	28
I don't think there is an answer to such a question	43	39

Sources: Bibby, Project Can75 and Project Canada 2000.

- Incidentally, people who are "no longer" asking the question feel reasonably certain that they have either found the answer (41%) or that no answer exists (42%). Those who "often" or "sometimes" think about the purpose of life are almost evenly inclined to take certainty, uncertainty, and no answer positions.
- Perhaps surprisingly, people who say they have "never" thought about the purpose of life are nonetheless not lost for an opinion: six in ten don't think there's an answer, while one in three think they have found the answer to the question that they seemingly haven't yet got around to asking . . .

As would be expected, there are some important variations in the levels of confidence people have about having uncovered life's meaning.

- *Weekly service attenders* stand out as being the most likely to feel they have found the answer (61%), while *never attenders* are the most inclined to say there is no answer to the question (56%); consequently, people in those two extreme categories are the least likely to still be raising the question. Illustrative of "nevers" who take the "no answer" position is a 22-year-old female student of mine who recently told me, "The purpose of life is to just live your life and enjoy yourself doing it and not worry about the purpose of life. Human existence is not that profound."
- *Conservative Protestants* are much more likely than others to maintain they have found life's meaning; my efforts to clarify their thinking show that many speak in clear-cut phrases

TABLE 4.4 **Meaning Question by Select Variables**

	FOUND ANSWER	UNCERTAIN	THERE IS NO ANSWER	NO LONGER ASK IT
NATIONALLY	33%	29%	38%	21%
Weekly	61	19	20	26
Monthly	41	32	27	10
Yearly	26	33	41	19
Never	18	26	56	25
Conservative Protestants	63	14	23	29
RCs in Quebec	39	27	34	13
RCs outside Quebec	29	21	40	21
Mainline Protestants	29	30	41	24
Other Faiths	42	14	44	7
No Religion	21	35	44	25
18–34	25	37	38	18
35–54	36	26	38	23
55+	38	21	41	23
Female	32	29	39	19
Male	34	27	39	24
Degree-Plus	36	29	35	22
Tech-Bus	29	36	35	21
HS or Less	32	21	47	21

Source: Bibby, Project Canada 2000.

such as "living to glorify God" and "serving and honouring the Lord." One 35-year-old woman from Edmonton who teaches Sunday school in her evangelical church puts things this way: "The purpose of life is to get to know Jesus Christ in a personal way and live out his expectations of us in the way we relate to others."[7]

• *Quebec Catholics* and people adhering to *Other Faiths* are particularly polarized between feeling they have found the answer and maintaining that there isn't one.

• Similar proportions of *Mainline Protestants* and *Catholics outside Quebec* express certainty or the lack of an answer to the meaning question. Among those in the latter category is a straight-talking Anglican from B.C., a retired professional, who says, "Meaning of life? Hey! We're all here. That's all there is to it."[8]

- *Younger adults* are somewhat less likely than others to feel they have found life's meaning. As one 20-year-old Catholic in his second year of university put it, "I have no idea what the purpose of life is. I believe when I get older and look back on my life, it might be clearer. Right now, I'm just gonna let it fly."[9]

- In all age and religious categories, *male-female* variations are very small.

- *Education* seems to make little difference in the certainty of having resolved the mystery of meaning, other than leading people to be more inclined to say an answer exists.

It all adds up to a lot of Canadians over their lifetimes raising the important question of the purpose of life — whether or not existence has meaning that precedes our appearance on the planet, or whether we are left to create meaning for ourselves. Their collective conclusion? Three in ten think they've found the answer, three in ten aren't sure, and four in ten say there is no answer to be found.

But we Canucks are a funny lot. Yes, many of us tell the pollster we don't think there is an answer to the question of life's meaning. Yet when he asks us point-blank to respond to the statement "*Life has meaning beyond what we ourselves give to it*" — as I did in 2000 — we capitulate: 86% of us agree, including 76% of those who indicate they don't think there is an answer to the question![10]

My interpretation of these seemingly contradictory findings is that Canadians know well that life is mysterious. We may not have discovered its purpose, but this doesn't mean we are comfortable saying, with confident finality, that the meaning we have tried to give to our lives is all there is. When push comes to shove, people defer to a sense that there is more to life than most of us can comprehend, that our goals are pretty finite when compared to the possibility that we could be spending our years on the planet for more lofty reasons.

In addition, it's pretty safe to assume that many people have not really carefully thought through life's meaning, even though they

"What Do You Think Is the Purpose of Life?"

In the winter of 2001–02, my research team and I approached a quota sample of two hundred diverse Canadians, asking them questions about purpose, suffering, life after death, God, experience, prayer, and the effects of September 11, 2001. What follows here and in subsequent sections are some of their responses. Randomly spliced in, courtesy of Doug Todd and his book Brave Souls*, are the thoughts of some well-known Canadian writers and artists.*

Growing, Doing, and Knowing

"The purpose of life is creation in every sense of the word. We create ourselves, our environment, our beliefs, our joys and, unfortunately, our sorrows. Then we create our children who create their own selves . . . and life goes on."
— *A 40-something Montrealer; she no longer practises the Catholicism of her youth.*

"To unite with our innate perfection and to share that with all beings."
— *A surgeon, 32, from St. John's; he is a practising Buddhist.*

"Loving. Doing. Creating."
— *An urban planner living in Vancouver; he describes himself as an atheist.*

"To experience the known and the unknown if we are lucky. The great mystery, of course, is the unknowable, which is saved for the end of life."
— *A 24-year-old Alberta university student; she identifies with the Nehiyaw, or Cree, religion.*

Living for God and Others

"The gospel is about trying to incarnate a love which is both radical and not stupid . . . There is a world we do not see. And there is a spiritual reality we cannot imagine. I believe the dimensions of that world are staggering."
— *New Brunswick–based author Ann Copeland, a former nun, who plays the organ in her Catholic church (Todd, 1996: 121, 117).*

"We are here to learn to have the pure love of Christ for everyone. Some need to be reprimanded, but still we need to love them."
— *A 24-year-old Latter-Day Saints homemaker from rural Alberta who is active in her church.*

"To allow each person I meet daily to witness the love of our Lord by sharing my example of respecting children and adults alike."
— *A former school administrator and teacher, originally from northern Ontario.*

Living to Eat, Drink, and Be Merry, plus Other People

"I think it is important to live life and enjoy life as much as possible. Sometimes it is equally important to take the foot off the accelerator, slow down and focus in on others. Life isn't always about yourself."
— *A non-active Lutheran, 49; he is in sales in Vancouver.*

"There's just one trip around the block and you better have as good a time as possible without hurting anybody else."
— *Canadian author and social critic Mordecai Richler (Todd, 1996: 17).*

"Life is an accident, not a purpose. Take the opportunity to enjoy it. Love yourself, your family and your neighbour; it's too short to fuss over the small stuff."
— *A single, 35-year-old, self-employed career woman in Calgary who says she has no religion.*

Source: Project Canada Quota Sample, Winter, 2001–02.

occasionally question what life is all about. As with those who acknowledge that they have "never" even raised the question, some of these people may simply be trying to save face by suggesting there probably isn't an answer to the query. And to be fair, some respondents undoubtedly find the item simplistic. Even if they have come to some conclusions, they don't think of the meaning of life in straightforward, succinct terms — so they can't really speak of having found "the answer" to the meaning of life. As one 19-year-old female put it, "That's far too complex a question to answer in two to three sentences."[11] Others are probably hesitant to sound too sure of themselves. In interviewing novelist John Irving, Doug Todd uncovered such a response:

> Now, if you push me to the wall, I'd say I'm not a believer. But it depends on the day you ask. It doesn't seem to me that doubt is the opposite of faith. Doubt is an integral part of faith. I'm not comfortable calling myself a believer, a Christian. But if somebody says, "Are you an atheist?" I'd back down from that question too. I'd say, "Listen, I've done a little too much reading and studying about religions in general to ever subscribe to such a simplistic view."[12]

Still, in agreeing that life "has meaning beyond what we ourselves give to it," close to nine in ten Canadians may be providing us with another hint that they sense there is Something back of their lives, as well as everyday life and history more generally. A theist might go so far as to say that the gods have been doing a pretty good job of alerting people to the fact that there is more to life than meets the eye.

Happiness and Suffering

It goes without saying that we all want to be happy, and we vary in how we conceptualize happiness. But what remains a mystery is how a person can find true and lasting happiness. Presumably, happiness is linked to clarity about life's purpose, which also gives meaning to suffering. In Nietzsche's words, "He who has a *why* to live can bear with almost any *how*."[13]

Some readers are familiar with the biblical book of Ecclesiastes, one of my favourite sources of thought. The writer portrays himself as someone who wanted to find happiness, raising the question of the ages: "For who knows what is good for mortals while they live the few days of their vain life, which they pass like a shadow?"[14] He relays to us some of the dead ends — notably hard work, successful work, and the pursuit of wealth and wisdom, which he poetically describes as chasing after the wind. In the end, his grand conclusion? "There is nothing better for mortals than to eat and drink, and find enjoyment in their toil," while relating to God: "This also, I saw, is from the hand of God; for apart from him who can eat or who can have enjoyment? For to the one who pleases him God gives wisdom and knowledge and joy."[15] Close to the famous dictum: "Eat, drink, and be merry, for tomorrow you die" — plus God.

But the writer reminds us that to live is also to experience pain: "For everything there is a season . . . a time to weep, and a time to laugh; a time to mourn, and a time to dance."[16] Life is far from easy, fair, or rational:

> . . . the race is not to the swift, nor the battle to the strong, nor bread to the wise, nor riches to the intelligent, nor favour to the skilful; but time and chance happen to them all. For no one can anticipate the time of disaster. Like fish taken in a cruel net, and like birds caught in a snare, so mortals are snared at a time of calamity, when it suddenly falls upon them.[17]

In the succinct words of Brian Stiller, "Inevitably on the human journey, life hurts."[18]

As with origin and purpose, approximately 90% of Canadians claim that they have raised the question of how they can experience happiness, with the question currently being asked by some 70%. An even higher 96% say they reflect on the question of why there is suffering in the world, nearly 80% "often or sometimes." Given such pervasiveness, variations by characteristics such as attendance and religious group, along with age, gender, and education, are very small. These kinds of questions are raised by virtually everyone. It therefore is not surprising that the happiness and suffering questions

"What Do You Think Is the Purpose of Life?" Some Further Thoughts

Positive Treatment of Others

"To do as much as you can, trying to be a good person, helping when needed, and showing respect and understanding to other people."
— *A Calgary financial consultant, 33; she is Greek Orthodox but not involved.*

"To break the pattern of re-birth by making Nirvana right here and now. To live with courage and grace and harm nothing. This is very hard."
— *A 31-year-old female from Ottawa who works in international development; a "practising Buddhist and United Church attendee."*

"Kindness seems to me to be the core of everything."
— *Douglas Coupland, author of* Generation X *and* Life after God *(Todd, 1996: 90).*

Tapping Our Potential

"Just like that army commercial, 'Be all that you can be.'"
— *A computer programmer from Burnaby, B.C., 38, who says he is United but hasn't been to church "in many moons."*

"To live and pursue experience."
— *An artist from London, Ontario, who describes himself as an agnostic.*

"To learn from our mistakes and be better on the next level."
— *A 25-year-old Presbyterian female who is currently a student in Saskatchewan.*

It Doesn't Include God

"Humans are an accident of evolution and as such will continue to evolve until either the sun implodes or humankind destroys itself, whichever comes first."
— *An administrator from Alberta, 35, who says she is a nonpracticing Christian.*

"It seems to me odd to require a force other than ourselves to make our life meaningful. I think what I believe is people have to invest meaning in life. I think of just being born as a colossal win."
— *Author Jane Rule, who describes herself as a nonbeliever (Todd, 1996:38,40).*

There Is No Purpose Beyond What We Ourselves Give to Life

"The purpose of life is to live, nothing more, nothing less."
— *A 21-year-old university student in Lethbridge who says she has no religion.*

"We are here to discover our own purpose for ourselves and, through the relationships we attract, to play out that purpose for the benefit of all concerned."
— *A 35-year-old in the film industry in Vancouver; raised United Church, studied theology, and now has "no fixed religion."*

"The universe we live in is so completely enthralling and exciting in the way it works itself out, one cog meshing with another. There is no need to plaster religious illusion over it."
— *West coast sculptor Bill Reid, credited with creating a global fascination with Native spirituality (Todd, 1996: 31).*

Source: Project Canada Quota Sample, October-December, 2001.

TABLE 4.5 **Happiness and Suffering, 1975 and 2000**
"To what extent do you think about the question 'How can I experience happiness?'"

	1975	2000
Often	31%	20%
Sometimes	46	48
No longer	13	22
I never have	10	10

"To what extent do you think about the question 'Why is there suffering in the world?'"

Often	44%	27%
Sometimes	43	52
No longer	10	17
I never have	3	4

Sources: Bibby, Project Can75 and Project Canada 2000.

are being raised by as many people today as in 1975. What has changed is the tendency of more people to say they no longer are asking the questions.

An important parenthesis. As I indicated at the outset of this chapter, ultimate questions get raised when social and personal events bring them to the fore. There is no doubt that the shocking developments of September 11, 2001, dramatically raised consciousness about suffering, death, and life as a whole among people worldwide. Many Canadians who told us in late 2000 that they were "no longer" raising the suffering question, for example, were undoubtedly thinking again. A national poll carried out in late November of 2001 for *Maclean's* and released in the magazine's year-end issue revealed that 23% of Canadians were feeling a stronger need for religious beliefs some two months following the attacks — although, unfortunately, the report does not tell us how devout those people were *before* the attacks.[19] We'll return to the issue of the impact of September 11th on religion in Canada in the Conclusion.

How have Canadians been resolving the happiness questions? Over the years we have been exploring what people across the country see as their key pathways to happiness by asking them about the things they have come to value most in life. The findings reveal a high level of consensus as to what people think will bring them happiness. Out of a list of some 15 traits, seven stand out. They encompass all levels of religious involvement.

- The top four valued goals for Canadians are freedom, family life, being loved, and friendship. Succinctly put, *freedom and relationships* are at the top of almost everyone's list. Young people are typically depicted as wanting freedom. That's true. But it's also true of adults. Teens further place supreme importance on good ties with others. As one 16-year-old teenager reminded us in our latest national youth survey, "All kids need love and support from someone or something."[20] So do adults. One 53-year-old woman from a small farming community in Saskatchewan expressed things this way: "The most important thing in life is relationships — relationships with God, with family members, and other people."[21]
- The next apparent key to happiness for most people is a *comfortable life*. People want to be well off materially.
- At a third level of importance is being *successful* at what one does, along with pursuing and achieving a measure of *creativity*.

TABLE 4.6 **Top Seven Values by Service Attendance, 2000**
Ranked by Importance

	NAT	WEEKLY	MONTHLY	YEARLY	NEVER
Freedom	89%	2	1	1	1
Family life	85	1	3	3	2
Being loved	84	4	2	2	3
Friendship	78	3	4	4	4
A comfortable life	64	7	6	5	5
Creativity	50		5	7	6
Success	49		7	6	7
Spirituality	34	5			
Religion	21	6			

Source: Bibby, Project Canada 2000.

- *Spirituality* and *religion* are of particular importance to people active in religious groups; in fact, among those who are highly involved, only relationships and freedom are ranked higher. Explaining the relationship between happiness and her faith, one 31-year-old mother of three from a small Alberta community commented, "I am happy, although at times life is tough and discouraging. It's hard to explain how these things can go together but my faith is the key for sure."[22]

In the minds of most Canadians, other characteristics such as recognition, excitement, involvement in their communities, their cultural group heritages, and having power have comparatively low levels of importance in their pursuit of happiness.

As might be expected, the people most likely to raise the question *"How can I experience happiness?"* at any one point in time are those who are not particularly happy with their lives generally and — consistent with the importance being placed on relationships — their marriages more specifically.

- Only about 15% of the people who are "very happy" or "pretty happy" are raising the question frequently, compared to some 55% of those who are "not very happy."

TABLE 4.7 **Happiness and Pursuit of the Happiness Question, 2000**
% Who Raise the Happiness Question

	OFTEN	SOMETIMES	NO LONGER	NEVER HAVE
All in All				
Very happy	14	32	37	17
Pretty happy	17	53	21	9
Not very happy	56	39	4	1
Marriage/Relationship				
Very happy	14	42	32	12
Pretty happy	17	53	22	8
Not very happy	46	33	18	3

Source: Bibby, Project Canada 2000.

- Among Canadians who are "very happy" or "pretty happy" in their marriages or relationships, a similar 15% raise the question often; by contrast, the level is almost 50% for those who are not very happy with such relational ties.
- Consistent with the overall pattern, in both the general and the relational instances, people who report that they are "pretty happy" are more likely than those who are "very happy" to raise the happiness question at least occasionally.

The inclination to raise the question *"Why is there suffering in the world?"* would be expected to be associated with a number of characteristics, including compassion and being troubled about what is happening in one's own life. Someone who claims to care about other people would be the kind of person who wonders why suffering takes place. The same query would be expected of an individual who is suffering personally. A look at some illustrative data from the latest *Project Canada* national survey bears out such ideas.

- Canadians who place a particularly high value on concern for others are somewhat more likely than others to raise the suffering question frequently.

TABLE 4.8 **Compassion, Health, and the Suffering Question, 2000**

% Who Raise the Suffering Question

	OFTEN	SOMETIMES	NO LONGER	NEVER HAVE
Concern for Others				
Very important	30	50	15	5
Somewhat important	17	57	22	4
Troubled about Own Health				
A great deal	42	47	9	2
Quite a bit	25	53	20	2
Somewhat	23	54	18	5
Little or not at all	16	53	23	8

Source: Bibby, Project Canada 2000.

- Similarly, there is a fairly pronounced tendency for individuals who are worried about their own health, for example, to raise the question, compared to people whose health is not a particular cause for concern.

The question of the meaning of suffering, of course, dates back to the beginning of time and is frequently accompanied by considerable passion and urgency. Renowned Harvard psychologist Gordon Allport once wrote that "to live is to suffer, to survive is to find meaning in the suffering. If there is a purpose in life at all, there must be a purpose in suffering and in dying."[23]

People who have believed in God, for example, have raised the obvious question of why bad things happen in a world created and controlled by a loving God. They also have been forced to ask a question that is even more pressing for them: "Why do the righteous suffer?" The answers have come in an array of explanations known as "theodicies." They variously emphasize issues such as human freedom, random existence, punishment, and lessons learned. Sometimes the explanations are satisfactory; sometimes they are not. We all know people who have experienced suffering and come through such times with their faith not only intact but enriched. A friend of mine with a United Church background who teaches at an Ontario university shared these personal thoughts a month ago:

> As I get older, I have experienced God during some dark times: the break-up of a marriage, turning 50, and dealing with a major life-threatening illness. These critical times have involved a basic choice: resign myself to the darkness and despair or surrender myself to a mysterious power that I have experienced as surrounding and sustaining me. I don't know whether this power can be called God in the traditional Western sense, because I have not experienced it as a Thou, rather as a source that helps me experience my soul as significant, loving and grounded.[24]

Another friend involved in Roman Catholic youth ministry told me recently, "This year I've been comforted, challenged, accepted, and loved by God. Sometimes I've been shocked by a sudden awareness that I'm in the presence of holiness. During times of intense suffering, I've been aware of God being the very ground on which I stand."[25]

For others, the experience of pain and suffering makes the idea of the existence of a loving God incomprehensible. One of our national survey respondents who lives in a small Ontario community told us, "I was a devout Anglican and very active in the church for many years. You will see by my answers on religion that I have pulled away from my church. Given what I see in the present day world, I cannot believe there is a caring God."[26] Children's author Robert Munsch, who was raised a Catholic and studied at a Jesuit Seminary, had twins arrive stillborn. He told Doug Todd, "I'm not saying there isn't a God. But there isn't a God who cares about people. And who wants a God who doesn't give a shit?"[27] Even John Stackhouse of Regent College, a former president of the Canadian Evangelical Theological Association, conceded in a recent interview with Bob Harvey, "the idea that God is all good and all powerful is really a hard position to defend in the light of nature and the newspaper, so much so that if I weren't a Christian, I would be an atheist."[28]

Vancouver-based journalist and broadcaster Susan Martinuk, in trying to reconcile a loving God and the reality of human pain, offers this observation: "Nobody gets a guarantee for a painless existence. Becoming a Christian or believing in a loving God doesn't change that. Suffering," says Martinuk, "is a consequence of living in a harsh, fallen world and it doesn't mean that God has moved from us. It just means that we are required to enjoy and reflect God's love while living through both the good and the bad."[29] Some people accept such a line of reasoning; others do not.

Todd, in his *Brave Souls*, relates the different responses of writers Peter Newman and Farley Mowat to World War II. Newman told Todd, "I found it very difficult to understand if there was a God, why he allowed six million Jews to be slaughtered who were totally innocent, including both sets of my grandparents, who died in concentration camps. It shakes the awakening of a faith. All of a sudden, somebody decided all these people had to die. It's ridiculous." In contrast, Mowat's primary response to the war was not to blame or reject God for such suffering, but rather to blame humans.[30]

In general, Canadians seem so consistent in how they interpret suffering that we have not repeated the question since asking it some two decades ago. When asked why people suffer, Canadians then — and I would maintain now — did not attribute suffering primarily to people or greed or economics or sin or God; they saw it as a fact of life, experienced by almost everyone in the course of a lifetime.

TABLE 4.9 **Why Do People Suffer?**

% Indicating Various Views of Suffering

Suffering is simply a fact of life, experienced by virtually all of us in the course of a lifetime.	91%
Suffering results from people today being greedy for riches and power.	58
People suffer because of the political and economic systems they have.	56
People usually bring suffering on themselves.	54
Suffering comes because people don't obey God.	23
People who suffer are being punished for their sins.	11

Source: Bibby, Project Can75.

The *Project Canada 2000* survey has found that, contrary to common belief, reflection on the reality of suffering does not lead most people to doubt the compassion of God. Some 84% of Canadians who say they "often" think about why there is suffering in the world "definitely believe" (48%) or "think" (36%) that "God or a higher power cares" about them. Only 6% of the remaining 16% definitely do not believe in a compassionate supreme being.

In his book *When Life Hurts*, Brian Stiller writes, "Belief in God doesn't mean the pain is less, rather it's that those who believe in a personal God have the capacity to feel the hurt within a larger framework of meaning."[31] For most, it seems, the use of that framework does not result in calling God's love into question. Sam Reimer, a sociologist who teaches in New Brunswick, may sum up the needs of many when he says, "I don't think we can have an answer to all kinds of suffering. But then again, people usually don't need an explanation for suffering as much as they need someone to cry with them."[32]

To the extent that Canadians over the years have seen suffering as having human sources, they have certainly wanted to see things made right. Right up to the present, close to 95% have maintained that people who cannot afford it have a right to medical care, while almost 90% have said that people who are poor have a right to an income adequate to live on. Reflecting world events, the proportion agreeing that "war is justified when other means of international disputes fail" has risen from around 20% between 1975 and 1985 to about 40% from the eve of the Gulf War in 1990 through the pre-terrorist days of late 2000.

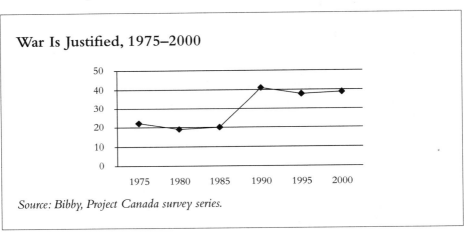

War Is Justified, 1975–2000

Source: Bibby, Project Canada survey series.

And what may be particularly telling about Canadian assumptions regarding suffering is that no less than 70% of adults and teenagers agree that "somehow, someday injustices will be made right." I'll return to the possible significance of that assumption in Chapter 6.

These findings show that the vast majority of Canadians raise the happiness and suffering questions in the course of living out their lives. The gods, it could be argued, are going well beyond existing churches and temples in stirring people up right across the country. But those stirrings hardly stop with queries about origins and purpose, happiness and suffering. They are particularly apparent in the case of reflections about death.

"Why Is There Suffering in the World?"

It's The Inevitable Result of Living

"On an individual level, doing the wrong thing at the wrong time for the wrong reasons causes suffering. We have some control over that. On a global scale, there's no real comprehending suffering. It appears randomly, as likely to strike good people as bad. It takes humility and forbearance to enjoy an ethical life in the face of cruel absurdity."

— A Toronto journalist and television personality, 47; he describes himself as an atheist.

"Suffering can be caused by natural or non-natural events."

— A 46-year-old artist who lives near Halifax; her background is Anglican.

It's Primarily Our Fault

"Some suffering comes to us from the way the world is meant to be: break physical laws and you can expect to suffer for it. Some suffering comes because the world is not the way it was meant to be: break moral laws and you will suffer for it."

— A professor who teaches at McMaster University in Hamilton.

"Much of it is due to 'man's inhumanity to man'; I suppose that's politically incorrect these days."

— A former moderator of the Presbyterian Church in Canada.

"There is suffering because human beings have disregarded God and tried to control everything with a selfish spirit often aimed at self-satisfaction rather than consideration for others."

— A high-ranking Lutheran church official in western Canada.

"More than 2,500 years ago, Prince Siddhartha said people suffer due to four great attachments to (1) physical pleasures, (2) views and opinions, (3) impermanent things that we imagine are permanent, and (4) the belief in self and mind for the gratification of self. I think he was right."

— A Buddhist and former university chancellor who says he is "a neophyte student of life."

"Suffering sometimes is the result of human wrongdoing and the result of the actions of evil spiritual beings. Yet, I recognize that the mystery involved in some forms of suffering probably cannot be resolved this side of heaven."

— A Toronto student, 27; she is involved with ministry to international students.

God Hurts with Us

"People blame God for suffering. God does not desire that we suffer. When we hurt, God hurts. The consequences of evil choices are the social conditions we live with: polluted water, toxic air, poisonous food, and cancer."

— A former Roman Catholic priest, now married and a member of the United Church; he lives in Ontario.

"People are wondering why God can allow something like September 11th to happen. God didn't allow it, but wept when men took it upon themselves to kill in His name and justify it with twisted logic and a religion of anger."

— A 30-year-old minister from P.E.I.; he is the minister of a rural Mainline Protestant church.

Source: Project Canada Quota Sample, Winter, 2001–02.

Life after Death

It remains one of the most basic questions we ask: "Is there life after death?" Even when we are seemingly consumed with day-to-day issues, the unpredictability of death — whereby death visits people around us in almost a roulette fashion, often with little regard for age — shakes us out of our normal routines. On those days when we sit together and remember the one who is now gone, for an hour or two everything else that matters to us is temporarily suspended. At such times, most of cannot help but raise "the question."

Perhaps what is particularly hard for us to accept is the sense that, when people die, they cross such a profound line — so here with us yesterday and so abruptly gone today, never to return to us again. Canadian author Jane Rule has commented, "The only one thing I don't like about death is that other people do it. I would like to pass a law that no one I love is allowed to die."[33] An articulate survey respondent from the Vancouver area offered the thought that "there is no beneficial reason to worry about death. But in the case of my children and grandchildren, I would hope it would not come for a long time and certainly not in my time."[34] In his memoirs, Pierre Trudeau offered these words about his feelings at age 15 when he learned of the death of his father:

> In the middle of the year I was fifteen, a winter night was interrupted by the terrible blow that left its mark on my adolescence and my life . . . I froze on the landing when I heard the awful words: "Your father is dead, Pierre." How can I describe what I felt at that moment? In a split second, I felt the whole world go empty. His death truly felt like the end of the world. That's the only way I can put it. My father had been a loving presence in my life, a reassuring force but also a stimulus, a constant challenge. He was the focal point of my life, and his death created an enormous void.[35]

Biographers Stephen Clarkson and Christina McCall have written that Trudeau's reaction to his father's death was "so profound and so far-reaching that he still cried uncontrollably at funerals when he was a grown man."[36] At the age of 78, Trudeau experienced the death of his youngest son, Michel, in an avalanche in British Columbia. According to people close to him, the loss had a devastating effect on the former prime minister through the last two years of his life before he himself died in 2000.

In light of how much we value relationships, how can we not wonder if, somehow and somewhere, we will see them again? If those who die are young, sometimes mere children or infants, their deaths seem so premature, their days on earth so incomplete. The need for them to have the chance to complete their abbreviated lives cries out for life after death. But who among those who have experienced a long life and a good life doesn't want the long and the good to continue?

As my mother, during her 70s and 80s, experienced the pain of so many of her friends and family members dying, I used to sometimes cautiously remind her that, ironically, her hurt was the mixed blessing of being fortunate enough to be living such a long life. But one doesn't have to live particularly long to experience the anguish of losing people of all ages.

This past year or so has been a time when an unusually large number of people around me have died, including a colleague down the hall, two others who had recently retired, the ten-year-old son of a close friend, and the 36-year-old former student I wrote about in *Unknown Gods.* Her sister-in-law had had that remarkable dream in which my former student's deceased husband had communicated words from Australia that only she would understand.[37] The diversity of how life ends was reflected in the fact that two of these five deaths involved cancer, one a heart attack, another an accident, the fifth suicide. And then there was the death of a very close friend's unborn child, about a month before he was to become the much-awaited companion of his Down syndrome brother.

I suspect that those blunt words from yesteryear are about as empirically sound as any statement ever uttered, that there's "*a time to be born, and a time to die.*"[38] Most of us, of course, hope this line is incomplete — that there's not only "a time to be born, and a time to die," but also "a time to live again." The theist cannot help but suggest that the fact so many people express the belief that "what is hoped for will in fact happen" may be yet another indicator of the gods moving among us.

If I Die Before I Wake

The question of what happens after death is raised by more than 90% of Canadians in the course of their lifetimes. Some 70% say they are currently asking the question "often" (18%) or "sometimes" (52%), while about another 20% report that they are "no longer" thinking about it. Just under 10% indicate that they have "never" reflected on what happens when we die. Consistent with what we have just seen with other "ultimate questions," people today are just as likely to raise the life-after-death question as they were in 1975. But more are now setting the question aside earlier, resolved or otherwise.

TABLE 4.10 **Life after Death, 1975 and 2000**

"To what extent do you think about the question 'What happens after death?'"

	1975	2000
Often	27%	18%
Sometimes	49	52
No longer	15	21
I never have	9	9

Sources: Bibby, Project Can75 and Project Canada 2000.

Perhaps some people in this latter category are like a 42-year-old Montreal woman in the aerospace industry who says, "I am so ambivalent about the whole question of life after death that I'll tackle it when the time comes." She describes herself as "a non-religious individual with faith." A 21-year-old Alberta university student with no religious ties similarly told us, "I'd like to think there is life after death and I will go to a heaven-ish place where I'll be happy. But I really have no idea. I guess I'll find out when it happens."[39] And a practically minded 72-year-old national survey respondent from a small town in Ontario simply informed us, "I'll wait to see what happens."[40]

- Still, that student notwithstanding, *younger adults* under the age of 35 are somewhat more inclined to be raising the question "often" or "sometimes" (81%) than 35-to-54-year-old Boomers (67%) or Boomers' Parents over 55 (64%).
- *Education* neither stimulates nor negates the raising of the

question: the inclination to ask it versus setting it aside differs little between university graduates (69%) and others (72%).

Since the mid-80s, we have asked respondents pointedly to what extent they are personally bothered about dying. In 1985, we found that 15% of Canadians said dying is something that troubled them "a great deal" or "quite a bit." The *Project Canada 2000* survey has found that the figure is now marginally higher, at 17%. Those who say the issue is of "little or no" concern to them have *decreased* from 56% to 49%.

- The 17% figure is slightly below concern about issues such as depression (23%) and loneliness (26%), fairly far below concern about marriage (31%), and well below the top three concerns — time, money, and health (just under 50%).
- Still, dying remains a serious concern for 21% of adults under the age of 35, 16% of 35-to-54-year-olds, and 15% of adults 55 and over. The key issue is health, but only 16% of Canadians over the age of 55 who describe their health as "fair" or "poor" express concern about dying, compared to 26% of those aged 35 to 54 and 25% of adults between the ages of 18 and 34.

These patterns are similar to what we found a decade ago; as I reminded readers at that time, when one is younger and health is a major personal concern, anxiety about dying is understandably higher than when one has had the chance to live a fairly long life. Words used at the funeral of an Ontario 21-year-old a few years ago sum things up well: "When death strikes the very old, it may break our hearts, but when death strikes the very young, it's enough to break our spirits. We want to scream our protests about all that could have been and should have been."[41]

I will never forget, as a 21-year-old, pressing the soft face of a whimpering baby who was only about five weeks old close to my own face, and feeling her little fingers gripping my finger — in her pain and confusion seemingly reaching out desperately, unable to fight off her spinal meningitis. Life had been particularly harsh for her; she was what was known then as "a welfare baby," and was being

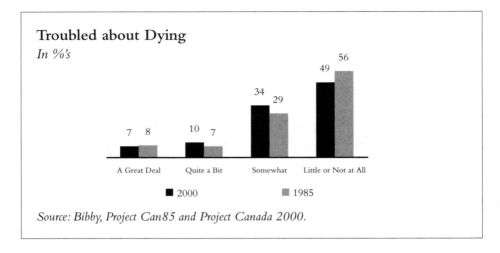

Troubled about Dying

In %'s

	A Great Deal	Quite a Bit	Somewhat	Little or Not at All
2000	7	10	34	49
1985	8	7	29	56

■ 2000   ▓ 1985

Source: Bibby, Project Can85 and Project Canada 2000.

cared for transitionally by my mother on her way to an adoptive home. She died about one week later.

"Pinball" Clemons relates his experience of speaking at the funeral of a 14-year-old boy named Danny who died of leukemia. "He was a wonderful person," says Clemons. "The other kids loved him, and his tutors and teachers had suffered immensely as they'd watched the disease progress in him. I stood there wondering what to say." He pondered addressing the question of "Why?" He says he instead "thanked God for allowing Danny to come into our lives, for his short time among us, for his not having to go through any more pain."[42] Still, the brevity of some lives is harsh beyond comprehension.

What's Going to Happen

Canadians have been very reluctant to rule out the idea of life after death. In 1945, Gallup found that only 16% indicated they definitely *didn't* believe in life beyond death, with the figure reaching 19% in 1960.[43] Our *Project Canada* surveys have found that, since 1975, the proportion of those offering a clear-cut "no" has actually decreased from 17% in the mid-70s to 10% as of 2000. Since 1975, a consistent majority of about 65% has asserted positive belief.

What has been changing over the years is the level of decisiveness with which Canadians both endorse life after death and reject it. They may be more reluctant to rule out the possibility, but they are also more reluctant to say they know for sure. In 1985, for example,

TABLE 4.11 **Belief in Life after Death, 1975, 1985, 2000**
"Do you believe in life after death?"

	1975	1985	2000
Yes	65%	65%	68%
I definitely do.	48	36	31
I think so.	17★	29	37
No	35	35	32
I don't think so.	18★	20	22
I definitely do not.	17	15	10

★*Estimate; response categories in 1975 were "Yes" (17%), "No" (17%), and "Uncertain" (35%).*

Sources: Bibby, Project Can75, Project Can85, and Project Canada 2000.

36% of the population said they "definitely" believed in life after death, while only 29% said, "I think so." As of 2000, things are reversed: now the 37% who "think" there's life after death exceed the 31% who say they are "definite" about it.

Many Canadians also subscribe to a number of other beliefs that confirm and help to clarify their belief in life after death.

- More than six in ten say they believe in *near-death experiences, heaven,* and *angels,* and the same proportion maintain that *how we live will influence what happens to us after we die.*
- Close to five in ten maintain that they believe in *hell* and our ability to have *contact with the spirit world,* with three in ten thinking, more specifically, that *we can communicate with the dead.*

When we focus specifically on those people who believe in life after death, some elements of their thinking become clearer. The vast majority also tend to believe in heaven and angels and near-death experiences. They further believe that our fate after death will be tied to how we have lived. Smaller majorities believe in hell and in our ability to have contact with the spirit world. A minority of life after death believers think it's possible to communicate with the dead.

In short, most Canadians who believe in life after death reflect their dominant Judaeo-Christian backgrounds in associating the afterlife with heaven, angels, and — to a lesser extent — hell. So it

TABLE 4.12 **Related Beliefs and the Extent to Which They Are Held by Those Believing in Life after Death, 2000**

% Indicating They "Definitely" Believe or "Think" They Believe

	NATIONAL TOTALS	HELD BY THOSE WHO BELIEVE IN LIFE AFTER DEATH
Life after death	68%	
Near-death experiences	68	80%
Heaven	65	84
Angels	64	83
How we live influences afterlife	62	79
Hell	46	61
We can contact spirit world	45	59
Communication with the dead	31	43

Source: Bibby, Project Canada 2000.

is that when we ask people for their views on what happens after death, they either respond in "heaven and hell" kinds of terms, or have fairly little to say.

- Seventeen percent maintain the afterlife will involve rewards and punishments; for a small number, there will be rewards but no punishments (3%). Illustrative of the former are the comments of a Gen X Edmonton communications specialist who is active in her evangelical church: "I know I am going to heaven. I believe there will be a Judgement Day and the Lord will determine everyone's future based on their commitment to Jesus Christ."[44]
- Close to another 10% of the population feel that we'll be reincarnated. Obviously, they include people in traditions such as Hinduism, which teach the idea. But belief in reincarnation is more pervasive than that. A small business owner in Vancouver, for example, who retains her United Church "ID" but is not actively involved, tells us, "When my physical body has given up, packed it in, died, I believe my spirit will continue to exist and that when the time is right, my spirit will be given another assignment and will be housed in another body."[45]

- Some 3% of Canadians offer other responses. A Muslim university professor from Manitoba offers insight into her personal view of life after death. She tells us she expects to be questioned and judged right after she dies. "I believe that after death my soul will become free from my body and my mere six senses. My soul will have the power of seeing and knowing in an unlimited way."[46]
- The dominant answer to our question, however — offered by some 40% — is that there is something beyond death, but respondents acknowledge they have no idea what it will be like. One 24-year-old university student sums up these common sentiments when she admits, "I have absolutely no idea what will happen to me when I die, although I do believe that there is something after this life."[47]
- Most of the remaining 30% of Canadians are either unsure about whether or not there is life after death or have concluded that things will end with death. A 56-year-old who teaches at York University in Toronto and says he has no religion expresses his thoughts this way: "It will be like before I was born — no consciousness."[48]
- A comparison with 1980 shows that there has been very little change over at least the past two decades in how Canadians view life after death.

While the majority of people across the country endorse a variety of views relating to life after death, they also differ to some extent along fairly identifiable lines. One is *religious group involvement*. Those most active in religious groups are, if anything, less likely to be currently asking the question about life after death — primarily because many feel they have resolved the matter. Yet to the extent that people are involved in groups, they tend to be more likely than less active individuals to believe in life after death, heaven, and hell, to believe that the way we live now influences what happens to us when we die, and to describe the hereafter as being characterized by rewards and punishments.

However, these various beliefs about life after death are hardly the prerogative of Canadians highly involved in organized religion.

TABLE 4.13 **Views of Life after Death**

"Which of the following comes closest to your view of life after death?"

	1980	2000
I believe there must be something beyond death, but I have no idea what it may be like.	40%	42%
There is life after death, with rewards and punishments.	19	17
The notion of reincarnation expresses my view of what happens.	7	8
There is life after death, with rewards but no punishments.	3	3
I am unsure whether there is life after death.	16	17
I don't believe that there is life after death.	13	10
Other	2	3
Totals	100	100

Sources: Bibby, Project Can80 and Project Canada 2000.

- When we look at people who *never attend* religious services, we find that some 70% are raising the life-after-death question, half believe in life after death, one in three in heaven, and one in five in hell. Among those who hold an array of ideas is a 35-year-old Vancouver environmental engineer who is articulate in laying out his thoughts: "I believe my soul (for lack of a better word) will remain somewhat intact. I believe I will be granted an altered state of being, which allows realization of lessons learned in mortal life and complete access to the subconscious. I also believe that I will take on new roles/responsibilities of guiding the mortal."[49]
- And being a regular worshipper does not bring with it a guarantee that one will be particularly well informed or convinced of what lies beyond the grave. Close to 30% of *weekly attenders* acknowledge that they have no idea what life after death will be like.

But I — like you — don't need survey data to be aware of such a fact. Over the years, I have been taken aback on several occasions by the limited extent to which highly involved people have thought about what will happen when we die. Moreover, it doesn't stop with the people in the pew. Perhaps a telling commentary on what religious groups have to say about life after death — or *don't* have to say about it — is what I have learned during the course of my fairly extensive journeys across the country over the past few decades: significant numbers of clergy agree with one Protestant minister who was honest enough to tell me on one occasion, "I don't know what I can say this Easter Sunday about life after death."

There are, however, noticeable differences in beliefs about what is going to happen, based on *religious group affiliation.* Conservative Protestants are more likely than people from other groups to endorse concrete life-after-death beliefs. They tend to be followed in order by Roman Catholics outside Quebec, Catholics in Quebec, Mainline Protestants, and people who identify with Other Faiths. Consensus between affiliates of various groups is high on the general belief in life after death and heaven, but drops off when it comes to ideas such as hell, and the idea that the afterlife will involve rewards and punishments.

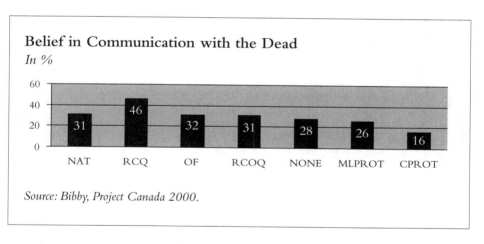

Belief in Communication with the Dead
In %

	NAT	RCQ	OF	RCOQ	NONE	MLPROT	CPROT
	31	46	32	31	28	26	16

Source: Bibby, Project Canada 2000.

- Differences between Roman Catholics in Quebec and Catholics elsewhere are interesting. While similar proportions — some 75% — believe in life after death, *Quebec Catholics* are much less likely than other Catholics to think that how we live will influence what will happen to us when we die, to believe in hell, or to think life beyond death will involve rewards and punishments.

- Two in three *Religious Nones* say they raise the question of what happens after death "often" or "sometimes," and just under half say they believe there is life beyond death. One in three think that what happens to us when we die will be influenced by how we live now, and one in four believes in heaven.

TABLE 4.14 **Life after Death (LAD) Items by Attendance and Group, 2000**

	ASKING LAD QUESTION	BELIEVE IN LAD	BELIEVE IN HEAVEN	BELIEVE HOW LIVE	BELIEVE IN HELL	NO IDEA	REWARD AND PUNISH
NATIONALLY	71%	68%	65%	61%	47%	35%	18%
Weekly	63	84	94	84	69	29	44
Monthly	76	83	85	88	69	31	31
Yearly	75	67	64	57	44	41	10
Never	68	49	33	42	22	29	4
CPROT	59	78	90	83	82	14	65
RCOQ	77	76	79	74	63	37	27
RCQ	79	75	72	58	41	41	12
MLPROT	70	68	69	64	48	39	11
Other Faiths	81	68	40	65	17	32	7
No Religion	63	44	24	34	13	27	5

Source: Bibby, Project Canada 2000.

Canadians of all ages, female and male, and of varying educational levels have very similar ideas surrounding life after death, with some minor differences:

- *Young adults* under 35 are slightly more likely than others both to reflect on what happens after death and to say they believe in life after death.

"What Do You Think Will Happen to You after You Die?"

Some Have Pretty Conventional Ideas

"I believe that we are placed on this earth through the miracle of birth given to us by our heavenly Father so when we die our spirit goes back to be with Him [and] all of those who have gone before us."
— *A 69-year-old female from near Montreal who is active in her United Church.*

"Because I have repented of my sin and placed my faith in Jesus, my soul will join, for eternity, all the believers from ages past. I hope it's exciting, because eternity is a long time."
— *A 35-year-old evangelical from Vancouver; she is a public relations consultant.*

"My soul will go to heaven. At the end of the world, my soul will be reunited with my renewed body and I will live in the new earth, this time not having to fight against sickness, suffering and sin."
— *A Reform elder from Hamilton in his mid-30s; he works in public affairs.*

Others Are a Bit Less Conventional

"Physically I will be put into a modest coffin and buried. Spiritually I 'believe' my spiritual energy will become the soul of a new person."
— *A Calgary administrator, 35; she says she is a nonpractising Christian.*

"I believe your essence lives on in the memories and hearts of those you touched in your life, and you go back to being a part of the sky, sea, and the sun."
— *A government worker in his late 30s; he doesn't attend services or identify with any group.*

A Good Number Are Thinking of Reincarnation

"Because I believe in reincarnation, I think I will come back in a different form that will be determined by karma and the life I lead now."
— *A 22-year-old university student in Alberta; a Hindu, she values her faith highly.*

"You get points for learning. Then, in death, you review the life you led. To me the ultimate reason for life is to learn and to perfect, so you're able to come back many times to learn something more."
— *Canadian Lynn Johnston, creator of the comic strip* For Better or for Worse *(Todd, 1996: 107).*

Some Have Little Idea — Maybe Hoping for Life after Death

"I don't know, though it would probably vary from day to day on how devout I'm feeling (you can tell I was raised in the United Church, right?)."
— *A 50-ish writer with a national magazine.*

"I cannot control what will happen when I die. I need to make the best use of my life now when I have some control of it."
— *A 73-year-old retired biological scientist and an active Buddhist.*

"Intellectually, I don't believe in living forever or in an afterlife. But I'd love to be proved wrong. In some sly little part of my brain, I think maybe I'm exempt."
— *Evelyn Lau, whose best-selling books include her autobiography* Runaway *and* Fresh Girls *(Todd, 1996: 71).*

Source: Project Canada Quota Sample, Winter, 2001–02.

- W*omen* are somewhat more inclined than men to endorse virtually all these beliefs. Consistent with the overall national pattern, women are more likely than men to say they believe in life after death, but they are also more apt to acknowledge that they have no idea what the afterlife will be like.
- *University graduates* are just as likely as others to believe in life after death; however, they are less inclined to believe in heaven and hell. Despite their higher level of formal education, they show no greater inclination to know what to expect from life after death. This finding is an important reminder that formal education, and science more specifically, has little to offer Canadians when it comes to comprehending the nature of life after death.

I want to come back to Pierre Trudeau. As most readers know, he was raised in a home where his mother was a particularly devout Roman Catholic, and even more so following the death of his father. Trudeau himself was married in a Catholic church, with Margaret converting to Catholicism. His three sons were baptized Catholic,

TABLE 4.15 **Life after Death Items by Age, Gender, and Education, 2000**

	ASKING LAD QUESTION	BELIEVE IN LAD	BELIEVE IN HEAVEN	BELIEVE HOW LIVE	BELIEVE IN HELL	NO IDEA	REWARD AND PUNISH
NATIONALLY	71%	68%	65%	62%	46%	35%	18%
18–34	81	72	65	61	49	36	16
35–54	67	69	65	61	47	37	18
55+	64	63	65	64	42	33	18
Females	73	72	71	68	49	41	18
Males	68	64	59	55	44	29	18
Degree-plus	74	66	56	59	39	33	16
HS-Some PS	69	69	65	61	49	37	16
Less than HS	69	68	76	65	53	36	20

Source: Bibby, Project Canada 2000.

and his funeral, of course, was a Catholic ceremony. Following his death, Margaret Trudeau maintained that her former husband had been a religious man who not only accepted death but also welcomed it without a fight. She maintained that he spent his last days talking about his imminent death — that he believed in resurrection and that "he knew Michel would be the first to reach him and then his mother would come and his father would come." Such were the thoughts and hopes of the highly respected former prime minister.[50]

Emotional Responses to Death

We have also attempted to probe the dominant emotional response people have to death by asking Canadians, *"What is your primary response to the reality of death?"* Five response possibilities have been posed: fear, sorrow, mystery, hope, and no particular feeling. In 2000, an open-ended opportunity was provided for respondents to cite any other response they regarded as primary. Obviously all of us respond to death with varied emotions. When we first ran this item back in 1975, a Roman Catholic woman from Drummondville, Quebec, who was 47 at the time beautifully summed up prevalent mixed emotions: "My response to death is sadness softened by hope."[51] Our interest nonetheless has been in the *primary* emotions that people tend to associate with death generally.

As of the latest survey, the dominant response to death people reported is sorrow (25%), followed very closely by mystery (22%). Those two responses are followed in turn by hope, no particular feeling, and fear.

Compared to 20 years ago, sorrow and mystery have supplanted mystery and "no particular feeling" as the sentiments most frequently reported. The proportion of people indicating their primary response to death is hope has remained about the same, while the percentage citing fear is down slightly from 1980.

What is especially noteworthy are the variations in these responses by service attendance. *Weekly attenders*, for example, are far more likely than others to say hope is their primary response, *monthlys* most commonly report mystery and hope, and *yearlys* and *nevers* say sorrow and mystery — with nevers also more likely than others to indicate "no particular feeling."

TABLE 4.16 **Primary Response to Death**

"What would you say your primary response is to the reality of death?"

	2000	1980
Sorrow	25%	19%
Mystery	22	23
Hope	18	17
No particular feeling	16	20
Fear	14	18
Other/Varied	5	3
Totals	100	100

Sources: Bibby, Project Can80 and Project Canada 2000.

Responses to death also vary considerably depending on the religious group with which one identifies.

- *Conservative Protestants* are considerably more inclined than others to say their dominant reaction to death is one of hope — followed by mystery.
- *Roman Catholics outside Quebec* most commonly cite hope and sorrow, *Catholics in Quebec* mystery, sorrow, and fear. One Roman Catholic university student from Alberta, a female who is 20, verbalizes the anxiety some feel: "I like to think that I will go to a better place. But generally I don't try to think about it because it kind of freaks me out."[52]
- Sorrow and mystery and no particular feeling are the most frequent responses of *Mainline Protestants*. One United Church woman from rural Saskatchewan expresses her primary feelings about death this way: "I feel a sense of mystery, and maybe a bit of apprehension about the unknown."[53]
- The dominant reaction of people who identify with *Other Faith* groups is one of mystery.
- And what about people who do not identify with any group — the so-called *Religious Nones*? They say that their two primary responses to death are sorrow and mystery, with no particular feeling a somewhat distant third. A 35-year-old arts fundraiser who works in western Canada illustrates the sense of mystery and adventure some such people experience

as they reflect on death. Describing himself as an agnostic, he proceeds to tell us, "I do believe in some type of afterlife, but not necessarily as depicted in any religious teachings. My ideal afterlife would have me re-experiencing all the great times both in my life and throughout history."[54]

TABLE 4.17 **Dominant Emotional Response to Death by Attendance and Group, 2000**

	SORROW	MYSTERY	HOPE	NO PARTIC	FEAR	OTHER
NATIONALLY	25%	23%	18%	16%	15%	3%
Weekly	18	16	43	9	9	5
Monthly	20	27	25	15	12	1
Yearly	26	26	11	17	18	2
Never	32	20	9	22	12	5
RCOQ	24	17	26	14	16	3
RCQ	24	28	12	12	22	2
MLPROT	27	20	17	22	10	4
CPROT	11	20	52	6	8	3
Other Faiths	15	36	15	15	18	<1
No Religion	32	29	6	19	10	4

Source: Bibby, Project Canada 2000.

Dominant responses to death do not differ very much by age, gender, or education.

- *Young Gen Xers* under 35 express marginally higher levels of mystery and fear and a lower level of hope than others. Slightly higher proportions of *adults over 55* report the polar responses of hope and no particular feeling.
- *Females* are a bit more inclined than males to cite fear and to have one main feeling.
- *Education* has little bearing on the primary emotional responses people have to death.

As we have been noting, despite the post-1960s attendance drop-off, Canadians continue to have a strong sense that the gods

TABLE 4.18 **Dominant Emotional Response to Death by Age, Gender, and Education, 2000**

	SORROW	MYSTERY	HOPE	NO PARTIC	FEAR	OTHER
NATIONALLY	25%	23%	19%	16%	14%	3%
18–34	26	26	12	14	18	4
35–54	26	22	19	14	16	3
55+	22	20	25	21	9	3
Females	27	21	19	12	18	3
Males	24	24	18	21	10	3
Degree-plus	28	20	21	19	10	2
HS–some PS	21	26	17	15	18	3
Less than HS	27	22	17	15	15	4

Source: Bibby, Project Canada 2000.

need to be brought in on critical life passages, including death. Since at least the 1980s, there has been no decrease in the inclination people have had to want funerals carried out for them by a religious group. Some 45% report that religious groups have performed funerals for them in the past, while 57% are saying that they anticipate approaching religious groups to have funerals carried out in the future. Perhaps significantly, this latter figure represents a jump from 44% in 1985.

- Future funerals performed by religious groups are envisioned by approximately 60% of *weeklys, monthlys, and yearlys,* along with about 40% of *nevers.*
- The demand for future funerals is in the 55% to 65% range for all *Catholic, Protestant, and Other Faith* affiliates — and characterizes one in three *Nones.*
- Many *older people* have already had funerals carried out for family members and friends in the past; *younger adults* are more likely to indicate they anticipate requiring religious groups to carry out funerals on their behalf in the future.
- Additional analyses not reported here reveal that there are no noteworthy differences in the anticipated demand for religious funerals by either the gender or educational level of individuals.

These findings point to a Canada where people are not merely fascinated with the question of whether or not there is life after death. Because of the value they place on both life itself and the relationships they cherish, the reality of death carries with it considerable significance. As they approach death, will they live again? As they watch relatives and friends die, only the most unreflective can help but wonder if this is a final farewell or just the end of one chapter in a continuing story.

The findings make it clear that the majority of Canadians believe there is something beyond death. But they also show that most people have no idea what it will be like. As a result, the majority are inclined to respond to death primarily in terms of sorrow or mystery, rather than hope.

The reality of death is a dramatic declaration that life is finite. Death is also a poignant event that calls Canadians to ponder the

TABLE 4.19 **Religious Funerals by Attendance, Affiliation, and Age, 1985 and 2000**

"Has a funeral been performed for you by a religious group in the PAST or, as you see it, will one probably be carried out for you in the FUTURE?"

	1985		2000	
	PAST	FUTURE	PAST	FUTURE
NATIONALLY	46%	44	44	57
Weekly	52	50	48	61
Monthly	55	40	55	61
Yearly	45	48	47	66
Never	37	28	35	38
RCs outside Quebec	50	44	44	64
RCs in Quebec	49	52	39	66
Mainline Protestants	52	43	57	58
Conservative Protestants	45	47	41	66
Other Faiths	43	27	48	54
No Religion	25	36	35	34
18–34	39	50	40	65
35–54	50	44	47	58
55+	55	37	47	50

Sources: Bibby, Project Can85 and Project Canada 2000.

"What Will Happen to You When You Die?"
Some Further Thoughts

Maybe It's an Energy Thing

"My energy will remain, though I'm not sure in what form. It may dissipate or it may remain intact waiting for an opportunity to become something living again."
— *A 31-year-old Ottawa writer, raised Catholic and interested in spirituality; she is now not practising any particular religion.*

"I will be cremated and my ashes spread from the top of some mountain. My energy will join and become part of the electricity around us."
— *A self-employed Calgarian, 35, who says she has no religion.*

"What is it that makes a human being go? It is energy. And the physicians tell us that energy never vanishes. So when the body is worn out and dies, where does the energy go? You should never rule out any possibility."
— *Writer Robertson Davies in 1994; unsure as to what happens after death, he maintained we need to keep our minds open (Todd, 1996: 138).*

Some Are Combining a Number of Ideas

"I like to believe my spirit will go to heaven, and that perhaps spirits become angels, or are re-incarnated. There is something very powerful out there and I know somehow we will all be a part of it."
— *A Roman Catholic banker, 42; she lives in a small city in Alberta.*

"I had a near-death experience as a teenager that changed my life. As I burst into the white light I was completely surrounded by a strong, soothing, serene, power-ful presence. I felt loved unconditionally, in my true essence, part of the Oneness."
— *A 59-year-old court worker from Dartmouth, Nova Scotia; raised Catholic, she hasn't been to church since she was 27.*

Others Say Death Is the End

"Only people who knew me will remember me. I think you are just gone."
— *A Vancouver teacher, 34; she says she is United but does not attend church.*

"My person shall be gone and my building materials will be recycled."
— *A Quebec professor, 64; he describes himself as a practising Catholic.*

"Nothing. Worms."
— *A 33-year-old urban planner on the west coast who describes himself as an atheist.*

"I certainly don't [believe in an afterlife]. It's just the same as when you squish an ant on the sidewalk. No one thinks ants go to ant heaven. It's sheer hubris that we would have the gall to think there's an afterlife for creatures like us."
— *Author W.P. Kinsella, whose works include* Shoeless Joe *(Todd, 1996: 26).*

"I don't believe I have a soul, and I don't believe in heaven or hell or a creator. When I die my brain and therefore my self-awareness will cease, and my corpse will eventually be recycled into the ecosystem."
— *A 34-year-old biologist from Cold Lake, Alberta; he is a nonpractising, nonconfirmed Protestant.*

Source: Project Canada Quota Sample, Winter, 2001–02.

possibility that existence more generally may not be finite. Here again, the theist would say that the gods seem to be stirring the souls of Canadians.

But as we will see shortly, the stirrings don't end there.

Earlier but Emptier Answers?

One important change that appears to have been taking place in recent decades is the tendency of people to "process" ultimate questions faster than in the past. As we have seen, Canadians today are just as likely to indicate that they reflect on origins, meaning, happiness, and suffering as people were in 1975. However, in each case, the proportion who are "often" thinking about these issues is down from the mid-70s, while the proportion who are "no longer" reflecting on them is up.

TABLE 4.20 **Processing of Ultimate Questions: Adults, 1975 and 2000**

	OFTEN		NO LONGER	
	1975	**2000**	**1975**	**2000**
Origins	18%	11%	27%	31%
Purpose	31	18	11	21
Happiness	31	20	13	22
Suffering	44	27	10	17
Death	27	18	15	20

Sources: Bibby, Project Can75 and Project Canada 2000.

This pattern is consistent with what we have observed for teenagers between 1984 and 2000. Here again, young people are still raising ultimate questions. But, as with adults, the "often" figures are down from 1984, and the "no longer" numbers are up.

An illustrative check of the questioning of purpose and suffering, comparing adult age cohorts in 2000 with those in 1975, confirms that a change has been taking place. There has been no significant decline in the inclination for Canadians in all three age groups — 18 to 34, 35 to 54, and 55 plus — to raise questions about life's purpose and the meaning of suffering. However, in the instance of each cohort, fewer people are raising those questions "often" and more people are "no longer" asking them.

TABLE 4.21 **Processing of Ultimate Questions: Teens, 1984 and 2000**

	OFTEN		NO LONGER	
	1984	2000	1984	2000
Origins	22%	17%	22%	24%
Purpose	30	26	13	17
Happiness	35	28	12	17
Suffering	37	25	12	18
Death	43	39	11	15

Sources: Bibby, Project Teen Canada 84 and Project Teen Canada 2000.

Such striking and consistent findings about the change in the way ultimate questions are being processed points to at least three possibilities. The first is that the questions are being resolved faster and at earlier ages. The problem here is that we have already seen evidence that "no longer" does not necessarily mean questions have been answered. This leads us to the second possibility: that the questions have simply been set aside. Canadians say that the pace of life has increased dramatically in the past ten years, that they seldom have time to do the things they want to do. Time and energy are being consumed by the pursuit of things like education and careers and family life. In the midst of it all, it may well be that people are not taking time to reflect on "life's big questions" to the extent that they did three decades ago.

There's a third possibility that is not exclusive from the second one. Perhaps Canadians are being nudged by the gods to raise such questions from the time they are fairly young, but they are lacking for answers. In Rodney Stark's market language, the problem may not lie on the demand side but on the supply side. There aren't a lot of clear-cut market offerings being made by religious groups and secular organizations.

What this situation suggests is that Christianity and Other Faith sources are not providing people with very much information on the nature of post-life existence, in particular. Religious groups are having at best a marginal influence on how Canadians see death and — presumably — on how they relate to it when relatives, friends, and others die. It is one thing for a 24-year-old university

TABLE 4.22 **Purpose and Suffering by Age, 1975 and 2000**

	1975			2000		
	18-34	35-54	55+	18-34	35-54	55+
Purpose						
Often	31%	28%	34%	19%	18%	18%
Sometimes	47	55	48	57	52	46
No longer	16	9	8	18	23	23
Never have	6	8	10	6	7	13
Suffering						
Often	40	42	54	27	25	31
Sometimes	45	45	44	54	51	50
No longer	13	10	7	15	20	14
Never have	2	3	5	4	4	5

Sources: Bibby, Project Can75 and Project Canada 2000.

student with "no religion" to say, "I have no idea what will happen to me when I die, but I hope that there is a heaven." It is another thing for another student, a 21-year-old Roman Catholic, to say, "I have absolutely no idea what will happen to me when I die. The question really troubles me because there seems to be no clear answer. Even with faith it is still scary not really knowing what is waiting for me."[55] It's apparent that she speaks for many people who have ties with religious groups, Catholic and otherwise.

Two Canadians who have had much to say about life after death are Tom Harpur and Brian Stiller. As the religion writer for the *Toronto Star* through the mid-80s and the author of many books since, Harpur has maintained that he feels "a deep, granite-like conviction that the hour of our death is indeed the gateway to a new adventure, a step to a fuller life beyond." The former Anglican priest feels the biblical writers "did their best, describing streets of gold and gates of sapphire," but "knew that the afterlife would be a reality beyond compare, and so they used the most valuable things they knew of to give it form." He thinks they came closest to describing what it will be like when they spoke "not so much of harps and precious stones as of healed relationships and an end to tears."[56] Brian Stiller, author and lifelong evangelical leader, has written, "If Jesus hadn't risen from the dead, the Apostle Paul would have thrown up his hands and said, 'Hey, let's go out and party, 'cause folks, this is all there is!' The reason he doesn't is that Christ's resurrection is proof that life doesn't end at death . . . Heaven is a real place where those accepted by Christ will live. It's a place where life is lived on a physical plane, where recreation and work aren't opposites as they are for us today . . . I live today knowing that I live forever."[57] More such voices need to be heard.

The current situation calls Canadian religious groups to ask themselves whether in fact the faiths they value have something decisive to say about ultimate questions relating to life and death. If so, they need to be doing a much better job of explicitly and effectively sharing their messages with people from Newfoundland to British Columbia.

In the midst of such an apparent lack of answers to the death question especially, there is good reason to believe that the "questions that only the gods can answer" will continue to be raised well into the new century and beyond. The reason? Sociologically speaking, people will feel the need to make sense of life and death. Theologically speaking, there is considerable evidence that the gods are taking matters into their own hands in trying to get through to Canadians. Perhaps because of their growing impatience with ineffective churches, they have been showing up in person.

CHAPTER FIVE

Relentless Gods

So far our examination of religion in Canada has turned up some important findings at both the group and individual levels. For all the talk about the demise of organized religion, we have found signs of new life among the country's established religious groups. We have also seen that people continue to pursue answers to the important questions concerning the meaning of life and death. However, in part because of the ongoing shortcomings of organized religion, growing numbers of people are putting the questions aside for lack of adequate answers.

I have been true to my word, playing the role of the sociological researcher in carefully looking at the observable side of religion. Those, after all, are the rules of the scientific game. As philosopher John Hick has put it, "God is not a phenomenon available for scientific study, but religion is."[1] At the same time, as I emphasized in the Introduction, to treat religion as if it is only a human phenomenon may be to ignore the key to understanding what is happening in reality's so-called observable realm. It's something like looking at the person on the ladder who has just got an electric shock while screwing in a light bulb — and trying to describe what happened without being aware of the electricity.

It's not, of course, scientific to *assume* that what people believe is true or that what they think they are experiencing is in fact what is taking place; those claims need to be verified. But when individuals make claims about realities relating to the nonobservable realm, it's also not good science to assume they can be reduced solely to social and personal factors. To return to the light bulb analogy, to do so would be to limit explanations to the person and fail to take into account the electric current. When people make claims involving the nonobservable, such ideas and events may be due to (a) human factors only or (b) factors that cannot be empirically known, but nonetheless are real.

This balance is particularly important to maintain as we turn to beliefs and behaviour relating to the gods. There's a whole lot of believing and experiencing and communicating going on. Maybe all this activity is telling us about people and the times. Then again, the theist who is sitting with us in the booth and offering colour commentary may have a different take on things. Perhaps the gods have grown impatient trying to reach Canadians through the churches and have now accelerated a supplementary strategy: relating to Canadians — directly.

Belief

God continues to do well in the polls. Back in 1975, we included a detailed item on belief in God in the first of our *Project Canada* surveys. We asked, *"Which of the following statements comes closest to expressing what you believe about God?"* and provided seven response possibilities, including an open-ended opportunity for respondents to say what they believe.

Some 91% of Canadians indicated that they believed in God or a higher power at least some of the time, 48% expressed unequivocal belief in "God," and a further 26% expressed tentative belief. Only 6% appeared to be agnostics, and just 2% atheists.

- An examination of the results by service attendance showed that *weekly* attenders were far more likely than others — including even *monthly* churchgoers — to express belief with no doubts.
- At the other extreme of service going, *nevers* were much more inclined than other people to take an agnostic or atheistic

TABLE 5.1 **Belief in God by Service Attendance, 1975**

	NATIONALLY	WEEKLY	MONTHLY	YEARLY	NEVER
I know God exists, and I have no doubts about it.	48%	77%	46%	39%	18%
While I have doubts, I feel that I do believe in God.	22	16	37	26	14
I don't believe in a personal God, but I do believe in a higher power of some kind.	17	3	12	23	28
I find myself believing in God some of the time, but not at other times.	4	2	2	6	7
I don't know whether there is a God, and I don't believe there is any way to find out.	6	<1	3	4	20
I don't believe in God.	2	0	0	<1	11
None of the above represents what I believe.	1	1	<1	2	2

Source: Bibby, Project Can75.

position, but 67% still asserted belief in either God (39%) or a higher power (28%).

- The diversity of responses could be seen in the observations of three Montrealers all around their late 40s — the first a Roman Catholic from a devout home but now attending only a few times a year, who commented, "Each of us creates God according to our own way of thinking." The second, who subscribed to No Religion, said, "God is an invention of the human race to explain what we cannot comprehend," and the third, a Christian Scientist, told us, "God is both a father and the essence of everything."[2]

I used the same item in the 1980 survey, but from 1985 onward, I've simply asked, *"Do you believe that God exists?"* — giving people the four response possibilities of "Yes, I definitely do," "Yes, I think so," "No, I don't think so," and "No, I definitely do not." The item obviously results in the omission of some who think in terms of "a higher power," but not all. A university student, 23, who says she has "no religion as of now," indicates she "believes in a higher being," adding, "if you call it God, Buddha, it doesn't matter."[3] A retired Windsor professor, 57, however, is among those who make the God–higher power distinction: "According to my religious beliefs, the universe does not have a God that is the Creator; it has no beginning and no ending but is ever changing and self-sustaining. I do, however, recognize the existence of Divinity or a Divine Force."[4] The item, then, misses some people who believe in a higher power; it does, however, give us information on "God" specifically.

Positive belief in God has remained very consistent over time, at just above 80%. However, similar to the trends with belief in life after death, people have shown signs of being a bit less decisive. Over the past two decades or so, there has been about a 10% drop in those who "definitely" believe in God, along with a very modest decrease from 1990s' levels in the proportion of those who "definitely" do not believe in God. Accordingly, the "think so's" have increased about ten percentage points since the mid-80s, and the "don't think so's" are up about three percentage points from 1985.

Illustrative of clear-cut belief are the observations of a 65-year-old journalist who is active in his Mennonite Brethren church in Winnipeg: "I do believe in God! I think of God primarily through the lens of Jesus Christ. But I also think of God as Sovereign spirit who stands above and beyond everything that exists."[5] An example of people in the "don't think so" category is a 24-year-old University of Lethbridge

TABLE 5.2 **Belief in God, 1985–2000**

"Do you believe that God exists?"

	1985	1990	1995	2000
YES	84%	82%	80%	81%
Yes, I definitely do.	61	56	57	49
Yes, I think so.	23	26	23	32
No, I don't think so.	10	10	11	13
No, I definitely do not.	6	8	9	6

Source: Bibby, Project Canada Survey Series.

student with no religious ties who says she is "undecided about whether or not there is a God — but leaning toward 'no.'"[6]

What do average people mean by "God"? The belief's high correlation with service attendance suggests most Canadians are thinking in fairly conventional, predominantly Judaeo-Christian terms. That said, considerable diversity obviously exists both between and within groups. Many may agree with the view of the Mennonite Brethren journalist just cited, who sees God as revealed through the person of Christ — and more. Others may be inclined, like this 26-year-old evangelical clerk from Alberta, to affirm belief in God almost solely in terms of Jesus: "My desire is to live a complete life close to my Lord Jesus Christ."[7] Some may be comfortable agreeing with a 41-year-old Catholic medical assistant originally from the Philippines, who told us the Apostles' Creed is pretty much her guideline — she believes "in God the Father almighty, creator of heaven and earth."[8] A good many others, however, may feel more affinity with the more complex statement offered by a United Church minister from Toronto:

> God, for me, is that power for which there are no adequate words; the creative source from which everything comes, which resides deep within everything. God is ultimate reality, the ground of all existence. God is Life, Breath, Spirit.[9]

What is widespread among Canadians is their belief that they matter to God — not merely that God cares about *people* but about *them* personally. The 2000 survey asked respondents if they *"believe God or a higher power cares about you."* No less than 73% say they either are definitely sure (41%) or think (32%) that God is concerned about them. The remaining 27% are divided between those who don't think that God cares about them (15%) and those who definitely do not think that's the case (12%). One First Nations university student, 24, speaks for many people when she says, "I believe that God exists in the form of a higher power greater than me, a God who cares about humanity and all creation."[10] A 50-year-old Presbyterian woman from Guelph comments,

I believe God to be a compassionate and caring God, One who hurts when we hurt, supports us when we need supporting and celebrates with us during our happy times and successes. God allows us to make our own mistakes and hopefully learn something from the process. I also believe God is understanding when we challenge and question. God is also FORGIVING![11]

Not everyone, of course, is quite so convinced of God's benevolent nature. A Unitarian in his 40s who lives in British Columbia acknowledges, "I am an agnostic. At the god I am agnostic about is close to the enlightenment 'deity' that, if it exists, plays little or no role in the day-to-day affairs of us mortals."[12] At the other end of the country, a 45-year-old nurse who was raised as a "fundamental/evangelical Christian" and now attends a United Church near Halifax tells us, "My 'spiritual thesis' is still in progress. But I believe god is a metaphor for the collective unconscious. I do not believe that god is a separate individual but still affects my life if I am able to plug into that collectivism. Therefore, god is not only love; god is also bad and the metaphor for satan is also the flip side of the same coin as god."[13]

As would be expected, there is a very high correlation between believing in God and believing in a caring God or higher power. Some 89% of Canadians who believe in God also maintain that God or a higher power cares about them; for those who "definitely" believe in God, the figure is 96%.[14] Interestingly, this means that about two in ten people who "think" God exists *do not* feel that God is particularly concerned about them. Conversely, reflecting the fact that some individuals differentiate between God and a higher power, about 2% of those who affirm the existence of a caring "God or higher power" do not believe in "God" as such.

The idea that God exists and cares is pervasive among people who attend services at least once a year and identify with any religious family. It is important to note that this view is also held by approximately one in two people who never attend services and by about one in three Religious Nones. Given the 1:3 ratio, diverse views are not uncommon in this "nothing" category. One 21-year-old Albertan

TABLE 5.3 **Beliefs about God**

	GOD EXISTS	GOD CARES ABOUT ME*
NATIONALLY	81%	73%
Weekly	99	97
Monthly	98	92
Yearly	81	72
Never	55	44
Conservative Protestants	93	92
RCs outside Quebec	91	85
RCs in Quebec	89	76
Mainline Protestants	85	78
Other Faiths	76	67
No Religion	40	36
Atlantic provinces	90	83
Prairies	84	80
Quebec	81	69
Ontario	79	73
British Columbia	77	68
55+	84	77
35–54	81	72
18–34	77	71
Females	84	79
Males	78	67

*Or "a higher power" cares about me.

Source: Bibby, Project Canada 2000.

with no religious ties claims to believe in God and to have felt God's presence "at times in my life when I needed help and support."[15] In contrast, another 21-year-old who describes her religion as "nothing" says, "I don't believe god exists, nor do I believe in a god who cares about me. My very reason for not believing is because what is happening in the world doesn't seem to make sense if there truly is a god."[16]

The prevalence of the twin beliefs in God and a God who cares is slightly higher in the *Atlantic* area and the *Prairies*, as well as among *older adults* and *women*. However, these minor demographic and social variations are not as impressive as the finding that these two beliefs about God are held by solid majorities of people across the country, regardless of region, age, or gender. Together, these responses about God point to an important, pervasive belief among Canadians today: "God exists, and God cares about me."

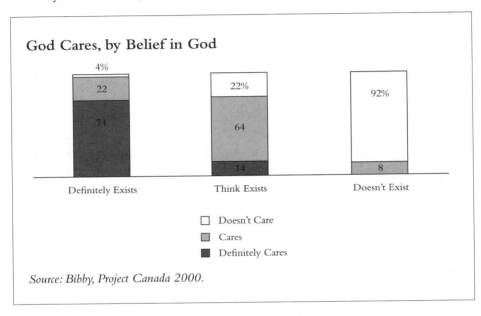

God Cares, by Belief in God

Source: Bibby, Project Canada 2000.

For the record, a Gallup poll conducted in early 1955 found that a higher level of 94% of Canadians claimed to believe in God, with only 6% having doubts.[17] Yet the item that was used read, "*Would you say that you, yourself, believe in God, or do you have doubts about it?*" Since the pollster offered only those two response possibilities, it was apparently not anticipated that people would question the existence of God, at least publicly. The only question was whether their belief in God was accompanied by doubts.

Today, people obviously have licence to think pretty much what they want to think, and to verbalize those thoughts in public. Couple that reality with the recent struggles of churches and one has to think that the heavens are probably fairly pleased with the results of our latest polls.

"Do You Believe in God?"

If so, what do you have in mind when you speak of God?

A Personal, Traditional God

"Yes, I believe in God. By 'God' I mean a personal mind of immense power and knowledge, who created the universe a finite time ago, and is the source of moral value. God, I am prepared to say, has decisively revealed himself in the person of Jesus of Nazareth."

— *A professor in his late 30s who describes himself as a "Christian theist."*

"Jesus has given definition with the human sphere. However, in praying I let my mind wander in holy imagination. I feel his presence every day, with moments when a consciousness of his love and care are so powerful as to be overwhelming."

— *A prominent evangelical leader and educator.*

"Yes. When I speak of God I picture the figure of a tall man with flowing white robes surrounded by a heavenly glow. His arms are open wide as if He is ready to embrace me. I know that I can bring anything to him without embarrassment. My God is also just and merciful. I also see his son Jesus with Him and the Holy Spirit who is in the shape of a dove. This to me also symbolizes the trinity — He is Three in One."

— *A CTV news personality in Ontario; he is a Gen Xer with a Christian Reform background.*

A Bit More Complex

"God is disembodied thought, pure and unlimited energy — light, fire."

— *A 40-year-old Moncton therapist and part-time student; she describes herself as "a non-churchgoing Anglican."*

"God is a non-matter, timeless, limitless and unchangeable existence. Although non-matter, 'The beautiful,' 'The compassionate,' 'The merciful,' and 'The love' are some of his material attributes! God's beauty, compassion, mercy, and love enlighten the 'purest hearts.' Only 'love' can purify hearts."

— *A Muslim professor in his 50s who teaches at a university in western Canada.*

Not God as Conceptualized by Most People

"I think of God as the benign creative intelligence that is creating and maintaining the universe in an ongoing process. The God written about in the Bible and most other religious texts I've read I view as a bad fairy tale."

— *A Saint John, New Brunswick, software specialist; he is 41.*

"'God,' for me, is a metaphor for what we cannot know. Can one 'believe' in a metaphor?"

— *A 70-year-old Unitarian who describes himself as a religious humanist; he lives in Saskatoon.*

"I believe in 'something,' and for lack of another word, and because there is a parallel of sorts, I use the word God. However, the God I've come to believe in is more akin to a universal 'intelligence,' a collective knowing of which we are all a part and into which we can tap. The old model does not 'do it' for me any longer."

— *A 52-year-old from Nova Scotia; she is the organist and choir director in her Anglican church.*

Source: Project Canada Quota Sample, Winter, 2001–02.

In some ways, the inclination of so many Canadians to believe in a God who cares about them personally is somewhat surprising, given that religious groups seem to have been of limited help in getting the word out. Our theist "in the booth" might argue that God has often had to take the initiative in finding other ways of getting the message through to people. If that's the case, based on what Canadians are saying — often fairly privately — perhaps the most effective method has been for God to show up in person.

Experience

To the extent that Canadians assert there is a God or a supreme being, there is probably no more convincing support for such a claim than personal experience — the sense that one has actually encountered that divine reality. Experience confirms that something previously held on an intellectual level actually exists. It's something like finally meeting a person one has heard about for years, and it is particularly important if one has sometimes harboured doubts that the individual really exists. Experiencing God's presence removes all doubt once and for all. It allows one to continue to believe in God, apart from one's involvement in a religious group.

Our surveys indicate that Canadians are convinced God has been showing up in their lives. Dating back to 1975, we have been asking the question, "*Do you believe that you have experienced God's presence?*" Just under 50% currently claim that they have — a level virtually unchanged since 1975. In addition, there have been only small variations in the inclination of people to express certainty about having had or not having had such an experience.

For some people, such as a 58-year-old Anglican priest from a small town in Ontario, the experience of God is both common and frequent: "Yes, I have experienced God many times and in many settings — alone in prayer and/or in the out-of-doors; in corporate worship in large and small groups while leading or while simply participating. It is usually as a sensation like heat, first, on the head and shoulders, often growing in intensity and then waning. However, that description is woefully inadequate."[18] A 22-year-old university student who is Catholic says, "I have felt the presence of God all over the place, including every time I get in my car."[19] A 47-year-old

United Church minister reports feeling God's presence frequently in the course of carrying out his work — including the vivid feelings surrounding his urgent baptism of a child as an emergency helicopter waited to airlift the infant to hospital. "I baptized the child and had an overwhelming feeling of peace. I learned later that the child was fine."[20] Award-winning Canadian Inuit singer Susan Aglukark told Doug Todd that she has "a constant discussion with God. When a decision comes up, the first thing that comes into my mind is, 'Okay God, what now?' That happens thirty to forty times a day."[21]

TABLE 5.4 **Claims of Experiencing God, 1975–2000**

"Do you believe that you have experienced God's presence?"★

	1975	1980	1985	1990	1995	2000
YES	48%	43%	44%	43%	41%	47%
Yes, I definitely do.	22	21	25	20	20	20
Yes, I think so.	26	22	19	23	21	27
NO	52	57	56	57	59	53
No, I don't think so.	–	–	32	31	33	31
No, I definitely do not.	–	–	24	26	26	22

★*In 1975 and 1980, the item read, "Have you ever had a feeling that you somehow were in the presence of God?" with the response options, "Yes, I'm sure I have," "Yes, I think I have," and "No."*

Source: Bibby, Project Canada Survey Series.

For others, the presence of God tends to be fairly dramatic and relatively rare. A 41-year-old woman from Ontario in ministry with the United Church recalls, "I was on a summer internship in northern Alberta and struggling with the question of whether or not I should proceed toward ordination. During a walk one evening, after a particularly stressful session with my supervisor, I felt a moment of peace envelop me and although I didn't hear anything with my ears, I felt like I heard the words, 'It will be all right.' My anxieties about ministry lightened and I knew that I could take the next steps along the path toward ministry."[22] Sometimes the experiencing of God is associated with traumatic events. A Baptist woman in her 50s who lives in Toronto describes a particular experience that

"Do You Feel That You Have Ever Experienced the Presence of God?"

Some Have Had Very Specific Experiences

"Yes. The first and most powerful experience took place more than 35 years ago when I was in second year university. My roommate and I went for a walk in the woods near our residence and then sat down to admire the woods and a marsh in the distance. We sat for perhaps half an hour in absolute silence, and then finally rose and walked quietly out of the woods. Our experience was that of changed perception and a sense of being part of a larger presence that included the whole world, and perhaps the universe. The very air and sky around me seemed golden, and glowing. Years later, we talked about it again after not seeing each other for decades. We both remember it as one of the most powerful experiences of our lives. He now attributes it to brain chemistry. I believe it was what most of us call God."
— *A 57-year-old journalist from Ottawa; he currently has no religious involvement.*

"For simplicity's sake, I could say yes, but it had such an inherently deep personal dimension that it doesn't lend itself to verbal descriptions. It took place in Java, Indonesia, when I was 26 years old, and was the culmination of a long and intense search for 'meaning.' To this day it still marks the pivotal event in my life, and is beyond the capacity of language or imagination to circumscribe adequately. It quenched and quenches my spiritual thirst, transcends the formulations of every religion I have studied, and continues to reveal itself as mystery."
— *A religious studies professor, 48, with a Hindu background; he currently does not identify with any religion.*

For Some, the Experience Has Been Associated with Trauma

"One particular time was in a head-on collision on a highway covered with thick slush. Realizing that I could not steer my car out of the ruts on the road as an out-of-control car was heading straight at me in my lane, my thought was 'I am going to die.' I have no memory of the crash itself, but do remember being completely safe and secure. It is as if giving up control offered me the gift of release and freedom."
— *A female minister to a Mainline Protestant congregation in Manitoba.*

"The death of a nephew ten years ago brought me to my knees in pain and despair, and my whole family was falling apart. Late one night, I took out a Bible (I had not cracked it open in many years) and asked God for help. I believe He heard me and I felt a warm calming presence in the room."
— *A woman from southern Alberta who is active in her local United Church.*

"Probably the most memorable of many experiences was a 'near-death experience' as I awaited surgery many years ago, when I sensed the bright presence of Christ as a shining, loving reality as near as the foot of my hospital bed that then enfolded me in love and peace."
— *A 59-year-old professor and media personality; she attends an Anglican church in Vancouver.*

Source: Project Canada Quota Sample, Winter, 2001–02.

took place "after an accident when my mother and I were hit and run over by a van. Perhaps I was in shock, but a friend came and prayed over us and we were at peace, no worries, no feeling of distress, just complete quietness."[23] A 26-year-old part-time university student told us, "I have experienced God in many different moments of my life. Last night I had my back healed; it was really bothering me and had it prayed for. God's hand came on me and took the pain away."[24]

The profound impact of people thinking they have experienced God can be seen when some individuals who don't even give credibility to the possibility find themselves trying to make sense of what appears to be a God-like encounter. A Unitarian minister told us that she identifies herself with the theological position known as *panentheism,* seeing a bit of divinity in every happening. "Occasionally in my ministry I have felt like the channel between 'something' — some kind of healing energy, God, whatever the language — and another person. It is as if something that needed to be communicated had to go through me. On one occasion ritual was

TABLE 5.5 **Some Correlates of Experiencing God**

	DEFINITELY OR THINK HAVE EXPERIENCED GOD'S PRESENCE
NATIONALLY	47%
Quebec	57
Atlantic provinces	51
Prairies	49
Ontario	41
British Columbia	37
55+	51
35–54	47
18–34	42
Females	52
Males	40
Less than high school	48
Degree-plus	47
Some post-secondary	43

Source: Bibby, Project Canada 2000.

involved; other times it has been more like counseling. But I said things that I didn't know could come from me!" She adds, "It's more than a bit eerie, especially when I don't know how to recognize this entity. I don't believe in a personal god of any kind, and so I do not know how to explain these rather fantastic incidents."[25]

There are some noteworthy variations among Canadians who think they have experienced God:

- *Quebeckers* are the most likely of all Canadians to maintain they have experienced God's presence, while *B.C. residents* are the least likely.
- *Older Canadians* are only marginally more inclined than their younger counterparts to claim that they have had such an experience.
- Five in ten *females* say they have experienced God, compared to four in ten males.
- The belief that one has been in the presence of God differs little by education: those with university degrees, for example, are just as likely as those who never finished high school to say they have had such an experience.

Experience of God Across Generations

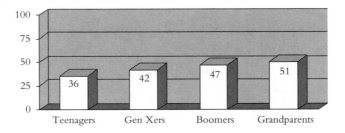

Source: Derived from Bibby, Canada's Teens, *2001: 52.*

The tendency to experience God is not strongly associated with service attendance, at least not regular, weekly attendance. In fact, what is striking is that claims of experiencing God have remained remarkably stable since the mid-70s, in sharp contrast to declining national attendance patterns. This is not to say, however, that the claim one has experienced God is not affected by religious group involvement — just to say that such an experience is hardly the exclusive claim of people who are actively involved in churches.

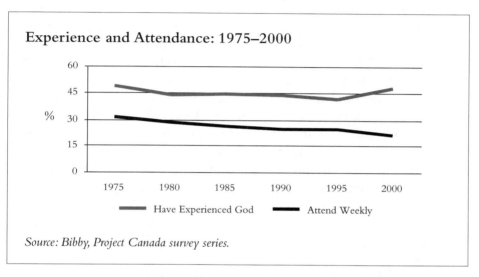

Experience and Attendance: 1975–2000

Source: Bibby, Project Canada survey series.

Prevalence of Experience among Religious Groups
Early thinkers such as Emile Durkheim, in his *Elementary Forms of Religious Life,* went to great lengths to show that the nature of religious experience is grounded in the groups involved.[26] His emphasis was reiterated in the 1960s by Berkeley sociologists Charles Glock and Rodney Stark. In their important pioneering work on the topic, they concluded that what people typically think happens is based largely on what groups tell them they are supposed to experience.[27] More recent work in the U.S. has similarly maintained that certain religious groups structure their activities in order to facilitate religious experiences, with the result that involvement in some religious groups is more conducive than others to religious experience.[28] The research that

Margaret Poloma has carried out on the "Toronto Blessing" charismatic church has served to illustrate and illuminate the role that groups play in cultivating religious experience.[29]

Consistent with such thinking, Canadians who identify with *Conservative Protestant* groups that place a strong emphasis on experiential religion and active involvement — such as Baptists, Pentecostals, Mennonites, and Nazarenes — are considerably more likely than others to maintain that they have experienced God's presence. Yet *Roman Catholics in Quebec*, despite being considerably less inclined than *Catholics in the rest of the country* to attend services regularly, are nonetheless more likely to say they have known God's presence (63% versus 52%). And close to half of those who identify with *Other Faiths* think they have experienced God, even though fewer than one in ten say they are weekly servicegoers. Some 40% of *Mainline Protestants* think they have experienced God's presence, as do about 20% of Canadians with *no religious affiliation* — well above the respective weekly attendance levels of both categories.

In addition to looking at the experience of God through the eyes of attendance and group identification, I have explored the possible importance of a large number of additional religious, social, and psychological factors that are seen by some observers as associated with experience. That analysis is found elsewhere for those who

TABLE 5.6 **Experience and Religious Identification**

"Do you believe that you have experienced God's presence?"

	TOTAL "YES"	DEFINITELY	THINK SO	ATTENDING WEEKLY
NATIONALLY	47%	20%	27%	22%
Conservative Protestants	71	54	17	58
RCs in Quebec	63	21	42	20
RCs outside Quebec	52	23	29	32
Other Faiths	47	22	25	7
Mainline Protestants	40	14	26	15
No Religion	19	6	13	0

Source: Bibby, Project Canada 2000.

want to examine the details.[30] The findings are important and can be summed up as follows:

- The importance of specific *group identification*, along with attendance, continues to be an important predictor of religious experience.
- However, what is surprising is the finding that people in all religious families who place a *high value on spirituality* are more likely than others to experience God. What it adds up to is this: if people who felt they have experienced God's presence gathered for a convention, those who registered would find themselves among some rather unexpected experiential partners ... to put it mildly.

Pervasive and Lasting Claims

Yes, God appears to have been showing up in a considerable number of people's lives. Incidentally, lest some cynics think such claims are atypical, they need to keep in mind that the direct experience of the supernatural has, of course, been widely claimed by adherents of a large number of religious traditions. Such a fact was acknowledged by Glock and Stark in their early efforts to identify key dimensions of religious commitment.[31] Experience, they maintained, is a key facet of commitment in virtually all major world religions, along with belief, practice, and knowledge. "To a greater or less extent," they wrote, "all known religious institutions have some expectation that the properly religious person will at some time or another achieve some sense of contact, however vague or fleeting, with a supernatural agency."[32] Theistic traditions continue to assume that their gods make themselves known.

During the 1960s, precisely at the height of the death of God movement, when some theologians were informing us that contemporary men and women could no longer think in traditional supernatural terms, Stark and Glock were finding not only that some nine in ten American church members *believed* in God but that more than seven in ten members felt that they had personally *experienced* God. Claims tended to be highest among evangelical groups such as Southern Baptists (94%), and somewhat lower but still high among so-called liberal groups such as Episcopalians (70%). The two sociologists commented, "There are few cues in the culture which would lead an observer to predict so high a rate of supernaturalism in what seems to be an increasingly modern, scientific, and secularized society."[33]

These early levels of documented religious experience claims have persisted through today in the United States, Canada, and elsewhere. If anything, the recent work of people like Harvey Cox, Robert Wuthnow, and Wade Clark Roof fuels the suspicion that levels of experience have risen in the past few decades, as spirituality in its ever-expanding expressions has become increasingly in vogue.[34] It all adds up to a lot of religious stirring.

What's more, when people think they have experienced God, the stirring doesn't tend to go away. We have already seen some evidence in the anecdotal accounts on page 148: the events may have happened years ago, but they made a lasting impression.

Consistent with such accounts, our effort to chart the changing beliefs and practices of Canadians, as reported in *Canada's Teens*, shows that as teens and young adults get older, their participation and belief levels tend to decline.[35] However, there appear to be two exceptions: *religious experience* and *prayer*. More Gen Xers and Young Boomers[36] now claim they have experienced God than was the case when they were younger, while private prayer levels have changed very little. Does this mean religious experience is fairly stable, that once people feel they have experienced God, for example, such a belief is not redefined and discarded later on in life?

On the surface, we don't know how much overlap we have. For example, we don't know if the 47% of Xers who thought they had experienced God in 2000 includes the 43% who said the same thing as teens in the 1980s.

However, as I noted in Chapter 2, our *Project Canada* national adult surveys spanning 1975 through 2000 have included some people who participated in the previous surveys, generating what is known as "panel data." For example, some 275 people who were part of the 2000 survey also took part in the 1985 survey. In response to the question, *"Do you believe you have experienced God's presence?"* 52% said "no" and 48% said "yes" in the year 2000. But

More People Who Believe They Have Experienced God's Presence

For Many God Is Experienced Frequently

"I cannot remember a stage of my life when experiencing God was not a common occurrence. Some have been profoundly physical sensations, usually during prayer, of being hugged. I have also felt a healing power flowing out through my hands during intercessory prayer."
— *A United Church minister; her congregation is located in a small community in southern Ontario.*

"Yes, I have experienced God on numerous occasions. One special time for me was when I was alone [in] Bolivia in a little church and was very much alone. While reading the Bible and meditating on it, I felt a very real presence envelop me with total love and peace. It was an experience beyond description!"
— *An evangelical youth worker in his late 30s who lives in New Brunswick.*

Maybe God via Other People

"Not necessarily God. I have felt that someone who was deceased has been present during my sleep, e.g. my father and grandfather. This has been during troubled times or just before something has happened. It was like they were there to reassure me, and this is why I think there is a place that your spirit goes to."
— *A 43-year-old executive assistant in Vancouver; she was brought up United, but no longer attends.*

"I left a downtown Calgary bar because I felt lost. On my way home I ended up having a conversation with an alcoholic bum. In this conversation I experienced the face of God."
— *A 24-year-old religious studies major; he has Christian and Missionary Alliance ties.*

Some Aren't Sure It Has Been God

"No, but on several occasions, I felt that someone protected me and the family from potential disasters. This someone may be one of my late grandmothers, who loved me very much."
— *A 56-year-old Toronto professor with Japanese roots who has "no religion."*

"Not God, but what I believe to be a friend reborn in the birth of our son. Our son was hours old when a friend (whose husband had died roughly nine months earlier) held him and the way he looked at her was like something I'd never seen before or seen since; it was him."
— *A 35-year-old administrative assistant who was raised in the United Church; she has "really lost belief in any organized form of religion" but feels her "faith and beliefs to be strong."*

"I'm not sure that I experienced God, but if I did it was not a very nice 'God.'"
— *A 19-year-old university student in Alberta; she describes her religious status as "None."*

"I can't say much about conventional mystical experiences. I may have had one as an adolescent, but in those days I certainly had many more religiously motivated guilt trips, which to me are not manifestations of the divine but rather reflections of the shortcomings of human groups."
— *A Quebec professor, 60, who had a Protestant upbringing but is now a practising Catholic.*

Source: Project Canada Quota Sample, Winter, 2001–02.

when we compared their responses in 1985 with the ones they gave in 2000, here's what we found:

- The 48% who said "yes" in 2000 consisted of 36% who *continued* to maintain, as they had in 1985, that they had experienced God. An additional 12%, led by people between the ages of 40 and 54, were making that claim by 2000.
- The 52% who said in 2000 that they had *not* experienced God were made up of 45% who had reported the same thing in 1985, and 7% who had previously thought they had experienced God, but by 2000 had changed their minds. Those who felt they had not experienced God, incidentally, were composed of some 55% of adults under the age of 40 versus about 45% of adults over 40.

In short, this "panel peek" suggests that as many as 85% of the people who think they have experienced God retain that belief over a considerable period of time — in this case, 15 years from the time we first asked. New claims of religious experience seem to be a bit higher among people in their 40s.

This brings us back to where I began in this section. There is probably no more compelling support for believing in God than feeling one has experienced God. While beliefs literally come and go — starting high in one's youth and frequently declining as one gets older[37] — the longitudinal findings indicate that experience is one of two characteristics that does not decrease to any great extent with the passage of time. The other is prayer.

Prayer

Canadians are not only believing in God and experiencing God; a startlingly large number also claim to be talking to God on a fairly regular basis. Such an activity speaks volumes about the possible effort of the gods to reach out to people. Ralph Milton, in his typical straight talk, puts it this way in his best-selling book *This United Church of Ours*: "One of God's favourite ways of communicating with individuals is through prayer."[38] Prayer also says much about a number of aspects of religiousness.

Think about it for a moment. When we look over in a restaurant, for example, and see an individual praying privately just before beginning a meal, the act speaks of far more than a person only "giving thanks" for food. We can make a number of fairly safe deductions about the person and his or her beliefs.

- First, as a private activity, prayer is noncoercive: a person prays because he or she wants to; it's not just a matter of sharing in a group activity. This is not like a public prayer at a wedding or a Christmas service. As such, personal prayer provides a unique look at *individual religiosity*.
- Second, prayer is what sociologists call *an unobtrusive measure*: it provides clues to a person's beliefs. The answers lie in the activity itself.
- Third, if a person prays, there is an assumption that Someone or Something is hearing the prayer — that it is being *directed toward some Other*. Webster's dictionary puts things bluntly: prayer is "the action or practice of praying to God."[39] We can deduce that most people who pray privately believe in God or some higher power.
- Fourth, to the extent that prayer frequently involves themes such as calls for help, forgiveness, expressions of gratitude, and reflections on life, a number of assumptions are being made about the *characteristics of the Listener*. For example, it is assumed that the One who hears cares about the person who is praying, is a good and willing listener, and is sufficiently in control of reality to be able to grant forgiveness, respond to other requests, and warrant the gratitude being expressed.

Consequently, I would argue that the voluntary act of private prayer signals that an individual believes communication is taking place with an all-powerful God or higher power who cares. If not, then why would a person bother to pray? Even the much-publicized prayers from foxholes and death scenes are uttered by people who at minimum *hope* there is a caring and capable Listener. Tom Harpur writes in his book *Prayer: The Hidden Fire* that his response to the sceptics' query "Why pray?" would simply be: "Most of the time, facing life's joys and dilemmas, I simply haven't had the foggiest notion of how else to respond, or of what else to do." He adds, "I don't like to think of prayer as a last resort, as a 'turn to prayer in foxholes once the shooting starts' type of approach. But honestly and practically, that's how it is."[40] Harpur seems to speak for many Canadians who, in the course of coping with life and death, reach out to a higher power — because it seems like the appropriate thing to do. Prayer seems to be almost our default mode. Who knows? In the process of finding ourselves turning to prayer, maybe we are stumbling upon an important clue that our existence is tied to the gods.

The Prevalence of Private Prayer

The latest *Project Canada 2000* survey has found that 74% of Canadians acknowledge that they pray privately — close to three in ten daily, two in ten weekly, and almost three in ten occasionally. The remaining 26% of the population say they never pray. The figure for private prayer is down slightly from 1975, when 81% of the populace said they prayed privately.

As with belief in God and the experiencing of God, it's intriguing to note that private prayer has such relatively high levels, well above the weekly service attendance levels of 31% in 1975 and 21% now.

- The proportion of people who are praying privately every day is up marginally from what it was in 1975.
- What has changed from 1975 is that fewer people are praying occasionally: they are more likely either to pray weekly (10% to 19%) or not to pray at all (19% to 26%). This is consistent with the involvement patterns I discussed in Chapter 3,

TABLE 5.7 **Private Prayer, 1975 and 2000**

"How often do you pray privately?"

	1975	2000
Daily	26%	28%
Weekly	10	19
Less than weekly	45	27
Never	19	26

Sources: Bibby, Project Can75 and Project Canada 2000.

where — especially among Mainline Protestants — fewer adults and teenagers are involved, but the "remnants" who have remained part of their churches show signs of being more active than people in the 1970s, 80s, or early 90s.

As would be expected, private prayer is most commonly practised by people who are active churchgoers. Contrary to stereotypes, they are frequently young. One 22-year-old Conservative Protestant who is very active in her church tells us, "I pray and experience God on a daily basis."[41] A young Mormon university student says that "God is a big part of my life and when I am praying, I know that He is listening to me."[42]

Yet, it's interesting to note that a majority of other people, including those who *never attend*, indicate they engage in private prayer at least occasionally. In fact, about one in five Canadians who never attend religious services say they pray privately once a week or more. Incidentally, in case someone is wondering, those "nevers" who pray weekly are not primarily devout older people who cannot attend services because of health problems. A comparison of never attenders and weekly attenders who are praying at least once a week shows the

TABLE 5.8 **Prayer by Attendance and Religious Group, 2000**
"How often do you pray privately?"

	DAILY	WEEKLY	MONTHLY	YEARLY	NEVER
NATIONALLY	28%	19%	9%	18%	26%
Weekly	66	21	5	7	1
Monthly	30	38	15	14	3
Yearly	20	19	11	24	26
Never	6	13	7	15	59
CPROT	61	13	5	13	8
Other Faiths	32	24	10	12	22
RCQ	31	20	9	21	19
RCOQ	30	31	9	14	16
MLPROT	24	19	13	22	22
No Religion	7	6	6	15	66

Source: Bibby, Project Canada 2000.

Prayer as Experienced Kapica-Style

A friend, Jack Kapica, known to Canadians from his years with the Globe and Mail, *offered these thoughts to me; I am sharing them with his permission.*

Yes, I pray privately. For about the past seven years I have been saying the rosary nearly every day. I carry this really neat little "finger rosary," a ring with ten nubbles on it with a cross at the 11th position. The whole thing turns, like a roller bearing. It stays neatly in my pocket, jostling with my loose change.

I started praying when I was helping my ailing parents, my father dying and my mother beginning a serious slide into Alzheimer's disease. An only child, I had little help, and needed all the help I could get, even if it was "only" spiritual help. In my mother's desk I found an old wooden rosary I had been given in high school, missing the eighth bead in the fourth decade. After many years of not praying, it felt strangely comforting to do so.

I wasn't really looking for anything, no answer or sign or anything. I just wanted to do something to keep my mind from skittering from one pointless and spooky thought to another. I wanted a little peace.

Eventually, I got it. In dribs and drabs, praying would clear my noisy mind, giving me maybe five or six precious minutes of calm each day. Occasionally, it would go to ten whole minutes, but that's rare.

Not every day either; sometimes the noise in my head is so insistent it is hard to ignore, and I hope I would be forgiven for the lack of full attention as I rattle off the old prayers. I pray God wouldn't be like my high-school algebra teacher, who had this uncanny ability to instantly identify a kid who had just allowed one irrelevant thought to creep into his mind while solving quadratic equations.

Weekends are tough, filled as they are with family duties from morning to night. When I miss praying for a day, I feel I've deprived myself of something.

I have no idea how much strength I get from prayer, nor do I know how I would even calculate it if I did. But I find that occasionally I get my best ideas while praying, ideas that are not really relevant to the Almighty or what I had been taught I should be thinking while I am praying.

At first I was guilt-ridden about these irrelevancies. But then I began to see them as little gifts.

From God.

As a sign he cares.

It's good to know that.

Jack also volunteered that he is Catholic who has "recently returned to attending church weekly after an absence of some 30-odd years."

never attenders are considerably younger: 42% are 18–34. Just 12% of weekly churchgoers pray that often.

The findings indicate that a sizeable number of those one in five Canadians who never attend services pray — some with considerable frequency. Among them is a 21-year-old woman from southern Alberta who told us, "I'm not a very religious person, don't attend services, and don't adhere to a specific religion. But I feel that I experience the presence of God whenever I pray, which is almost every day."[43] A 24-year-old male who does not attend services and has no religious affiliation similarly acknowledged, "I feel I have been given comfort at times when I have asked for it — although I am not 100% sure it was God."[44]

These two people also serve to remind us that prayer is found among the "Religious Nones." While two in three people with no religion acknowledge that they never pray, the flip side is that one in three do — 13% of them weekly or more.

People involved with *Conservative Protestant* groups are approximately twice as likely as other affiliates to pray privately on a daily basis (61%). When the cut-off point is extended to weekly-plus, *Roman Catholics outside Quebec* (61%) move into second place behind *Conservatives* (74%). People identifying with *Other Faith* groups (56%), *Quebec Catholics* (51%), and *Mainline Protestants* (43%) are third, fourth, and fifth, respectively.

Regionally, people living in the *Atlantic provinces* (59%) are the most likely to engage in private prayer frequently, and *B.C. residents*

TABLE 5.9 **Prayer by Region, Age, and Gender, 2000**
"How often do you pray privately?"

	DAILY	WEEKLY	MONTHLY	YEARLY	NEVER
NATIONALLY	28%	19%	9%	18%	26%
Atlantic provinces	38	21	7	19	15
Prairies	31	19	7	18	25
Quebec	28	19	9	17	27
Ontario	26	21	11	17	25
British Columbia	17	17	8	21	37
Females	33	21	10	15	21
Males	22	17	8	21	32
55+	41	19	7	14	19
35–54	26	19	8	22	25
18–34	16	20	13	16	35

Source: Bibby, Project Canada 2000.

are the least likely (34%). Daily to weekly prayer is also quite a bit more typical of *older adults* than younger people and somewhat more common among *females* than males.[45]

Yet the differences are relative. The majority of Canadians, regardless of region, age group, or gender, are praying at least sometimes. And that finding says much about their ongoing inclination to believe in God, their views about God, and their sense that they have experienced God.

The Predictive Power of Private Prayer

The argument I have been making for private prayer's predictive value is readily borne out by the survey findings:

- To the extent that people pray on a *daily* basis, they are inclined to believe in a God, believe God cares about them, think they have experienced God, see themselves as spiritual, and — in one in two cases — attend services on a weekly basis.
- Most people who pray only *occasionally* believe in God and maintain that God cares about them; however, fewer see themselves as spiritual, or believe they have experienced God's presence, and just one in ten are weekly service attenders. For many individuals in this category, prayer may well be largely a utilitarian, "extrinsic" activity, rather than something that is particularly relational in nature.
- A minority of Canadians who *never* pray privately believe in God, but even fewer in this group believe that God cares about them or that they have experienced God. Just one in four see themselves as spiritual, and only one in a hundred attends a religious service every week.

These findings about God, experience, and prayer show that religion is strongly rooted in group participation. People who are actively involved in groups are more likely than others to believe in a caring God, to think they have experienced God, and to communicate with God through prayer. That relationship should not surprise too many people.

"Do You Ever Pray Privately? If So, Why?"

It's a Source of Comfort

"Prayer is a communication tool for me to express myself to my God. It helps me to alleviate stress and trust that God is in control."
— *A 31-year-old director of human resources in Toronto; she attends an Alliance Church.*

"When I was a young girl, my mother taught me a bedtime prayer and it helped me whenever I was deeply afraid. I believe in the mysteries of prayer. I'm not overly consistent, but something always draws me back."
— *A Nova Scotia mother of two who is 39; her religious journey has included gospel, Baptist, United, and yoga experiences.*

"Yes, I pray privately. I am better able to concentrate and to keep all of my focus on Him when I pray privately. I usually pray just before bedtime. This calms my mind and puts my body in a state of ease and extreme comfort."
— *A student and part-time security guard, 23, from Moncton; he attends a Baptist church.*

It Provides Direction

"I feel that there is a God and I need help and guidance in my life. I also pray for God to help others and quite often name whom and what the problem may be. I pray throughout the day and always when I retire at night."
— *A recently widowed Guelph female in her early 50s; she regularly attends a Disciples of Christ church.*

"Yes. I need someone to talk to, to help me to find my way. I also pray to talk to my father who passed away a few years ago."
— *A Roman Catholic, 40, who works as an administrative assistant in Montreal.*

"I pray privately every day. It helps me keep in tune with God so that I have a better idea of what he wants of and for me."
— *A Mennonite national office worker who is in her 40s; she lives and works in Winnipeg.*

It Is Really about a Relationship

"I think it is important to commune with God on a regular basis. I need to invest time into my relationship with God just as I would with any friend."
— *A 23-year-old administrative assistant to a dean at a Christian school in Toronto; she describes herself as "a born-again evangelical."*

"Yes, on a weekly if not daily basis. I have learned that prayer prepares me for that which I will encounter. Prayers of intercession for people who are suffering prepares me to be involved in their suffering, and the suffering of others; prayers for my 'enemies' prepares me to be present to them."
— *A United Church minister, 45; his congregation is west of Toronto.*

"I pray regularly — several times a day at length, and many short prayers during the day as well. Prayer lets me talk to God — to God! God cares about me, I care about him, and we both care about the world — so of course we talk all day."
— *A 41-year-old theology professor; he describes himself as an evangelical who regularly attends an Anglican church in Vancouver.*

Source: Project Canada Quota Sample, Winter, 2000.

TABLE 5.10 **Private Prayer as a Predictor**

PRAY PRIVATELY	BELIEVE IN GOD	BELIEVE GOD CARES	HAVE EXPERIENCED GOD	SEE SELF AS SPIRITUAL	ATTEND WEEKLY
NATIONALLY	80%	73%	46%	58%	21%
Daily	99	97	80	88	51
Weekly	99	93	63	76	23
<Weekly	84	74	34	48	9
Never	43	31	12	23	1

Source: Bibby, Project Canada 2000.

However, these findings also unveil another important and more intriguing reality: significant numbers of people who are not actively involved in groups are also believing and experiencing and communicating. Our theistic colour commentator might well suggest that the gods are using both *the church route* and *the direct route* to get through to Canadians — and in the process are enjoying considerable success.

The empirical data are decisive: God has not disappeared from the lives of the vast majority of Canadians. The average people we pass on sidewalks and roadways and see in supermarkets and malls may not often say it out loud, but most of them believe in God, converse with God, and in nearly one in two cases think they have experienced the presence of God. That's a lot of people. These are not anomalous beliefs, practices, and experiences.

We have suggested that a significant amount of spiritual restlessness is evident in the widespread tendency of Canadians to raise questions about origins and purpose, happiness and suffering, and life after death. And we have observed the prevalence of God in people's lives. But the relentless pursuit of the Gods may not stop there.

CHAPTER SIX

Rumours
and Revelation

A restlessness for the gods is apparent in Canadians' asking ultimate questions, believing in God, and experiencing and communicating with a God who they are convinced cares about them.

But the restlessness goes further. Sometimes, sociologists maintain, the best pieces of evidence for what is taking place are less obvious — something like clues in a detective story — what they call "unobtrusive" indicators.

So far we have been relying on direct evidence, whereby people tell us about their yearnings, their beliefs and experiences, and their practices. Some time ago, one of my favourite sociologists, the provocative Peter Berger, suggested that by looking at people rather than to the heavens, we might see a number of clues that point to the existence of Something Else. Following Berger, if the gods are restless and moving among us, they might be placing some hints of their presence in virtually every one of us.

A prolific author over the years, Berger taught at schools that included Hartford Seminary, Rutgers University, and Boston College. In 1969, he wrote a stimulating book that I think has never received the attention it deserves. I suspect it was overlooked mainly because it was regarded as too theological by sociologists and too sociological by theologians. Berger anticipated the problem and wrote in the preface:"I can claim no authority as a sociologist for a good deal of what follows here. This means that I'm sticking my neck out in the most blatant way." He added that the book "is not particularly addressed to sociologists" but "to anyone with a concern for religious questions and the willingness to think about them systematically. I hope that it may have something to say to theologians, though I'm fully aware of my lack of expertise in theology." He concluded the preface by saying, "I suppose one sticks one's neck out when it comes to things one deems important. I think that religion is of very great importance at any time and of particular importance in our own time."[1] The book is seldom cited and is now out of print, although it is available at many libraries — thanks to librarians who ordered the book because Berger was a best-selling author at the time of its release.

The important work that fell between the cracks of sociology and theology is entitled *A Rumor of Angels*. As with so many Berger books, it raises a number of stimulating ideas that people need to go out and test, but to the best of my knowledge, this has never been done. That's unfortunate because it has much to say about "latent religiousness" and offers much as we explore the restlessness of the gods. So let's blow the dust off *A Rumor of Angels* and revisit some of Berger's ideas that are particularly important to our examination of supernatural activity in Canada.

Rumours Berger Style

"A few years ago," writes Berger, "a priest working in a slum section of a European city was asked why he was doing it, and replied, 'So that the rumor of God may not disappear completely.'" The word, Berger said, aptly expressed what the supernatural and its indicators had become: "rumors — and not very reputable rumors at that."[2]

When Berger penned the book in the late 1960s, many observers — led by the "God is dead" movement among theologians — were maintaining that belief in God and supernatural phenomena were in severe decline.[3] Contemporary men and women allegedly could no longer think in traditional supernatural terms. "If commentators on the contemporary situation of religion agree about anything," writes Berger, "it is that the supernatural has departed from the modern world."[4] It was a time when religious leaders were being urged by writers like Harvard's Harvey Cox and Britain's Bishop John Robinson to translate their messages into new thought forms that people could comprehend.[5]

Berger notes that for all the debate about the term "supernatural," it has denoted the belief that there is *an other reality* that "transcends the reality within which our everyday experience unfolds." Ancients, for example, assumed another, supernatural world of divine beings and forces existed that influenced this one. "It is this fundamental assumption," Berger maintains, "that is allegedly defunct or in the process of becoming defunct in the modern world."[6]

According to Berger, the embracing of modern science had resulted in a secularization of consciousness, whereby individuals were no longer thinking in supernatural terms as they lived out their lives. Those who continued to believe in supernatural things constituted, in Berger's phrase, "a cognitive minority." By that, he meant they held views that differed significantly from those prevalent in a society and relied on the support of like-minded people in order to sustain their ideas and to make them plausible.[7] He refers to such sources of support for ideas of all kinds as "plausibility structures." Modern men and women, he writes, are typically exposed to structures that do not acknowledge or support belief in the supernatural.

Berger reminds readers that in the midst of it all, "a little caution is in order. There is scattered evidence that secularization may not be as all-embracing as some have thought, that the supernatural, banished from cognitive respectability by the intellectual authorities, may survive in hidden nooks and crannies of the culture." Citing a variety of studies of belief, he suggests that "these subterranean rumblings of supernaturalism can, it seems, coexist with all sorts of upstairs rationalism."[8]

People who want to know whether the gods exist invariably start by looking to the heavens. Berger maintains that another possible starting place for theologians and others might be to look earthward at the human condition — something of "an anthropological starting point" that he refers to as "inductive faith." To do so, he says, is to observe some intriguing "signals of transcendence," which he defines as "phenomena that are to be found within the domain of

our 'natural' reality but that appear to point beyond that reality."
According to Berger, there are some fundamental human traits or
"prototypical human gestures" that may constitute such signals. These
"reiterated acts and experiences express essential aspects of our
being. They are not unconscious, requiring excavation from the
depths of the mind; rather they belong to ordinary everyday life."[9]

Consistent with the title of his book, the tone of *A Rumor of
Angels* is not one of a dogmatic theist who is trying to document a
point. On the contrary, it is one of a sociologist who looks at personal and social life and says, "I wonder if . . . ?" As for where he
stood personally, Berger confessed, "For better or worse, my self-
understanding is not exhausted by the fact that I am a sociologist. I
also consider myself a Christian, though I have not yet found the
heresy into which my theological views would comfortably fit." He
took the position that "in the religious view of reality, all phenomena point toward that which transcends them."[10] To look at people,
he maintained, is to observe a number of possible "signals of transcendence" that seem to point toward something beyond them.

Damnation
Some acts of brutality, writes Berger, seem so excessively cruel that
we as humans lack for an adequate response that enables the scales
to be balanced. These are "experiences in which our sense of what
is humanly permissible is so fundamentally outraged," he says, "that
the only adequate response to the offense as well as the offender
seems to be a curse of supernatural dimensions."[11] Berger empha-
sizes that he is purposely choosing this negative form of reasoning
over a positive sense of justice and natural law, believing it more
sharply illustrates a signal of transcendence "over and beyond
socio-historical relativities."[12]

Atrocities such as those that occurred in Nazi Germany, or the
massacre of children, are examples of deeds that not only "cry out to
heaven" but also "cry out for hell."[13] These days one only has to think
of young children being raped and murdered or terrorists killing four
thousand innocent civilians to get Berger's point. It's not just a case of
people failing to be good; there is an element of evil in what takes
place. As New York Rabbi Marc Gellman put it in the aftermath of

the September 11, 2001, terrorist attacks on New York and Washington, "People now understand there is radical evil in the world."[14]

In such instances, any societal response in the form of punishment or retaliation seems inadequate; any societal response in the form of forgiveness seems incomprehensible. More is required. In Berger's words, "These are deeds that demand not only condemnation but *damnation* in the full religious meaning of the word — that is, the doer not only puts himself outside the [human] community; he also separates himself in a final way from a moral order that transcends the human community, and thus invokes a retribution that is more than human."[15] Such deeds call for Someone or Something to make things right. Perhaps Rabbi Gellman summed up the sentiment with his words at the New York memorial service on September 23: "We believe a good God will not allow evil to win out over goodness."[16] In Toronto, Msgr. Samuel Bianco, rector of St. Michael's Cathedral, told his congregation: "Justice will be brought to the terrorists, and they will be held in account, just as we all will one day." [17]

Such a human reaction, a sense that somehow, someday, such gross injustices will be made right, says Berger, provides us with what he calls "an argument from damnation." It is not a rational assumption: there is no reason to believe that, at our hands or in this life, such an equalizing of things will take place. However, the fact of people having intense feelings that things *need* to be balanced out and indeed *will be* balanced out at some point and somewhere is, for Berger, a signal of transcendence. Sentiments like these provide a possible hint that Someone or Something exists that will one day make things right.

Hope

Human existence is always oriented toward the future, says Berger, and a key dimension of such an orientation is hope. Most people are intensely hopeful, even when circumstances don't particularly warrant any optimism. A pervasive response to adversity is the assertion that things will get better. Berger reminds us that such hope is not particularly rational; there is no guarantee whatsoever that things will actually improve.

I remember as an undergraduate being asked to visit a 19-year-old woman at the University of Alberta Hospital who was battling cancer. When I arrived at her room, I was surprised to find that she was someone in one of my classes. I had assumed she'd been hobbling on crutches and attending class only off and on because she'd injured an ankle. But she had undergone surgery and was now receiving cancer treatments. I vividly recall how, with confidence and defiance, she told me she would "beat this thing" and be out of hospital in a few weeks. She died within a month. People who say they will fight severe illnesses frequently die. Individuals who say they "will get back on their feet financially" often don't. People facing emotional pain and strain who say they "will get through this okay" sometimes crumble.

Yet in the midst of struggle and pain and disappointment, people invariably declare hope. We see it and hear it daily: "Tomorrow's a new day"; "We'll turn things around"; "We're not giving up"; "I'm going to get better"; "New Yorkers will rebuild the towers"; "We're going to move forward." Mere clichés from people trying to put up a brave front? Not according to many reputable observers of human life. Brian Stiller is among those who have stressed that hope is the key to healing: "Hope helps us see outside our hurt, past the plaguing fear, gripping dread, unnerving anxiety and paralysing despair."[18] He recalls Victor Frankl's much-cited observation of fellow prisoners in concentration camps: "The prisoner who has lost faith in the future — his future — was doomed. With his loss of belief in the future, he also lost his spiritual hold; he let himself decline and became subject to mental and physical decay ... We all feared this moment — not for ourselves, but for our friends."[19]

Berger also recognizes the essential nature of hope, not only as one lives life but also as one confronts death. The willingness to virtually forfeit the present — to risk one's life for the saving of another, to finish a book or a painting when one is near death, or to find meaning in the face of severe pain — points, he says, to the possibility of something beyond life as we know it. Berger sees particularly profound meaning in the ability of people to deny the reality of death, to have positive hope as they confront dying — a defiance that is expressed by the Apostle of old: "Where, O death, is your victory? Where, O death is your sting?"[20] Such hope, says Berger, speaks particularly loudly when people we love die.[21]

Earlier, I mentioned my friend Stan and his wife, Jan, who lost their much-awaited son one month before he was born — a son who would have been the brother to Jonathan, born some seven years before with Down syndrome. In the face of such disappointment and pain, Stan shared these words with some friends:

> Jonathan led our families to his little brother's basket with a tiny carnation and whispered, "Bye Paul," caressing his tiny head for the first and last time. We can both tell you that notwithstanding this great disappointment, God is good and we know that He will be with us all as we work through the pain in our lives. Your prayers have transformed heart, home, and hospital into sacred places. Our confidence in the love and wisdom of God is profoundly intact. Anticipation of the future is filled with hope. God sends us Angels who wake us up and say, "Behold I am with you always, even unto the end."

Berger is not naive; he readily acknowledges that hope in the face of both life and death can be explained empirically. Experience informs us that, for better as well as for worse, life is not a straight line: if things are not going well, there is a good possibility that they will get better. Similarly, he is well aware of the argument of sceptics like Freud that belief in life after death has been the eternal wish of humankind.[22] It may also be that we learn to cultivate hope because it is functional, rather than because it is necessarily grounded in reality. This reflects the idea of French existentialist Albert Camus that we must learn to live without hope, but conduct our lives as if there were hope.[23] Still, says Berger, "there is something in us that, however shamefacedly in an age of triumphant rationality, goes on saying 'no!' and even says 'no!' to the ever so plausible explanations of empirical reason."[24] Hope is posited by Berger as a second signal of transcendence — another possible innate hint from the gods that they exist.

Order

A third signal that Berger discusses is the widespread human propensity for order. He argues that, throughout most of history, people have believed the desire for social order corresponds to an underlying belief in the order of the universe. Such faith, says Berger, is "grounded in a faith or trust that, ultimately, reality is 'in order,' 'all right,' 'as it should be.'"[25]

He notes faith in order is experienced not only in the history of societies and civilizations, but also in the life of each individual. It can be seen in the simple words of a mother trying to comfort her child with the words "Everything is all right." The fact of the matter, of course, is that everything is not necessarily okay. The world is the same one in which the child will experience suffering and eventually die. Unless there is something beyond this world in which we can trust, that is in ultimate control of life and history, he says, the statement is a lie.

The fact that this mother and so many of us readily maintain "all is well" in the face of a world in which all is *not* well may be highly telling. Such reassurance, Berger says, assumes the existence of a transcendent order that allows us to trust ourselves and our destinies to that order. In his words, our "ordering propensity implies a transcendent order, and each ordering gesture is a signal of this transcendence."[26]

This signal of order may also be evident in the widespread belief that there is structure to the universe. Things are not chaotic. Such belief in an orderly universe is perhaps suggested by the widespread belief that life has meaning beyond any purpose we may give to it. As discussed in Chapter 4, the very fact so many people are raising the question of the meaning of life seems to indicate a pervasive sense of something back of life that gives it meaning — and order.

Humour and Play
Further signals of transcendence, according to Berger, can be found in humour and play. We often talk about humour being "good for the soul," about "needing a good laugh." When we laugh — really hard — it's as if we "escape this world" momentarily. When we can laugh at ourselves and what we do, and not take ourselves so seriously, we see things for what they really are. Humour allows us to put life into perspective. In his *Invitation to Sociology*, Berger criticized his sociology colleagues for often going about their tasks with a grim humourlessness, adding that they needed to learn to

laugh at themselves.[27] One of my three sons, when he was in his preschool years, used to provide me with needed perspective when he would greet my excessive declarations of achievement with the simple line *"What's so dreat about it?"* Then there are eccentrics like bestselling Canadian author W.P. Kinsella, who says, "I like to be able to laugh at people who take my work seriously."[28]

But humour does more than just provide perspective. Humour makes it possible to temporarily transcend life and imminent death. Many of us have seen people who, although close to death, have joked and clowned in a manner that has seemed almost death-defying. A few years back I watched the father of a close friend dance and laugh in the hallway of his palliative care unit about two weeks before he died; maybe his perspective had been altered forever by the fact that he'd spent some three years as a Polish POW at Auschwitz. Another friend with a wacky sense of humour kept that wacky humour intact right up until he died. And Paul McCartney commented that during his last visit with George Harrison a few weeks before the former Beatle's death, Harrison "was obviously unwell but he was cracking jokes like he always was."[29]

Doug Todd, in writing about best-selling children's writer Robert Munsch, tells us that the author "is a paragon of goofiness" as he performs in front of thousands of children. "Most of his children's books are outrageous fun," says Todd, while noting that Munsch's most famous children's book, *Love You Forever*, was written when he was grieving for his two babies who were born dead. "As with many comics," writes Todd, "you wonder whether, if Munsch wasn't laughing so much, maybe he'd be crying."[30]

Berger also notes that people who are in the presence of others who die — even on battlefields — have been known to use humour as a means of coping with tragedy, as something of a means of moving life to another level. Victor Frankl writes that "the attempt to develop a sense of humor and to see things in a humorous light is some kind of a trick learned while mastering the art of living." Even in a concentration camp, he recalled, "a very trifling thing can cause the greatest of joys . . . We laughed and cracked jokes in spite of, and during, all we had to go through . . ."[31]

You, like I, have seen people vacillate between tears and laughter during times of mourning and strain. For me, a night in 1968 in a Louisville hospital now seems like part of an earlier incarnation. As a young student minister, I was sitting with a couple from about 11:00 at night to 6:00 in the morning — slow and painful hours during which their 15-year-old daughter lived out her last hours following a car accident. You can imagine how difficult it was for them — and for me as a neophyte clergyman. At about three in the morning, a drunk wandered into the emergency room waiting area and, of all things, started telling jokes. My first reaction was, "Oh no, what a time for such a bizarre thing to be happening!" But in retrospect, it was as if the whole thing had been staged by Someone. The harmless, remarkably coherent drunk managed to get a mild smile or two from the three of us. Then he succeeded in breaking us up. And three weary and worn people began to laugh their heads off — a remarkable, temporary reprieve from reality. Then, apparently having done his job, he wandered back into the night.

Like humour, play, according to Berger, suspends the time and space structure of everyday life: "Play always constructs an enclave within the 'serious' world of everyday social life."[32] It is typically a joyful activity which appears to suspend or bracket time and space. When we "goof off" with our friends, "lighten up," or poke fun at circumstances, we seem to step outside of everyday life and everyday things. When we are playful, it is as if we temporarily step into a different realm, where life seems as if it has somehow been put in parentheses and for the time being is almost irrelevant. Official roles and statuses and rules are often momentarily suspended as we share in the mood of the moment. At 2:00 a.m. in a restaurant, when giddiness and laughter are overflowing, people are all temporarily equal. We often describe people during these times as being "down to earth." Maybe it's more accurate to say that the entire experience seems to be removed from this earth. It is this curious quality of bracketing reality that helps to explain the liberation and peace that play provides.

During times when we play and laugh, says Berger, we may be experiencing emotions that further point to the possibility of a realm that transcends our everyday existence. Here again, the gods may be providing signals of transcendence.

Spirituality

I have little doubt that if Berger were writing a new edition of *A Rumor of Angels*, he would also take note of the increasingly overt expression of spiritual need that has received so much attention over the past decade or so. Frankly, he didn't foresee it. Though cautious about predicting the future, he ventured the opinion that "an impressive rediscovery of the supernatural, in the dimensions of a mass phenomenon, is not in the books."[33] As it has turned out, Berger missed a section of the library. The fact that so many people today openly acknowledge their spiritual needs points, it seems to me, to a desire for something or someone that can satisfy deep and personal longings. Why else do so many Canadians, young and older, so readily express needs that are specifically "spiritual" in nature? Even though they often have difficulty expressing exactly what those needs are, what *is* clear is that large numbers of people feel compelled to reach out beyond themselves — perhaps in the process providing still another signal of transcendence.

Rumours Canadian Style

Armand Mauss, one of my mentors, who taught for years at Washington State University, would often listen patiently while I enthusiastically threw out "Berger this's" and "Berger that's." Then he'd say calmly, "Berger's certainly got some interesting ideas. But what we need to do is go and find out whether there's any truth to what he's saying."

It was good advice. In planning the *Project Canada 2000* survey, I decided we were well overdue to check out Berger's rumours. It was time to take something of an aerial photograph of the extent to which Canadians are exhibiting these alleged signals of transcendence. Keep in mind that the purpose was not to validate Berger's argument — to confirm that these beliefs and attitudes are actually pointing to something transcendent. That is and presumably always will be a faith issue. As Berger put it, "Needless to say, there is no empirical method by which this faith can be tested."[34] Instead, we attempted to explore the extent to which the rumours are found in Canada today by including pertinent items in the survey. Here's what we found.

Justice and Hope

The idea that there are some deplorable acts for which human forms of *justice* seem inadequate is held by 91% of Canadians, with little difference by gender or age. Some 70% of people across the country agree with the statement, "Somehow, some day, injustices will be made right." This belief is held by slightly more women than men, and by marginally more Gen Xers than older adults. This same statement, incidentally, was endorsed by 70% of 15-to-19-year-olds in our national survey of teens completed in late 2000.[35] Together, these findings indicate that a solid majority of Canadians — well beyond the 20% or so who are actively involved in religious groups — have a strong sense of both the need and the prospect of some kind of "ultimate justice."

In the case of *hope*, Canadians are almost unanimous in acknowledging that, even when life has not been going well, they have still believed things would get better. And, as seen in our detailed

TABLE 6.1 **Signals of Transcendence: Justice and Hope**

	NAT	WOMEN	MEN	18–34	35–54	55+
Justice						
In the case of some deplorable acts, such as the raping and murdering of children, no human form of justice seems to be enough.	91%	92%	90%	96%	89%	90%
Somehow, some day injustices will be made right.	70	75	64	73	70	66
Hope						
Generally speaking, when life has not been going well, I have still believed that things would get better.	94	93	94	89	95	95
I believe in life after death.	68	72	64	72	69	63

Source: Bibby, Project Canada 2000.

examination of the subject in Chapter 4, about 70% believe in life after death, led by slightly larger proportions of women and young adults than others.

As Berger noted, the pervasiveness of hope regarding life is surprising, given the fact that it is frequently not warranted. The finding that seven in ten people believe in life after death, in an age when we look to science to validate many of our ideas, is also quite remarkable. Then again, science is still unable to say virtually anything about what happens after we die. The fact that such large numbers continue to believe in the possibility of life after death in lieu of concrete supporting evidence suggests, at minimum, a pervasive yearning among Canadians for life to continue.

Order and Humour/Play

Canadians believe in an *orderly universe*. Close to 90% endorse the idea, with that level slipping to 81% in the case of adults under 35. Almost 70% acknowledge that when they have tried to comfort someone, they have sometimes used the phrase "Everything is okay." Here, younger adults and males lead the way. Such findings point to the widely held assumption that all is right with creation, that things are orderly. Consciously and unconsciously, the majority of us are even telling troubled children and friends, not that "everything *will be* okay," but that "everything *is* okay" — when we know that, objectively speaking, life is often not okay. Maybe the line says little about the assumption of transcendence, but maybe it says a lot.

As for *humour* and *play*, I would again remind you that I can't and am not trying to draw any clear lines here from people to the gods. The question is, Do humour and play provide people with resources that sometimes elevate them to what seems like almost another sphere?

Canadians readily acknowledge that sometimes, when they have faced difficult situations, they have found that they may as well laugh as cry. The fine line between sadness and humour is confirmed by some 90%, with little variation by either gender or age. When asked to respond to the statement "When I am in a situation where my friends and I are laughing and joking, it sometimes seems as if we are temporarily in a different world," some 60% agreed. Again, there is little

TABLE 6.2 Signals of Transcendence: Order and Humour/Play

	NAT	WOMEN	MEN	18–34	35–54	55+
Order						
There is basic order to the universe.	86%	86%	86%	81%	89%	88%
When trying to comfort someone — a child, a friend — I sometimes have said to them, "Everything is okay."	67	62	73	76	64	63
Humour and Play						
Sometimes in difficult situations I have found I may as well laugh as cry.	88	90	86	92	85	89
When I am in a situation where my friends and I are laughing and joking, it sometimes seems as if we are temporarily in a different world.	58	57	58	63	53	58

Source: Bibby, Project Canada 2000.

difference between females and males while, in terms of age categories, adults under 35 are slightly more likely than others to report such feelings.

Spirituality
The *Project Canada 2000* survey asked Canadians a number of questions about spirituality, including these three: *"Do you yourself have spiritual needs?" "How important to you is spirituality?"* and *"Do you see yourself as a spiritual person?"*

Almost 75% acknowledge that they have spiritual needs and 70% say spirituality is important to them. A somewhat lower proportion of about 60% indicate they see themselves as "a spiritual person." Spiritual needs and viewing oneself as spiritual obviously overlap: three in four people with needs also see themselves as spiritual. But clearly, those who feel spiritual needs exceed the number who have a self-image of being spiritual.

TABLE 6.3 **Signals of Transcendence: Spirituality**

	NAT	WOMEN	MEN	18–34	35–54	55+
Have spiritual needs	73%	81%	65%	71%	74%	74%
Spirituality important★	70	77	62	66	69	75
Am a spiritual person	58	66	49	54	60	59

★"Very Important" (34%) or "Somewhat Important" (36%).

Source: Bibby, Project Canada 2000.

- *Women* are more likely than men to score higher on all of these three measures, and further analyses not reported here show the differences by gender persist, regardless of age group. Still, a majority of men indicate they have spiritual needs and note that spirituality is important to them, with five in ten saying they see themselves as spiritual.
- Differences by age are minor for spiritual needs and the self-image of being "a spiritual person," although there is a slight positive relationship between age and the importance placed on spirituality.

In short, spiritual interest and claims are literally all over the place. If the gods are using spiritual quest to point to transcendence, they are having a great deal of success.

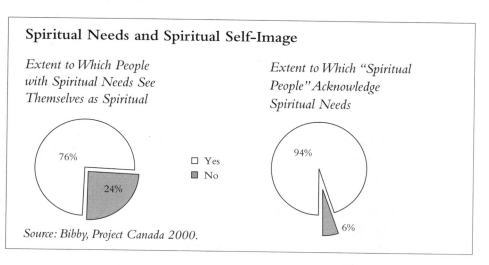

Spiritual Needs and Spiritual Self-Image

Extent to Which People with Spiritual Needs See Themselves as Spiritual

76%
24%

□ Yes
■ No

Extent to Which "Spiritual People" Acknowledge Spiritual Needs

94%
6%

Source: Bibby, Project Canada 2000.

Rumours among Nevers, Nones, and Nots

Following Berger's musings, if there are signs that Someone or Something beyond us is trying to plant some clues of transcendence, it is worth seeing to what extent those hints are evident in the lives of Canadians who are the least conventionally religious. These are presumably the toughest people in the religious market for both the churches and the gods to reach. We have been looking at some of them throughout this book. But now we want to bring these people together, formally introduce them, and see to what extent the possible signals of transcendence we have been examining are evident in their lives.

Three categories that have been standing out as including people on the edges or beyond the edges of organized religion are the "Nevers," "Nones," and "Nots." The three labels refer, respectively, to (1) those who never attend services, (2) those who do not claim any religious affiliation, and (3) those who do not believe in God. Nevers make up about 21% of the national population, Nones 14%, and Nots 6%.

TABLE 6.4 **Overlapping of Nevers, Nones, and Nots**

	N	% OF POP	NEVERS	NONES	NOTS
Nevers	265	21%	—	44%	14%
Nones	172	14	63	—	30
Nots	69	6	52	74	—

The correlation coefficients (r's) = nevers-nones .42; nevers-nots .18; nones-nots .42.

Source: Bibby, Project Canada 2000.

Obviously, they are not mutually exclusive groups of people. A quick background check that reads something like Abbott and Costello's "Who's on First" — except that it's even more confusing — shows the following:

- almost half the *Nevers* (44%) are also Nones, but only about 15% are Nots;
- some 60% of the *Nones* are Nevers, but only 30% are Nots;
- about half the *Nots* are Nevers, and around 75% are Nones.

If I were to try to redeem myself for all that confusion and put things more clearly, I would simply say that *Nevers* are not usually anything else, while *Nones* tend to be Nevers, and *Nots* tend to be Nevers and Nones. Or better still, just glance at Table 6.4 and things should be perfectly clear . . .

So what about it? Are signals of transcendence evident in the lives of people in these three categories? The short answer is "Yes" — frequently in the lives of Nevers and Nones, and sometimes in the lives of Nots as well.

TABLE 6.5 **Transcendence among Nevers, Nones, and Nots**

	NAT	NEVERS	NONE	NOTS
Justice				
Deplorable acts/no human form of justice enough	91%	90%	86%	85%
Somehow, some day injustices will be made right	70	53	51	30
Hope				
When life not well, have believed would get better	94	94	88	94
I believe in life after death	68	49	44	14
Order				
There is basic order to the universe	86	78	75	58
Trying to comfort, have said, "Everything is okay"	67	69	57	56
Humour and Play				
Sometimes have found I may as well laugh as cry	88	89	89	84
When laughing and joking, sometimes seems as if we are temporarily in different world	58	61	58	42
Spirituality				
"Very" or "Somewhat Important"	70	47	48	19
Have spiritual needs	73	55	54	18
Less conventional	47	91	98	93★

★N (15) too small for stable percentaging; 14 people less conventional. Included for heuristic purposes.

Source: Bibby, Project Canada 2000.

- Large majorities in each category feel that no form of human *justice* provides an adequate response to some deplorable acts. Half of the Nevers and Nones, along with 30% of Nots maintain that "somehow, some day injustices will be made right."
- *Hope* that things will get better is almost unanimous among people in all three categories; belief in life after death is held by close to half of the Nevers and Nones, and only about one in seven Nots.
- A majority in each grouping feels there is basic *order* to the universe, and find themselves saying, "Everything is okay."
- *Humour* is acknowledged by most of the people in the three categories as having been a resource in difficult times. And about 60% of Nevers and Nones and 40% of Nots identify with the sense of play having created a sense of temporarily being in a different world.
- The importance of *spirituality* as well as the existence of spiritual needs are acknowledged by about 50% of Nevers and Nones, but only 20% of Nots. However, in all three categories the kind of spirituality they have in mind is invariably less conventional than the spirituality of Canadians more generally.

Signals of transcendence? Simple socialization? Who knows for sure? But what these findings do confirm is that, beyond conventional conceptions and expressions of religiousness, Canadians demonstrate a remarkable penchant for the supernatural. Sometimes the restlessness is explicit; sometimes it is far less obvious. But it is evident in the lives of almost everyone — even many atheists. Our theistic commentator would undoubtedly be taken by the effectiveness of the gods in shaking up the nation.

What remains to be seen is what Canada's churches can do with all this.

CHAPTER SEVEN

What People Want from the Churches

Let's be brutally honest from the outset. Canadians may be hungering for the gods but that is hardly to say they are hungering for the churches. As one Gen Xer told me recently, "Of course I'm interested in meaning and spirituality. But to be honest, I really don't like churches and church people all that much."[1] Yes, people are asking the age-old questions about life and death. Most believe in God, and very large numbers are both experiencing God and privately communicating with God. In addition, people from British Columbia to Newfoundland are providing some interesting evidence of the existence of God, on something of an unconscious level.

These kinds of findings point to a great opportunity for religious groups who have something to bring. After all, as I emphasized in Chapter 4, religion historically has had much to say about God, depicting God as the creator who brought everything into being, sustains it, and will be there at the end of individual lives and human history.[2] Religion has also had much to say about individuals, asserting that they find their purpose, resources, hope, fulfillment, and happiness in God. Religion has further maintained that God calls people into good relationships, beginning with family and friends, extending to our communities and societies, and reaching further to embrace everyone everywhere. God, self, and society —

these have been the three great emphases of religion. They continue to be the emphases that Canadians expect from the churches.

However, far from everyone feels these themes are being addressed well by the country's religious groups — so much so that it can sound presumptuous to entitle this chapter "What People Want from the Churches." The facts confirm what most of us know well from encounters with people in everyday life: many don't want much of anything from the churches. Such people are not associating their life and death and spiritual needs with religious groups.

Nevertheless, I would argue that the primary reason significant numbers do not *want* much from the churches is because they are not *expecting* much from the churches. That could change if people came to believe that religious groups have significant things to offer. We want to try to clarify what Canadians, in theory, think churches should be doing and proceed to ask them directly what it would take for them to give groups a closer look.

The Canadian Wish List

In our *Project Canada 2000* national survey, we asked people across the country, *"Do you think that religious groups still have a role to play in Canadian lives?"* Seventy-six per cent said "Yes"; 24% answered "No."

- As would be expected, *weekly attenders* are almost unanimous in maintaining that groups have a role to play. But it's intriguing to note that they are joined by some nine in ten *monthlys*, seven in ten *yearlys*, and more than six in ten *nevers*.
- A solid majority of people across the country who identify with Protestantism, Catholicism, and Other Faiths feel religious groups have a contribution to make to Canadians — although the figure slips to 65% for Roman Catholics in Quebec. Religious Nones are divided equally on the question.
- *Adults under the age of 35* are less likely than others to think groups have a role to play (60% versus about 80%), while males and females are equally likely to endorse their contribution.

Looked at slightly differently, 94% of the one in four people who *do not* think that religious groups still have a role to play in individual

TABLE 7.1 **Groups Have a Role to Play**

"Do you think that religious groups still have a role to play in Canadian lives?"
% Indicating "Yes"

NATIONALLY	76
Weekly	96
Monthly	92
Yearly	69
Never	63
Conservative Protestants	90
Mainline Protestants	84
RCs outside Quebec	83
Other Faiths	79
RCs in Quebec	65
No Religion	51
Atlantic Provinces	83
Prairies	82
Ontario	82
British Columbia	75
Quebec	61
55+	84
35–54	81
18–34	60
Females	76
Males	74

Source: Bibby, Project Canada 2000.

lives are attending services yearly (61%) or never (33%). No surprise there; if they thought the churches were pertinent, they'd be showing up. Almost half (49%) of those who question the need for religious groups are under the age of 35, 33% are 35 to 44, and 18% are 55 or older. Obviously, these characteristics overlap. For example, 20% of those who say groups no longer have a contribution to make to Canadian lives are people under 35 who attend yearly or less.

But these variations describe a view held by a minority. A solid majority of Canadians continue to think religious groups have a role to play in individual lives, including Catholics in Quebec, people who never attend services, young adults under the age of 35, and one in two people with no religious affiliation. It's also important to remind everyone of the findings discussed earlier indicating that a majority of these younger adults who are numerically dominant in the "None" and "Never" categories can be expected to reaffiliate and/or become more involved and more favourably disposed to religious groups as they age.[3] Moreover, it is also important to remember that people who feel groups no longer have a role to play say so on the basis of their perception of what groups are doing right now. Apart from some becoming more positive as they get older, at least some of the critics would presumably be less negative if they had reason to change their perception — a possibility that seems to be largely up to the churches.

One further point: a measure of disenchantment with current developments and leadership does not translate into many critics writing off religious groups. People with high levels of confidence in religious leaders predictably are more likely than others to feel that groups still have a contribution to make. But even among those who have limited confidence, one in two maintain that "religious groups still have a role to play in Canadian lives." This strikes me, at least, as a pretty encouraging sign of consumer resilience. Other "companies" should be so lucky.

Those survey respondents who told us they think religion has

Belief Groups Have a Role to Play, by Level of Confidence in Religious Leaders

CONFIDENCE:

A Great Deal	86%
Quite a Bit	90%
Some	80%
Little or None	51%

Source: Bibby, Project Canada 2000

---

a role to play were then asked, *"What do you consider that role to be?"* We provided four possible responses:

1. They should be addressing all of life — *spiritual, personal, and social issues.*
2. They should focus on *spiritual and personal issues* — and stay out of social issues.
3. They should focus on *spiritual and social issues* — and stay out of personal issues.
4. They should focus on *spiritual issues only.*

The most common single response, offered by 43% of Canadians overall, is that groups should be addressing all of life. Smaller proportions say the focus should be spiritual issues only (17%), spiritual and personal matters (9%), or spiritual and social concerns (7%).

- Seven in ten *weekly attenders* and six in ten *monthlys* cite "all of life."
- "All of life" is also the most common response of people in all religious group categories, led by *Conservative Protestants* (68%). Individuals identifying with *Other Faiths* are the single exception: here an equal proportion indicate they favour a spiritual emphasis only.
- Despite the perception that *Mainline Protestants* give major attention to social issues, less than 10% of their affiliates feel the focus of ministry should be on social issues only, compared to almost 50% who say ministry should address all of life — a level similar to that of *Roman Catholics outside Quebec.*
- *Catholics in Quebec* are particularly polarized: one in three think religious groups should speak to *all of life,* but another one in three feel groups no longer have *any* role to play. Most of the remainder favour churches having a more specialized and limited role.

Men and women differ little in their views of what religious groups should be doing. However, there are some noteworthy differences across the country, as well as among older and younger Canadians.

TABLE 7.2 **What the Role of Religious Groups Should Be, by Attendance and Affiliation**

	ALL OF LIFE	SPIRITUAL ONLY	SPIRITUAL AND PERSONAL	SPIRITUAL AND SOCIAL	NO ROLE
NATIONALLY	43%	17%	9%	7%	24%
Weekly	71	14	7	4	4
Monthly	61	14	6	11	8
Yearly	35	16	10	8	31
Never	27	22	7	7	37
CPROT	68	11	7	4	10
RCOQ	49	19	9	6	17
MLPROT	49	16	11	8	16
RCQ	36	13	6	10	35
Other Faiths	29	31	12	7	21
No Religion	23	17	7	4	49

Source: Bibby, Project Canada 2000.

- An emphasis on religion addressing all of life is pervasive in the *Atlantic region* and, to a lesser extent, in *Ontario* and on the *Prairies*. *Quebec*, as already noted, is polarized between emphases on "all" or "nothing." In *British Columbia*, the three dominant roles cited — apart from "no role" — are (1) all of life, (2) the spiritual, and (3) the spiritual and personal.
- *Adults under 35*, similar to people living in Quebec and B.C., tend to think the contribution of groups should be either "all" or "nothing."

How strong is the mandate for social ministry? In the 1970s, 63% of Canadians felt that ministers *should* be involved in social, economic, and political issues. Those who opposed ministers' involvement were led by Nevers, Nones, and Roman Catholics in Quebec — who, of course, had just witnessed the province taking over many tasks previously carried out by the Church. Conversely, Catholics in the rest of the country were more likely than other Canadians to feel ministers should be involved in such matters.

TABLE 7.3 **What the Role of Religious Groups Should Be, by Region, Age, and Gender**

	ALL OF LIFE	SPIRITUAL ONLY	SPIRITUAL & PERSONAL	SPIRITUAL & SOCIAL	NO ROLE
NATIONALLY	43%	17%	9%	7%	24%
Atlantic	55	15	5	8	17
Ontario	50	18	9	5	18
Prairies	48	17	8	9	18
Quebec	33	15	5	8	39
B.C.	28	20	18	9	25
55+	48	19	8	9	16
35–54	43	21	9	8	19
18–34	38	9	8	5	40
Women	45	16	7	8	24
Men	40	18	10	6	26

Source: Bibby, Project Canada 2000.

By the 1980s, those supporting religious involvement in public affairs had dropped 12 points to 51%, with disapproval up considerably among infrequent attenders and affiliates of all groups, with the sole exception of Conservative Protestants.

Today the trend toward wanting religious leaders to be involved in public life is showing some signs of reversal. Currently, 56% of Canadians favour such involvement.

- Similar to the case in the 1970s, current "pro-involvement" advocates are being led by *weekly* and *monthly attenders*, a majority of *Catholics outside Quebec*, and almost half the *Catholics in Quebec.*
- But unlike the 70s scenario, those supporting social involvement are much more likely to be *Conservative Protestants* (74%) than Mainline Protestants (59%). This tendency of evangelicals to combine an emphasis on social change with personal change is a major change worth underlining.
- In terms of age, *adults under 55* continue to be marginally more likely than those over 55 to favour ministers dealing

TABLE 7.4 **Religion and Social Involvement by Attendance, Affiliation and Age**

"Ministers should stick to religion and not concern themselves with social, economic, and political issues."

% Disagreeing

	1975	1985	2000
NATIONALLY	63	51	56
Weekly	68	63	70
Monthly	75	56	67
Yearly	63	47	52
Never	52	45	45
RCs outside Quebec	72	57	62
RCs in Quebec	53	37	46
Mainline Protestants	67	57	59
Conservative Protestants	66	64	74
Other Faiths	62	37	52
No Religion	49	44	51
18–34	67	52	58
35–54	65	56	56
55+	56	44	53

Source: Bibby, Project Canada Survey Series.

with social issues, but the differences by age cohort have become increasingly small over the past two decades.

In summary, more than one in two people across the country today — led by those who are most actively involved in their groups — feel religious leaders should be addressing social, economic, and political issues. Relatively few want social ministry to be the exclusive focus of churches. But there is a widespread sense, particularly among those most involved, that faith has to address not only spiritual and personal matters, but social issues as well.

Spiritual Issues

We have already seen that Canadians, in large numbers, are expressing spiritual needs and interests, with many seeing themselves as spiritual.

Such findings are consistent with widespread impressions. As I reminded readers in *Canada's Teens*, from about the early 1990s onward, the American media led the way in creating the perception that many people who are not particularly interested in organized religion are nonetheless openly searching for ways to meet their spiritual needs.[4] Major magazines such as *Time*, *Newsweek*, and *Life* proclaimed the new interest in spirituality, while best-selling books ranging from James Redfield's *The Celestine Prophecy* and Thomas Moore's *Care of the Soul* to Betty Eadie's *Embraced by the Light* seemingly provided evidence of the pervasive quest for spirituality.[5]

Respected trend gazer John Naisbitt forecast the rebirth of spiritual interest in 1990 in his book *Megatrends 2000,* and this renaissance was confirmed by highly regarded researchers such as Wade Clark Roof and Robert Wuthnow.[6] Congregational gurus such as Lyle Schaller, Bill Easum, George Barna, and Tom Bandy made themselves available to churches that attempted to respond to the need at hand.

In fairly predictable fashion, the Canadian media have assumed that if it is happening in the U.S., it must be happening in Canada as well. Highly regarded journalist Ron Graham spent two years travelling the country looking for Canada's soul and concluded in his 1990 book *God's Dominion* that increasing attention was being given to spiritual issues.[7] *Maclean's* magazine proclaimed in an October 1994 cover story that "a massive search for spirituality is gripping North America."[8] In 1996, Doug Todd unveiled his book *Brave Souls* and announced, "Something big is going on in contemporary spirituality."[9] I myself, in books like *Unknown Gods* and *There's Got to Be More!*, have maintained on the basis of my national surveys that there is widespread receptivity to spirituality in Canada; in the process, my research has been readily co-opted by a media anxious to document their spirituality claims. Academics and the media alike have continued to make the case for the ongoing interest in spirituality, providing the public with updates. By way of example, *Maclean's* ran an April 13, 2001, cover story on "The New Spirituality," David Lyon of Queen's University analyzed the nature of contemporary spiritual quest in his *Jesus in Disneyland* (2000), Roof followed up his earlier work on spirituality among Baby Boomers with the publication of *Spiritual Marketplace* (1999), and Wuthnow looked at how spirituality has changed since the 1950s in *After Heaven* (1998). And the gurus are still writing "how to respond" books and making the congregational and denominational rounds.

For all the speculation and American research, however, Canadian religious groups that are attempting to respond to the interest in spirituality need to understand more clearly what is actually happening in Canada. Some basic questions need to be answered. For example, is there something new about widespread interest in spirituality? What do people today mean by the word? And who do they share their spirituality with — if anybody? Our national surveys have attempted to probe each of these three questions.

The Spirituality Surge
The prevalent assumption is that there has been an acceleration in spiritual quest in recent years, specifically since about the late 1980s. We have checked out this perception with Canadians. The *Project Canada 2000* survey asked, *"Thinking back over the past ten years, would you say there has been an increase, a decrease, or no particular change in your interest in spirituality?"*

Some 26%, led by women, reported their interest in spirituality had increased during the 1990s, and 14% said it had decreased; the remaining 60% said their interest level had remained essentially

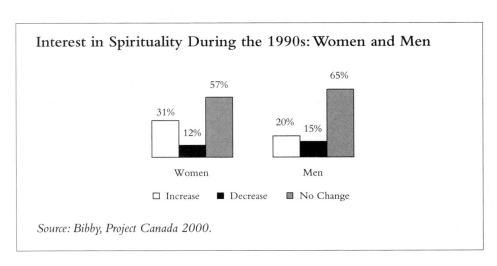

Interest in Spirituality During the 1990s: Women and Men

Women: 31% Increase, 12% Decrease, 57% No Change
Men: 20% Increase, 15% Decrease, 65% No Change

☐ Increase   ■ Decrease   ▨ No Change

Source: Bibby, Project Canada 2000.

the same. The net gain in interest was therefore 12%, or about one in ten people.

However, the increase may not really be linked specifically to events that occurred during the 1990s. A closer look at those increases by age shows the figures to be 31% for 18-to-34-year-olds, 24% for those 35 to 54, and 23% for adults 55 and over. When younger adults, 18 to 34, are comparing their interest now to what it was a decade ago, they are talking about the days when they were anywhere from about 10 to 25 years old. Our national surveys of teenagers suggest that when people are younger, their interest in spirituality is lower than it is later on.

TABLE 7.5 **Spirituality and Age Variables**

	SPIRITUALITY INTEREST INCREASE IN PAST DECADE	HAVE SPIRITUAL NEEDS	SPIRITUALITY IMPORTANT
Teenagers	—	48%	60%
18–34	31	71	66
35–54	24	74	69
55+	23	74	75

Sources: Bibby, Project Teen Canada 2000 and Project Canada 2000.

Consequently, a net increase in spirituality would probably be found in any "one-time survey snapshot." For example, in 1995, we asked Canadians to compare their current interest in spirituality with what it had been *five years earlier*. Some 26% of 18-to-34-year-olds said it had increased, compared to 21% of those 35 to 54, and 17% of people 55 and older.

Further, as we saw in Chapter 6, there is little difference by age in the expression of spiritual needs or in the belief that one is spiritual. Those findings point to the possibility that large numbers of people have valued spirituality for some time. The latest Gen Xers, for example, show no signs of being more interested in spirituality than their Boomer parents or their grandparents.

In short, for all the media hype, it may well be that public openness to spirituality has been there "all along." To the extent that the media have played up spirituality and entrepreneurs have accelerated their efforts to respond to "the spirituality market," interest has been high. But our findings suggest the media haven't so much created that market as responded to it.

What all this adds up to is the conclusion that the market for spirituality has been and continues to be extensive. As Canadians look at churches, they assume those institutions will be giving primary attention to spirituality.

What Do People Have in Mind?
Although the term *spirituality* is widely used by average citizens and everyone else, it isn't at all clear what people have in mind when they use the word. In the 1995 national survey, we followed up the question "*Do you yourself have 'spiritual needs'?*" with the obvious query: "*What do you mean by 'spirituality'?*" A preliminary examination of the open-ended responses revealed that a large number of ideas were fairly conventional in nature.[10] For example, some people suggested that their views of spirituality involved belief in God, praying, and their "relationship with Jesus." A Baptist from Prince Edward Island who is 79 commented, "As a Christian, I believe that when we are born again we are indwelt with the Holy Spirit, so my spiritual needs are met through the spirit." A 45-year-old Roman Catholic from Oakville, Ontario, said that for him spirituality means "being in communion with our Lord Jesus Christ and the Holy Spirit."

Other responses were less predictable and less conventional, including themes such as "inner awareness," believing in "a force that controls the universe," and "thinking outside the material levels of life." A 56-year-old Anglican from Victoria who attends services about once a year told us that his spirituality involves "the belief that somehow there is some influencing force — that we are not all generic vegetables." A 66-year-old Catholic from a Montreal suburb who attends services weekly described her spirituality succinctly but vaguely as "inner life." A 42-year-old who works in finance in Toronto reported that he never attends services, although he was raised Catholic. He described his view of spirituality this way: "To search for Truth, which lies in the ability to perceive, feel, and acutely sense the reasoning behind events which may not be obvious to the conscious mind and may defy logic."

In trying to classify these extremely diverse responses, we first divided them into "conventional" and "less conventional" categories, then further divided them into five sub-categories each. Some illustrative responses are as follows.

Conventional
Belief: God, Jesus, life-after-death
"Believing in God and the Bible"
"Belief in God's ability"
Practice: attendance, prayer
"Communication with God through prayer"
"Going to church on weekdays and always on Sunday"
Experience: God, relationship, resource, peace, ecstasy
"Living in fellowship with Christ"
"Having a proper relationship with God"
Knowledge: inner awareness, external awareness
"Knowing God is there, hears our prayers, and answers them"
"A feeling of being whole and at peace with life"
Behaviour: self, others
"Being a good Christian"
"Whenever you do God's way, help others, there is life"

Less Conventional
Outlook: beyond material, value human spirit, soul-focus, greater power
"A matter relating to your inner self or soul"
"Belief that somehow there is some influencing force"
Practice: group involvement, meditation, discipline, reflection
"Peace of mind, meditation"
"Seeking answers to the purpose of life"
Experience: peace, nourishment, connection, wholeness, ecstasy
"Nourishment for our souls"
"Feeling of oneness with the earth"
Knowledge: inner awareness, external awareness
"A knowledge of all living things seen and unseen"
"Needing to know there is a power greater than me"

Behaviour: self, others

> "Being accepting of others and one's self"
> "Nurturing the needs of the soul"

Overall, just over half the responses were judged to be conventional in nature. In turn, close to 50% of these had a strong experiential and relational emphasis, while another 35% were heavily cognitive, involving belief and outlook. In the case of less conventional responses, the most prevalent were cognitive, in the form of outlook, followed fairly closely by those with experiential and knowledge emphases.

TABLE 7.6 **Types of Spirituality Responses**

	CONVENTIONAL RESPONSES	LESS CONVENTIONAL RESPONSES
NATIONALLY	53%	47%
Experience	44	26
Belief/Outlook	36	32
Practice	10	9
Knowledge	5	22
Behaviour	2	4
Other	3	7

Source: Bibby, Project Can95.

What is particularly apparent is that large numbers of Canadians do not see spirituality in the same way as most of their compatriots who are highly involved in the country's religious groups.

- To the extent that people *attend* services regularly, they hold conventional views of spirituality; to the extent that they do not attend, they hold less conventional views.
- *Conservative Protestants* tend to have the most conventional views of spirituality; *Religious Nones* and to a lesser extent affiliates of *Other Faiths*, the least conventional. Roman Catholics and Mainline Protestants are located between the two extremes. It's worth noting that *Catholics in Quebec* exhibit lower levels of conventional spirituality than Catholics elsewhere.

There are also significant gender and age differences in the way Canadians conceptualize spirituality.

- Conventional responses tend to be offered far more often by *men* than by women.
- *Older adults* likewise are considerably more likely than either Boomers or Gen Xers to see spirituality in conventional ways.

We consequently have a situation in which interest in spirituality is very high among people involved in religious groups and also among those who are not. At first glance, this would seem to add up to an obvious opportunity for religious groups. More than one in two Canadians expresses spiritual needs, with those numbers readily exceeding the one in five people who are actively participating in religious groups.

TABLE 7.7 **Types of Spirituality Responses, by Attendance, Affiliation, Age, and Gender**

	CONVENTIONAL RESPONSES	LESS CONVENTIONAL RESPONSES
NATIONALLY	53%	47%
Weekly	77	23
Monthly	52	48
Yearly	34	66
Never	9	91
Conservative Protestants	88	12
RCs outside Quebec	64	36
RCs in Quebec	56	44
Mainline Protestants	56	44
Other Faiths	26	74
No Religion	2	98
55+	71	29
18–34	48	52
35–54	47	53
Men	62	38
Women	46	54

Source: Bibby, Project Can95.

What People Mean by "Spiritual" When They Speak of Spiritual Needs

Conventional

". . . living in fellowship with Christ . . . believing in God and the Bible . . . that God is there for us, hears our prayers and answers them . . . communication with God through prayer . . . need to know there is a power greater than me . . . need God's spirit to guide, protect, and support me in good times and bad . . . building a personal relation with Jesus Christ . . . nourishing our souls so we can be closer to God . . . the need to reconnect with my religion . . . the need for strength, comfort, and courage available from a power beyond ourselves . . . to be a good Christian . . . believing in a higher power . . . acceptance of a higher being with which our spiritual side communicates something greater than me or mankind . . . to pray and commune with my heavenly father . . . a devotion to things of God and not material things . . . Christianity . . . a belief in a presence beyond our bodily beings . . . someone is out there to help you deal with things . . . a loving God . . . having faith in God and being in tune with your-self and your faith . . . needing to know the heavenly father lives and loves me personally . . . knowing there is a God and a guardian angel that looks after us . . . being aware of God and his relationship with the world . . . being in touch with God . . . the need to attend mass more often . . . believing in a supreme being . . . the human spirit maintaining contact with God through his spirit . . . "

Less Conventional

". . . a matter relating to our inner-self or soul . . . peace of mind . . . a feeling of oneness with the earth and with all that is within me . . . the existence of an immortal soul that has to be cared for . . . our relationship with god or nature or the universe . . . positive thinking and excitement . . . someone to confide feelings with . . . can be religious or the beauty of nature of the love of family and friends . . . a feeling that a force controls the universe . . . the human spirit and goodness of humankind that ultimately triumphs over evil . . . searching for meaning . . . a deeper appreciation and understanding of myself, others, and god . . . recognition and nurturing the needs of the soul . . . a feeling of being whole and at peace with my experiences in life . . . inner awareness . . . an experience without physical origin . . . having some religious feelings and thoughts . . . belief that somehow there is some influencing force . . . my presence and communication with the world around me . . . feeling there is some-thing more to life than the obvious here and now . . . belief my existence will continue in another dimension . . . "

Source: Bibby, Project Can95 National Survey.

But it's not quite that simple. While much spirituality is highly conventional, especially in the case of people who are already involved in the churches, it also is clear that, the less people are involved, the less likely they are to hold conventional views of spirituality. Significantly, the uninvolved are particularly inclined to hold views of spirituality that are at odds with the beliefs of the group that is officially the most eager to "reach" them — Conservative Protestants.

And so a dilemma appears to exist. Many Canadians have conceptions of spirituality that are fairly foreign to religious bodies and especially to Conservative Protestants. The two sides may have little more than a word in common. Yet maybe that common word is enough. Perhaps it will allow the churches and Canadians outside the churches to at least converse. At a Project Canada consultation in Vancouver a few years back, Wade Clark Roof suggested that religious groups might consider providing environments where people with spiritual interests might come together and talk, in order that religious groups and "outsiders" might learn from one another and that churches might find creative ways of responding with integrity to "less conventional" spiritual needs. It might be a good start.

The Social Side of Spirituality

No one seems to know very much about the social dimension of spirituality — for example, whether or not people share their understanding and nurturing of spirituality with others or essentially go it alone. We attempted to get some preliminary answers to the question by asking those 58% of Canadians who indicated they see themselves as "a spiritual person,"

> Which of the following best describes you?
> 1. I find I can relate my spirituality to others in my religious group.
> 2. I share my spirituality with some people close to me, outside of a religious group.
> 3. Actually, I keep my spirituality pretty much to myself.

The responses reveal that spirituality is something highly private for most people — more so, perhaps, than any of us realize — including tose who are highly involved in churches.

- More than five in ten inform us that they keep their spirituality pretty much *to themselves.*
- Better than three in ten say they *share their spirituality* with some people who are close to them, outside of a religious group.
- Only about one in ten indicate they can relate their spirituality to others *in their religious groups.* Those who can include only about 30% of weekly attenders. Illustrative of this apparent anomaly is a 49-year-old nondenominational evangelical from Truro, Nova Scotia, who says his spirituality is very important to him and that he receives a high level of enjoyment from his church. He conceptualizes being spiritual as "believing in and participating in the unseen part of life — to walk with God."[11] Yet he acknowledges his spirituality tends to be shared with people other than those in his religious group. Individuals who relate their spirituality to people in their churches range from a high of 25% for Conservative Protestants to lows of 8% for both Mainline Protestants and those identifying with Other Faith groups.
- Perhaps surprisingly, older people are just about as likely as younger people to keep their spirituality to themselves, despite the fact that they are over-represented in religious groups. Among them is a 78-year-old Catholic who lives in a small Atlantic community and attends services every week. She says, "my being appears human but my being is more — it is also spiritual! Both must be nurtured to make my being whole and meaningful."[12] Interesting thoughts; yet she says she doesn't tend to relate them to the people in her Catholic parish.
- Differences in how spirituality is shared or not shared are small between females and males.

There's little doubt about it. Canadians not only have an interest in spirituality, but a solid majority also say they have spiritual needs, and more than half see themselves as spiritual. Yet when it comes right down to sharing their sense of spirituality, a remarkably small number are relating what they understand and feel to others in religious settings. Their preference, even when they are actively

TABLE 7.8 **Private and Public Expressions of One's Spirituality, by Attendance, Affiliation, Age, and Gender**

	KEEP IT PRETTY MUCH TO MYSELF	SHARE IT OUTSIDE A RELIGIOUS GROUP	CAN RELATE IT TO OTHERS IN MY RELIGIOUS GROUP	TOTALS
NATIONALLY	53%	35%	12%	100%
Weekly	33	38	29	100
Monthly	47	40	13	100
Yearly	60	37	3	100
Never	80	20	0	100
RCOQ	57	32	11	100
RCQ	54	30	16	100
MLPROT	59	33	8	100
CPROT	26	49	25	100
Other Faiths	38	54	8	100
No Religion	62	38	0	100
18–34	50	37	13	100
35–54	56	36	8	100
55+	52	30	18	100
Females	54	37	9	100
Male	52	33	15	100

Source: Bibby, Project Canada 2000.

involved in a group, is either to keep their spirituality to themselves or to share it with people who are close to them, outside of a religious group.

But then again, some of our illustrative comments suggest that maybe even the more involved Canadians and religious groups are not really talking about the same thing. At minimum, the current situation points to the need for churches that believe they have something to bring to conversations about spirituality to find creative ways of opening up the communication lines on spirituality — beginning with their own people.

What People Mean When They Say "I Am a Spiritual Person" — and the Extent to Which They Relate Their Spirituality to Others

Conventional Responses
Keep It to Myself
". . . believing in God . . . the belief we have a soul . . . having beliefs and practicing them . . . believing in something beyond the things created by mankind . . . praying to a supreme being . . . feeling we are all guided by a supreme being . . . doing unto one another as you would have them do unto you . . . believing that the spirit lives after the body dies . . . full commitment to God . . . having the presence of God with me and near me . . . being a good person and following the Ten Commandments . . ."

Share It with Some People Outside of a Religious Group
" . . . concern for more than the physical part of life — trying to see what lies beneath . . . being plugged into a higher power at all times . . . belief in a divine being who will provide grace to carry on, especially during time of illness, death, etc. . . . constantly questioning the meaning of life and struggling for certainty about God and resurrection . . . belief in God and the justice of karma through continuous life experiences until you get it right . . . respect for others and being part of a community that helps one another . . ."

Relate It to Others in My Religious Group
" . . . looking for the meaning of life with God . . . communion with God, Jesus and the Holy Spirit . . . relatedness to god . . . god's spirit gives direction for life — god speaks by this world and I speak in prayer . . . seeing God in all things . . . loving God with heart, soul, mind and loving my neighbour as myself . . . nourishing my Spirit and my body and mind . . ."

Less Conventional Responses
Keep It to Myself
". . . talking to god, seeing god in others . . . I am deeply affected by human expressions of music, dance, ballet, and the arts . . . inner peace . . . I believe the spirits are found all around us . . . I don't like the word 'spiritual' — a person with good values and an empathy for other people's conditions; I like to help others be calm . . . all caring humans have a certain spirituality . . ."

Share It with Some People Outside of a Religious Group
". . . believing in our personal truths . . . being conscious of life and those around you . . . being one with the universal energy and cosmic power . . . believing in a power above and beyond things earthly . . . believing in an energy and order greater than ourselves . . . knowing humans and animals are more than just physiology and brain; each has its own spirit or soul and all are connected spiritually to other beings living or dead . . ."

Source: Bibby, Project Canada 2000.

Personal Issues

For years I have been repeating the observation of an extraordinary mentor of mine — sociologist Gwynn Nettler, who taught at the University of Alberta. In trying to synthesize what people want out of life, Nettler drew on international polling to claim that people in the 1970s essentially wanted two things: to stay alive and to live well.[13] There's no reason to believe things have changed.

It goes without saying that people want to be happy, but, as stressed in Chapter 4, the eternal question has been how to find happiness. Our surveys through 2000 have been asking Canadians about their values and their sources of enjoyment.

- Invariably they place the greatest importance on freedom and relationships, along with privacy and, of course, a comfortable life. In the youth surveys, teenagers cite the same factors. Like them, most of us deeply value good ties with the people we care about. At the same time, we don't want to sacrifice our individuality and autonomy. The trick is finding out how to get it all. Relationships are great, but so is freedom.
- Such values are reflected in Canadians' top sources of enjoyment: family and friends, their houses and apartments and jobs, and freedom reflected in leisure time given to music, television, and sports. Good health and life itself, of course, are assumed to be in place.[14]

Yes, Nettler has pretty much summed it up. We want to stay alive. And we want to live well. The problem, of course, is that we don't always or even typically get what we want. We have a lot of concerns. Consistent with what they see as their sources of happiness, Canadians also have anxiety about a lot of things, especially money, health, and time, which are at the top of their lists. Among their other prime concerns are their children, their jobs, their lack of recognition, and the feeling that they want more out of life.

To live life and to get to know people is to find people experiencing a lot of pleasure and also a lot of pain. There is no need for me to pontificate here: I know that your experience has been mine. To get to know individuals well is to find that everyone has days — often

TABLE 7.9 **Top Ten Sources of Enjoyment**

% Receiving "A Great Deal" or "Quite a Bit" of Enjoyment

1. Family life	86%
2. Friends	83
3. Music	77
4. My house or apartment	77
5. Marriage/relationship	75
6. Children	69
7. Siblings	64
8. City/town I live in	61
9. Being by myself	58
10. Mother	57
Some Significant Others	
Television	56
Job	53
Father	47
Pets	46
Sports	40
Household work	29
Internet	22
Religious group	22

Source: Bibby, Project Canada 2000.

weeks, sometimes months, even years and lifetimes — when they are deeply troubled, feel anxiety, experience anguish, and even enter into times of despair that come from a sense of helplessness and lack of hope. In the words of a wise former minister of mine, "Life is tough and people get hurt."

I could offer detailed illustrations, but in addressing people over the years on the point of personal struggle and pain, I have found it unnecessary. Every listener and every reader only needs to briefly scan their own biographies and the lives of people with whom they are close to know only too well what I am speaking about. Friends and relatives suffer in any number of ways. Disappointments and dreams are decimated. People, including young people and infants, die. Scott Peck wasn't exaggerating: life is difficult.[15]

TABLE 7.10 **Top Ten Personal Concerns**

% Concerned "A Great Deal" or "Quite a Bit"

1. Never seem to have enough time	48%
2. Lack of money	47
3. Health	47
4. Children	42
5. Job	39
6. Lack of recognition	35
7. My looks	33
8. Should be getting more out of life	32
9. Marriage/relationship	31
10. Wondering about life's purpose	28
Among the Less Common	
Sex life	27
Loneliness	26
Getting older	26
So many things changing	24
Depression	23
Feelings of inferiority	21
Dying	18

Source: Bibby, Project Canada 2000.

Where do people turn? We asked Canadians that question in our most recent survey. Many, as would be expected, indicated that they turn to more than one key source for help.

- Some 55% say that when they face a serious problem, their resources include their *family* — most often a spouse and frequently parents.
- About 20% report that they look to *friends*, while close to another 20% say that *God* is at least one source of help, with some emphasizing the importance of prayer.
- Another 15% indicate that they rely totally on *themselves* to deal with serious problems.
- A smaller number — about 5% — indicate their resources include *specialists*, such as counsellors or physicians. Perhaps

TABLE 7.11 **Sources of Support**

*"When I face a serious problem, I turn to . . ."**

Family	55%
Husband/wife	27
Parents	10
Other family	18
Friends	19
Friends generally	18
Boyfriend/girlfriend specifically	1
God or prayer	18
Myself	15
Specialist	5
Other	2

Up to two sources could be cited.

Source: Bibby, Project Canada 2000.

significantly, very few ministers, priests, or other religious figures were mentioned. However, as will be evident shortly, Canadians sometimes find their religious groups to be a personal resource via friends and certainly via faith.

In exploring personal resources, we asked Canadians who are currently attending services at least once a month about the help they have received from their groups in times of need. The question read:

Generally speaking, when you have encountered personal problems over the years, have your religious groups:
1. Been aware, and given you the support that you have needed.
2. Been aware, but not given you the support you have needed.
3. Not been aware, but still have given you the support you have needed.
4. Not been aware, and have not given you the support you have needed.
5. Other.

Overall, religious groups receive reasonably high grades.

- Some five in ten people across the country say that, in general, religious groups have been aware of times when they have had personal problems and have given them support.
- More than another two in ten say that, even when groups have not been aware of what they have been going through, they still have been a source of support. Perhaps, for example, a person has benefited from worship services even though his or her problems were not made public.
- On the negative side, two in ten people claim that groups have tended not to be aware of their personal problems, and have not given them support.
- Yet less than one in ten say that groups have been aware of what they were experiencing, but failed to give them support.

Not surprisingly, more active attendance is associated with greater awareness of problems and a positive congregational responses to them. There are, however, noteworthy differences between Protestants and Roman Catholics.

- Despite having similar proportions of people attending either weekly or monthly, some 72% of Protestants say their groups have been aware of their problems, compared to only 37% of Catholics.
- Consequently, Catholics are far more likely than Protestants not so much to fault their parishes for failing to respond to their problems as to say that their churches have been unaware of their difficulties and therefore have not provided them with the support they have needed (34% of Catholics versus 9% of Protestants).

One obvious explanation would seem to lie in the fact that local Catholic churches are frequently larger than Protestant congregations. For example, 43% of Catholics attending services monthly or more say that their parishes have five hundred or more active people, while only 12% of Protestants report being part of congregations

TABLE 7.12 **Role of Religious Groups in Providing Support for Active Affiliates in Times of Need**

	N	AWARE AND SUPPORTED	UNAWARE AND SUPPORTED	UNAWARE AND DID NOT	AWARE BUT DID NOT
NATIONALLY	287	50%	23%	20%	7%
Weekly	204	56	22	16	6
Monthly	82	37	25	32	6
Protestants	157	64	19	9	8
Mainline	82	60	26	8	6
Conservative	46	59	13	13	15
Roman Catholics	117	32	29	34	5
Outside Quebec	76	32	30	34	4
In Quebec	41	34	27	32	7

Source: Bibby, Project Canada 2000.

that large. As a result, Catholic parish priests and lay leaders may be having severe difficulty keeping in close touch with the lives of so many parishioners.

But size may be only part of the story. The large differences in both awareness and support between Protestants and Catholics, regardless of age and gender, suggest that Protestants may be putting more emphasis than Catholics on goals such as fellowship versus attendance and ministering to one another versus ministry to oneself. Clearly, such news calls for thought and response.

The findings about variations by age in awareness and support may be highly significant for both Catholics and Protestants. A cursory glance at the patterns shows that — among these monthly-plus attenders — adults 35 and over are considerably more likely than younger adults to say their groups have been aware of their personal problems over the years, and have given them support. It is easy to dismiss this difference by age as a reflection of youthful cynicism. However, we need to remember that these are the 18-to-34-year-olds who are *still attending services* at least once a month.

A loud alarm bell should be going off: it is safe to assume a good number of people who did not have their personal needs addressed by religious groups are no longer actively involved. Conversely, by

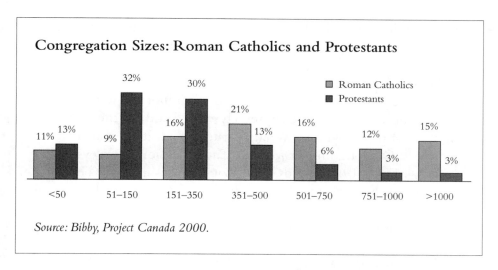

Congregation Sizes: Roman Catholics and Protestants

Roman Catholics
Protestants

	<50	51–150	151–350	351–500	501–750	751–1000	>1000
Roman Catholics	11%	9%	16%	21%	16%	12%	15%
Protestants	13%	32%	30%	13%	6%	3%	3%

Source: Bibby, Project Canada 2000.

saying that groups were responsive, older adults have indicated that they have been satisfied with the ministry they have received. Many adults under 35 who are currently attending services need to be similarly convinced that their lives and their concerns matter to their congregations. Otherwise, many of them can be expected to join the ranks of the inactives. The window of opportunity for groups to minister to the needs of some of their young adults may soon be closing.

Clearly, many Canadians facing personal problems, especially Catholics, have been slipping through the ministry cracks of religious groups. These findings signal the need, in many congregational instances, for leaders to be far more effective at being in touch with

TABLE 7.13 **Awareness of Personal Problems:
Protestant and Roman Catholic Monthly-Plus Attenders**

	AWARE		AWARE & SUPPORTED	
	PROT	RC	PROT	RC
ALL	72%	37%	64%	32%
55+	79	53	70	47
35–54	71	29	64	42
18–34	55	17	43	10
Female	73	36	65	34
Male	71	36	63	31

Source: Bibby, Project Canada 2000.

their people, especially their younger people, in order to help their members and adherents cope with life's difficulties.

Relational Issues

As we have just seen, there is nothing more important to Canadians than relationships. They are supremely valued and are the source of high levels of enjoyment. What is true for adults is also true for teenagers. Our ongoing *Project Teen Canada* national surveys of the country's 15-to-19-year-olds show that relationships have been and continue to be the number one source of enjoyment for young people.[16]

But all is not always well on the relational front.

- While friendship is highly valued by 78% of adults and 85% of teens, family life is seen as extremely important by 85% of adults — but just 59% of teenagers.
- Although 94% of parents say they are getting high levels of enjoyment from their children, a much-lower 71% of teenagers say the same thing about their mothers and 62% say this of their fathers.
- Parents might be enjoying their offspring, but that doesn't mean they are not worried about them: as we just saw, no less than 42% say they worry about their children "a great deal" or "quite a bit." Among parents with at least one teenager, the figure jumps to 48%.

Such "hard data" serve as a reminder of what seems to be an age-old reality: teens and parents value good relationships. But in a good many cases, they are failing to have those kinds of good ties with each other. In our latest youth survey, for example, about 15% of teens report that they have arguments with their parents every day, while another 40% or so report that arguments take place at least once a week. Family life can be great, but as one 16-year-old from a small northern Ontario town reminded us, it's not always that way: "The family adds a lot of stress to teenagers' lives," she says.[17]

Some other adult survey findings illustrate how elusive satisfying relationships can be:

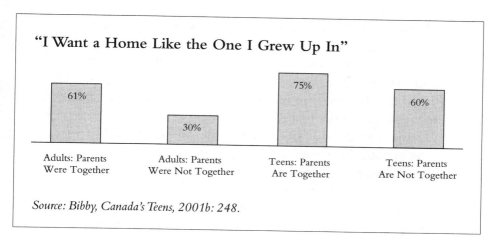

"I Want a Home Like the One I Grew Up In"

| 61% | 30% | 75% | 60% |
| Adults: Parents Were Together | Adults: Parents Were Not Together | Teens: Parents Are Together | Teens: Parents Are Not Together |

Source: Bibby, Canada's Teens, 2001b: 248.

- Close to one in three Canadians (31%) say problems in their marriages concern them "a great deal" or "quite a bit."
- Our 1975 survey found that 7% of Canadians had been divorced; that figure now stands at 16%.
- Among people who have never married, 48% say they are troubled about the inability to find the relationship they want, while 33% express concern about not being married. Contrary to widespread thinking, incidentally, in both cases the levels of concern are higher for males than for females.[18]

In short, Canadians want good relationships. Sometimes they are finding them, sometimes they are not.

The surveys also document what most of us assume — that people want to be able to experience good interpersonal relations that extend well beyond immediate relationships to our communities, regions, and nation, and, for that matter, around the globe. It's all part of wanting to stay alive and live well. Who needs conflict at any level? Here again, Canadians are enjoying varying levels of success.

- About 60% are unsure about the reliability of people in general, with 20% even feeling that a stranger who shows a person attention is probably up to something.
- Close to nine in ten feel people have a right to an income that allows them to live.

- Almost 90% of Canadians who live outside Quebec want the province to remain in Canada.
- A two in three majority *do not* think we should focus on our country to the exclusion of the needs of the rest of the world; they also see no reason why another world war needs to take place in the relatively near future.
- On the positive side of interpersonal values, about 70% to 80% of Canadians are placing high value on such key traits as kindness and concern for others, politeness, and forgiveness.
- On the negative side, just under half the population view generosity as "very important," while an appallingly low 16% place that kind of importance on involvement in their communities.

The irony, as we all know well, is that optimum social life involves some give and take. Enhanced living at the collective level requires a measure of civility at the individual level. People can say they want good relationships and a civil society and planet. But if basic traits such as concern for others and generosity are not valued and practised, an enriched collective life will never be realized.

Does religion have any role to play in instilling characteristics that make for good interpersonal life? Presumably so. All major world religions have strong ethical components — and in some cases, such as Confucianism, ethics are the prominent feature of the faith. The Judaeo-Christian tradition that continues to be so dominant in Canada is clearly one that calls people not only into a relationship with God but also into living in ways that improve relationships between people.

It can be argued that, historically, Canada has benefited considerably from the ethical and moral contributions of religion. Whatever their shortcomings, religious groups have called on people to exhibit characteristics that foster civility — honesty, compassion, generosity, and forgiveness, to name a few. If we are a nation that has known a measure of success in realizing our desire to be gentle and caring, religion deserves some of the credit for getting us there. Gentleness and caring did not come out of a social vacuum.

Religion's contribution to civility continues to be needed. For

TABLE 7.14 **Interpersonal Attitudes and Values by Region**

	NAT	BC	PR	ON	PQ	AT
Attitudes: % Agreeing						
These days a person doesn't really know who can be counted on.	59	62	66	60	53	56
A stranger who shows a person attention is probably up to something.	20	20	16	17	28	13
People who are poor have a right to an income adequate to live on.	88	87	89	86	88	97
I want Quebec to remain in Canada.	84	86	88	89	67	94
We need to worry about our own country and let the rest of the world take care of itself.	37	40	35	35	40	39
There will likely be another world war within the next 25 years.	34	47	37	31	28	38
Values: % Indicating "Very Important"						
Politeness	76	78	77	74	74	85
Concern for others	71	67	72	76	61	83
Kindness	81	80	84	83	72	91
Forgiveness	70	66	75	73	61	85
Generosity	47	40	48	48	43	61
Involvement in your community	16	15	17	16	11	24

Source: Bibby, Project Canada 2000.

some time now, I have been among those who have maintained that many observers superficially dismissed the drop in national service attendance in the post–1960s as simply "the problems of organized religion."[19] What was not sufficiently examined by academics and media alike were some of the possible implications for civility in Canada.

Over the years, the dominant Christian tradition and other traditions stressed the importance of interpersonal traits that make for enhanced social life. Children who attended Sunday schools, for example, were exposed to the importance of basic characteristics such as honesty and concern for others — so much so that peers who chided such kids for being part of church activities added the derogatory term "goody-goody" to the cultural vocabulary. As critics are quick to point out, the values didn't always translate into corresponding behaviour. Ideals weren't always realized, and people who failed to match values with performance were readily dubbed "hypocrites." Yet, even if behaviour often left something to be desired, large numbers of young people and older people were at least being exposed to interpersonal ideals. Seemingly, such a situation was preferable to people not being exposed to the ideals at all.

As service attendance dropped in the last half of the 20th century, fewer and fewer Canadians of all ages were being exposed to interpersonal values by religious groups.

- In the mid-1970s, 32% of Canadians with school-age children said that they themselves were attending services on a weekly basis, with 38% enrolling their offspring in Sunday schools and similar programs in religious groups on a regular basis.
- As of 2000, the good news may be that fewer parents are "dropping off the kids." The bad news is that only about 20% of parents and their school-age children are showing up on close to a weekly basis.

Those developments are not in themselves socially fatal, providing that alternative sources of such values are being found. If people can learn social civility through the schools or the media or the family, for example, little is lost. What is disturbing, however, is this: there is good reason to believe that we may not have been doing a particularly good job of finding equally effective alternatives. Some say that schools should pick up the interpersonal value slack. But the fact of the matter is that our Canadian schools operate in a milieu that is highly conscious of cultural diversity, where people are extremely suspicious of anyone who wants to postulate values. "Whose values?" is the predictable objection to "values education."

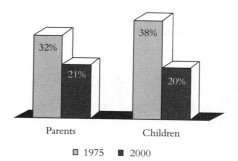

Weekly Attendance: School-Age Children and Their Parents

32% | 21% | 38% | 20%

Parents　　Children

■ 1975　■ 2000

Sources: Bibby, Project Can 75 and Project Canada 2000.

The media, North America—wide, are also positioned to play a powerful role in imparting values to Canadians. In their diverse print, sight, and sound forms, the media are today's primary mindmakers. But it can be argued that media profit margins seem to depend as much on the depiction of incivility as the promotion of civility. If anything, critics of the media are concerned about the media's contribution to violence, anxiety, distrust, and individualism, rather than their conscious attempt to enhance social life. It's difficult to make a convincing case that the media will be leading the way in enriching the interpersonal life of Canadians.

As for parents filling the void left by the disappearance of the churches, the problem here is that moms and dads don't live on a cultural island. There is no guarantee that, just because they are parents, they are personally committed to interpersonal values and to instilling them in their children — any more than members of the media, for example, can be expected to somehow hold and disseminate such ideals. And, as we all know, parents who do instill values of civility are far from the only strong influence on their children's lives.

The latest *Project Canada* findings suggest something of the costs that we may be paying as a result of our inability to find adequate replacements for organized religion when it comes to instilling values.

TABLE 7.15 **Values: Weeklys and Nevers**

% Indicating "Very Important"

	ADULTS		TEENS	
	WEEKLYS	**NEVERS**	**WEEKLYS**	**NEVERS**
Valued Goals				
Family life	91	80	74	49
Friendship	85	74	85	84
Being loved	83	79	85	70
Concern for others	77	64	71	59
A comfortable life	49	70	66	75
Valued Means				
Honesty	96	89	78	70
Politeness	78	75	65	55
Forgiveness	82	63	72	50
Generosity	66	37	51	36
Community involvement	28	10	★	★

★Item not included in Project Teen Canada 2000 survey.

Sources: Bibby, Project Canada 2000 and Project Teen Canada 2000.

- Canadian adults and teenagers who attend services weekly tend to be more likely than their counterparts who never attend services to place a high value on family life, being loved, and concern for others.
- Weekly attendance is also positively associated with interpersonal values such as honesty, politeness, forgiveness, and generosity. Obviously, many adults and young people who are not involved in religious groups likewise place high value on such characteristics. The point, however, is that proportionately they finish behind churchgoers.

As I have pointed out in *Canada's Teens*, today's emerging young people are somewhat more inclined than adults to have a personal, relativistic view of morality — consistent with the predictions of postmodern thinkers.[20] Asked pointedly, *"On what do you base your views of what is right and wrong?"* greater percentages of teenagers than adults cited personal factors over external sources, including religion. Their Boomer parents and Gen Xers base their moral views almost equally on external and personal sources, with fewer drawing on religion than do grandparents. Only a minority of teens claim to have moral criteria that resonate, for example, with those of a retired 58-year-old Presbyterian in Thunder Bay who says he relies on "Biblical teachings tempered by common sense" or the 56-year-old Pentecostal from rural Nova Scotia, who informs us that she bases her views of right and wrong on "community and biblical standards."

There is little difference, however, in the inclination of generations to assert that everything is relative. This suggests that relativism has become extremely pervasive in our culture, to the point where the phrase has become something of a truism. No less than 65% of teens agree with the statement "*What's right or wrong is a matter of personal opinion.*" Yet, at the same time that large numbers of young people and adults endorse relativism, more than half say values in Canada have been changing for the worse.

What seems to be happening here is that young people in particular are increasingly interpreting values and morality in a very individualistic rather than a communal manner. Their values tend to be derived from what they've experienced personally, rather than from broader systems such as religion, which define what is ethical or moral in terms of the collective good.

It might be argued that since values are increasingly the product of

TABLE 7.16 **Moral Attitudes across Generations**

	ADULTS	TEENS	GRAND-PARENTS	PARENTS	YOUNG ADULTS
Basis of my moral views:					
Personal factors, including values	35%	49%	35%	35%	39%
External factors	42	28	34	44	43
Religion specifically	17	16	26	16	12
Other	6	7	5	5	6
"I believe . . ."					
Everything's relative.	70	65	65	72	72
In general, values in Canada have been changing for the worse.	56	53	58	56	57

Source: Derived from Bibby, Canada's Teens, *2001b: 249.*

personal experience and personal gratification, young people may be more inclined to expand their circle of compassion as they become older. Maybe so, but then again, maybe not. The surveys have found that as adults get older, many confess it doesn't always work that way. With the passage of time, those who say they have become less honest actually outnumber those who say they have become more honest.

Journalist Jenefer Curtis has recently written, "Our wired globalized world needs ethics. Combine globalization, pluralism, a decline in institutionalized religion and intensive individualism and you come up empty in terms of fundamental values, values needed to provide spiritual sustenance and to inform public policy."[21] At this point in time, it is not clear where such values and ensuing ethics will come from. One can place little hope for a more civil and kind world in individuals who base their behaviour primarily on what they happen to feel or want.

In short, growing percentages of Canadian parents have not been active in religious groups, nor have they been encouraging their children to participate. Such patterns may involve a noteworthy social price. These days there is widespread concern about such issues as teenage crime, violence in schools, violence against women and children, and social fragmentation. Each of these issues obviously contains strong interpersonal elements. Motivating people to be kinder and more considerate in their dealings with others was a role that was centrally important to the churches.

The decline in participation in organized religion is nothing less than a serious problem for life in Canada if equally effective new players that foster civility have failed to appear. To date, their arrival is in question. One is hard-pressed to locate religion's successor. It is consequently not surprising that 50% of Canadians agree that "*the decline in the level of participation in organized religion has had a significant impact on the quality of life in Canada.*"

- They include 43% of people who attend services on a yearly basis and 30% of those who never do.
- Even 15% of the Nones agree with the statement.

TABLE 7.17 **Organized Religion and Quality of Life**

"The decline in participation in organized religion has had a significant negative impact on the quality of life in Canada."

% Agreeing

NATIONALLY	50%
Weekly	81
Monthly	62
Yearly	43
Never	30
Conservative Protestants	78
RCs outside Quebec	60
Mainline Protestants	56
RCs in Quebec	49
Other Faiths	40
No Religion	15
55+	62
35–54	51
18–34	37
Men	52
Women	48
Atlantic provinces	67
Prairies	59
Ontario	49
Quebec	44
British Columbia	42

Source: Bibby, Project Canada 2000.

Our findings suggest that a large number of Canadians continue to look to religious groups to play a major role in instilling values that make for good interpersonal life. They are expecting organized religion to have something decisive to say about how people should relate to each other, be the nature of those relations immediate or community, national or global. Of course, there are some people who want religious groups to stick strictly to the spiritual realm. But the survey results show such individuals are in a minority.

Getting Down to Specifics

We saw in Chapter 2 that 55% of adults who are currently attending services less than monthly say they would "consider the possibility of being more involved in a religious group if [they] found it to be worthwhile for themselves or their families." Clearly they have to be shown: the fine-print of the finding reveals that 15% offer an unequivocal "Yes" to the receptivity query, while 40% say, "Perhaps." However, the good news for religious groups is that only 45% of Canadians who attend services less than once a month say they are *not open* to the possibility of greater involvement.

The *Project Canada 2000* survey followed up the question of receptivity by asking the obvious, important question: *"What kind of things would make it worthwhile?"* Responses were open-ended. About two in three people who had indicated receptivity offered their thoughts.

Close to 40% cited *ministry factors*, particularly relating to themselves personally, such as the meeting of personal needs, personal fulfillment and growth, and affinity with others; some want activities and programs and ministries aimed at specific age and family cohorts.

A 23-year-old from a small town in Ontario with a United Church background said she would consider participating in a religious group "if it would bring serenity to my family." A 61-year-old business manager in Vancouver — a current Religious None with Anglican and Baptist roots — indicated that he might be open to involvement if he could see "a focus on family and spiritual values — with no hypocrisy."

These ministry factors are similar to what the late esteemed Queen's historian George Rawlyk found using national poll data gathered in the mid-90s. A few months before his death, Rawlyk commented,

> A large number of Canadians would return to the church if they were given specific guidance on how to live their lives — two or three specific things they could remember from a church service concerning how they should live their lives. A large percentage [also] would return if they felt that their spiritual needs would be met in the church. When you get down to it, they're looking for guidance and there is this aching for spirituality.[22]

Some 30% of our survey respondents who reported that they would be open to greater involvement drew attention to *organizational factors*. They would like to see changes in style and outlook, including, in some cases, better ministers, priests, and other leaders. As one woman in her 70s exclaimed to me at a United Church Presbytery gathering in northern Ontario a few years back: "You know the main reason why people don't want to come to church? We don't have any good preachers anymore!" A 31-year-old Anglican from Calgary says he would perhaps consider being more involved "if the

TABLE 7.18 **What Would Make Greater Involvement Worthwhile**
Factors Cited by People Attending Less than Monthly Who
Say They Would Consider Being More Involved (N=257)

Ministry Factors	37%
Self	21
Society	5
God	4
Activities and Programs	4
Specific Ministries	3
Organizational Factors	30
Changes in Style and Outlook	23
More open to diversity	5
More contemporary	5
More positive	5
Less formal	2
Less conforming	2
Other	4
Better Leadership	3
Other	4
Respondent Factors	30
Getting older, having children, etc.	7
Involvement of family and friends	6
Schedule changes	5
Relational problems	3
Other	9
Other Factors	3

Source: Bibby, Project Canada 2000

church were less condemning." In Dieppe, New Brunswick, a 44-year-old Catholic who infrequently attends mass maintains that he would be open to greater involvement but the demands are high: "Allow priests to marry," he says, adding that this is essential in order for priests to be available for Catholic ministry. A recent university graduate from Ontario, 24, who comes from a home with no religious affiliation, says she would perhaps consider involvement if there was "no hypocritical treatment of people and more liberal views of women, minorities, sex, birth control, abortion, etc."

Some of these organizational and ministry factors are similar to those identified about a decade ago by the respected veteran pollster George Gallup. Drawing on his extensive surveys of Americans, Gallup offered the observation that the vitality of religious groups will greatly depend on how effectively they respond to six basic needs of people. He listed them as (1) the need to believe life has a purpose; (2) the need to have a sense of community and deeper relationships; (3) the need to be appreciated and respected; (4) the need to be listened to — to be heard; (5) the need to feel one is maturing spiritually; and (6) the need to receive practical help in closing the gap between belief and practice. Gallup cautioned that religious groups are not necessarily meeting these needs very well. Organizational issues are a common problem: "70% of Americans interviewed believe that most churches and synagogues today are not effective in helping people find meaning in life . . . The fact is, significant numbers of people find churches irrelevant, unfulfilling, and boring."[23]

Another 30% noted the importance of factors pertaining to *themselves* rather than religious groups as such — including having children, the participation of family and friends, and changes in their work schedules. A single 34-year-old who lives in a small town in Ontario informs us that she might consider becoming involved when she marries and has children: "If I had children I might consider Sunday School so they would learn and understand something of their Anglican heritage." Similarly, an Alberta woman who currently attends United Church services about once a year says things could change down the road: "If I had children, I would be more involved in a religious group. I believe it provides a good moral upbringing." She herself attended services "nearly every week" when she was growing up. A mother of three in a small town in New Brunswick who also identifies herself as United Church is waiting for her remaining preschooler to age a little: "When the youngest child is old enough for Sunday School, then the whole family can go rather than just some."

An examination of these three categories of "worthwhile factors" by religious families reveals some important variations. Ministry factors seem to be slightly more important for those of *No Religion* than for others, organizational factors are more salient for *Roman Catholics* — particularly those outside Quebec — and respondent issues are somewhat more important for *Mainline Protestants* than for other people who are receptive to greater involvement.

These are potentially significant variations with major policy implications. For example, Nones may need to be convinced that their needs can be met; Catholics that the Church is capable of change, openness, and flexibility; and Mainline Protestants that particular emphasis to their children, partners, and friendship networks will be given. These factors need to be looked at in more detail in future research with larger samples that will also permit an examination of variations among Conservative Protestants and Other Faith groups.

TABLE 7.19 **Factors That Would Make Involvement Worthwhile by Religious Families**

	N	MINISTRY FACTORS	ORGANIZATIONAL FACTORS	RESPONDENT FACTORS	OTHER FACTORS	TOTALS
NATIONALLY	255	37%	30%	30%	3%	100%
RCs outside Quebec	47	36	41	19	4	100
RCs in Quebec	40	38	30	25	7	100
Mainline Protestants	84	36	22	42	0	100
No Religion	45	44	22	31	3	100

Source: Bibby, Project Canada 2000.

What Would Make It Worthwhile to Be More Involved in a Religious Group

Ministry Factors

". . . support and comfort . . . a strong moral environment . . . firmer direction . . . providing peace of mind . . . helping me find a job for my spouse . . . singing . . . addressing social, emotional, and health concerns . . . support during tragic times . . . if it added to the well-being of my children and family . . . providing a sense of fulfillment . . . greater friendship and togetherness . . . if I felt that I could grow as a spiritual person . . . having activities for the family together . . . being more attuned to everyday community well-being . . . if it would make people happy . . . child-centered activities . . . improved closeness with my spirit, a true alignment with my spirit . . . if it were fun and fulfilling . . . a focus on saving our children and teens . . . relating to my life more closely . . . a blend of spiritual and social involvement of people my age . . . a more down-to-earth approach to everyday problems . . . if religion dealt more with the reality of problems we experience and how to cope . . . the religious education of my children . . . more life in the services . . . theology from the pulpit as developed as mine or that provided some thoughtful challenges . . . benefiting my family and community, such as instilling respect and providing help . . . help in dealing with trauma . . . social contacts . . . having help looking after elderly parents . . . spiritual deepening . . . if it were more relevant to today's families . . . providing a sense of belonging . . . community-oriented and child-friendly atmosphere . . ."

Organizational Factors

". . . enjoyable services . . . more open to modern culture and issues facing people today . . . less abstract . . . treating all people as equal . . . allowing priests to marry . . . interactive programs . . . encouraging more family involvement . . . absence of conflict over sexual lifestyles and more joyful spontaneous worship . . . more on day-to-day issues and less about heaven and hell . . . a sense of community and less emphasis on status . . . dropping the formality and ceremony, and bringing it down to the human level . . . recognizing that women are significant . . . less involvement in controversial social issues . . . making it interesting, trying new things instead of the same old preaching . . . a strong focus on spirituality, greater acceptance of and harmony with other religious groups, less politics and power struggles . . ."

Respondent Factors

". . . being married and raising a family . . . having more time . . . if my kids lived with me . . . my family becoming more involved with church activities . . . if I had children I might consider Sunday School so they would learn and understand something of their heritage . . . will likely be more involved as my kids become involved . . . a change in my shift work . . . couldn't tell you — just seems that at some point it will be the right thing for my family . . ."

Source: Bibby, Project Canada 2000.

Possible Convergence: A Match Made in Heaven?

The findings point to a situation where the majority of Canadians say religious groups have a role to play in Canadian life — with that role involving the addressing of spiritual, personal, and relational needs.

Spiritual interest across the country is widespread, in large part, it would seem, because the gods have been stirring among Canadians, leading them to ask questions about life and death and God. Many have privately concluded not only that there is a God but also that they have experienced God. Moreover, most people converse on more than infrequent occasions with a God they think cares about them.

Personal needs are also readily acknowledged; the desire for good relationships are paramount, along with the desire for good interpersonal life, beginning at home and spreading outward.

These three themes — God, self, and society — are precisely the three emphases that have been central to religion throughout history. Religion has much to say to people who are trying to come to grips with spiritual restlessness, who are looking for personal hope, resources, and the possibility of new beginnings. Religious groups also have much to say about how interpersonal relations at all levels of social life can be enriched. As we have just seen, significant numbers of Canadians who are receptive to greater involvement say that these are precisely the kinds of things they would like to find in the churches. It sounds like a match made in heaven!

A decade ago I wrote in *Unknown Gods* that churches are going broke at a time when the population is going hungry. The situation appeared absurd to me at the time. Maybe I continue to miss something, but the new data only confirm that things are not the way they should be. All is well on the demand side. It's the supply side that poses the problem. The belief systems and programs offered by churches and other religious groups are simply not connecting with the people who need them or think they might need them at some point in the future.

There is consequently a great need for Canadians and religious groups to discover each other, for a connection to take place. The paradox is that at a time when numbers and morale are sagging in many congregations, current cultural conditions point to the intriguing possibility that the country's churches could grow by responding to the population with integrity. The steps that groups must take are by now obvious: they must find their affiliates, explore their interests and needs, and minister to them as possible.[24] No need for visions, no need for revelations, no need to be paralysed by the excuse that groups don't know how to proceed. In the no-nonsense words of old: "Let anyone with ears to hear listen!"[25]

The opportunity is there, the needs are there, and the strategies that are required are clear. What is needed now is a response. Restless churches and restless Canadians badly need to find each other.

Conclusion

To return to where we began, there are signs of significant spiritual restlessness in Canada. After a few decades of slumber, there appears to be a stirring among the country's established churches — those same groups that Canadians have been so reluctant to abandon. There is also a stirring among large numbers of people outside the churches, who are pursuing answers about life and death and spiritual needs with more openness than at perhaps any time in our nation's history. Much more private and much less publicized is the fact that three in four people are talking to God at least occasionally. Even more startling, two in four Canadians think they have actually experienced God's presence. And then there are those "haunting hints" of a Presence — the cry for wrongs to be made right, the sense that things are ultimately under control, life-giving hope and humour, the need for spiritual fulfillment.

All of this takes us back to the intriguing question raised at the beginning of the book: How much of this restlessness is strictly human and how much of it reflects the activity of the gods? Is it simply a matter of cultural and social and personal factors leading churches to experience a measure of rejuvenation, or are individuals being more compelled to reach out for something beyond themselves? For example, could it be, as some observers have maintained, that some unique features of postmodernism are altering institutions, organizations, and individuals?[1] Or could it be that we will not be able to understand our times adequately without pondering the possibility that more is happening — that "the Spirit of God is moving upon the face of the waters" and that maybe St. Augustine was right when he maintained "our souls are restless" this side of God?

As I have mentioned earlier, science, unfortunately, is a limited instrument for studying the totality of reality, relying as it does on our five senses. When it comes to religion and supernatural claims, science can look at response, but it is limited to social and personal explanations when trying to account for stimulus. In methodological terms, such a delimitation amounts to premature closure — the failure to consider the full range of possible pertinent factors that are contributing to what is happening. The old analogy still applies: limiting religion's potential fullness to science's eyes is like searching for a lost key only under a light because the lighting is better there, or like searching for handwritten material on a computer because it's easier than going through an endless number of file cabinet drawers.

The insistence on limiting one's view of reality to that which can be known through the senses may be key to understanding why some highly influential people made some serious mistakes when they speculated about religion's future.

Why the Wise Men Were Wrong

Hindsight, of course, allows any of us to appear a lot brighter than we are. Living now versus then makes it relatively easy to pronounce judgement on those who have gone before us — luminaries who looked into the future based on what was happening then, and took some big chances.

Still, courtesy notwithstanding, it's time we said it: when it came to predicting the future of religion generally and Christianity specifically, Karl Marx, Emile Durkheim, and Sigmund Freud were wrong.

- Societies and individuals have not ceased to have a need for religion with the dissipation of social inequalities and personal forms of deprivation, as Marx envisioned.
- The problems of the Christian Church in late-19th-century

Europe did not result in the demise of Catholicism, which Durkheim assumed was imminent.
- The accomplishments of science have not resulted in people being less inclined to look to the heavens to deal with the harsh realities of life and fate, as Freud predicted would happen.

Organized religion — and, in the Western world, Christianity specifically — has continued to have a significant following. The vast majority of people in countries like Canada and the United States, as well as those in Britain and continental Europe, continue to embrace supernatural ideas. Rodney Stark and William Bainbridge have summed things up this way:

> At least since the Enlightenment, most Western intellectuals have anticipated the death of religion as eagerly as ancient Israel awaited the messiah . . . The most illustrious figures in sociology, anthropology, and psychology have unanimously expressed confidence that their children, or surely their grandchildren, would live to see the dawn of a new day in which, to paraphrase Freud, the infantile illusions of religion would be outgrown. But as one generation has followed another, religion has persisted."[2]

The Need for the Supernatural

Freud was particularly vocal about the fact that religion had no future in the face of the ongoing advance of science. In his book *The Future of an Illusion*, he maintained that religion was needed at a point in historical development when civilization knew no better. But with the passage of time, such childish things needed to be put away and replaced with reality, as revealed by science. It was not that religion lacked for some appealing things — such as the assertion of life after death. The problem was that such ideas reflected what humans hoped for versus what is real. For Freud, there was no such thing as a supernatural realm, and he claimed it would only be a matter of time before such a fact was accepted.[3]

Marx, of course, saw the supernatural realm as an illusory dimension, invented by humans, that provided hope for the hopeless. He argued that, rather than encouraging people to alter their oppressive social conditions, religion provided them with an alternate reality that made them accept their subordinate position. It functioned like a drug, as an opiate, blinding them to the conditions at hand and bottling up their creative energies. Marx consequently saw his critique of religion as an attempt to remedy the condition that required the drug. Using another lesser-known metaphor, he wrote that religion functioned liked flowers covering a chain. His critique of religion was an attempt, he said, to remove the flowers from the chain, so the chain itself could be removed, allowing people to experience true, rather than illusory, happiness.[4]

Durkheim personally believed there was no such thing as a supernatural realm. His classic work, *The Elementary Forms of Religious Life*, gave much attention to how such ideas, complete with the belief in religious experience, are created by groups — in their own images, as a reflection of their own collective thoughts and emotions.[5]

Unlike Freud and Marx, however, Durkheim anticipated that supernatural beliefs would persist indefinitely. Science, he maintained, provides a better means of understanding than religion — and progressively replaces it. However, scientific thought "is fragmentary and incomplete; it advances but slowly and is never finished; but life cannot wait." We are impatient and "rush ahead to complete it prematurely."[6] As a result, religious explanations may be forced to retreat in the face of the steady advance of science. But religion never surrenders. In Durkheim's thinking, people would use the gods indefinitely to fill the holes in their understanding.[7]

However, contrary to Durkheim's claims, religion persists not only because scientific explanations aren't available just yet. Beliefs in the supernatural have not disappeared because some questions cannot be resolved by using scientific methodology — dependent as it is on empiricism, or sense-based reality. What lies beyond death is such an issue, as are other questions regarding God, including the activity of God in life. As we have seen, these are questions to which people are seeking answers. As long as there is death, people are going to be asking, "Is there life after death?" And science will have little if anything to say. Science will also be unable to offer the final word when people try to make sense of their feelings of having experienced

God. Put succinctly, we sometimes look to nonscientific explanations because the question being asked cannot be addressed by science. It is sometimes not impatience but necessity that leads people to supplement science with other kinds of explanations.

Berger is among many observers who have maintained that science and other secular theodicies — explanations for suffering and dying — "fail in interpreting and thus in making bearable the extremes of human suffering. They fail notably," he says, "in interpreting death . . . Most people, it seems, want a greater comfort, and so far it has been religious theodicies that have provided it."[8] In an interview with Bob Harvey of the *Ottawa Citizen*, Britain's Karen Armstrong, author of the best-selling book, *The History of God*, offered the observation, "We don't necessarily need a God or a supernatural personality, a sort of cosmic big brother. But we are creatures that need meaning in our lives, and if we can't build a faith into our lives we seem to fall into despair."[9]

As I have reminded readers in both *Fragmented Gods* and *Unknown Gods*, the inclination to look beyond science for answers is hardly new. Since the birth of science, people have readily supplemented scientific explanations with supernatural, or "non-naturalistic," ones. In fact, it might be more historically accurate to say that they supplemented supernatural explanations with scientific ones.

Freud was wrong because he failed to understand that science cannot move fast enough to fill holes in knowledge. Durkheim was wrong in assuming that, theoretically, science would be able to fill the holes. Marx was mistaken in asserting that the resolution of inequality and deprivation would result in people's no longer needing religion. The limitations of science, as well as the limitations of material well-being, mean that religion has a significant place in people's lives.

Organizational Resilience

Marx and Freud assumed that, as the need for religious and supernatural ideas dissipated, so would religious organizations. In contrast, Durkheim's thinking about religion centred on his belief in the indispensability of the group. He saw the group as the source of religious ideas, and he maintained that religion carries out an array of important collective and individual functions. Consequently, despite the problems of Christian organizations in the Western world, notably the Roman Catholic Church, Durkheim believed that religion would survive. In his much-quoted, poetic words, "The old gods are growing old or are already dead, and others are not yet born . . . There are no gospels which are immortal, but neither is there any reason for believing that humanity is incapable of inventing new ones."[10]

Where Durkheim erred, like so many others during his time and since his time, was in underestimating the staying power of the existing Christian Church, including its potential to reinvent itself. As I emphasized in Chapter 3, organizational structures that have come into being to express and support religious traditions — and have lasted for years and even centuries — do not readily disappear. They have the benefit of not being dependent merely on financial resources and consumer whims for sustenance. There are at least significant pockets of people who are intensely committed to those organizations and to their renewal. It is not wise to minimize either their chances for survival or their potential for significant resurgence. As Anglican Primate Michael Peers put it so well a few years back in paraphrasing a former Archbishop of Canterbury, we are "in for the long haul."[11]

Somehow, despite the fact that the Catholic Church, for example, had survived for some 18 centuries, the wise men of old bet against it. They lost.

Science or Nothing

All three of these influential thinkers also made the fatal error of overclaiming. It is one thing to acknowledge — as I have been doing throughout this book — that science relies on sense-based information. That's just to accept that science's method is empirical. It is quite another thing to take a positivistic position, maintaining that if something cannot be known empirically it does not exist.

Reflecting in large part the intellectual climate of their times, Freud, Marx, and Durkheim were all positivists. As a result, in examining religion, past, present, and future, they *assumed* that the explanations for religious belief and behaviour were found in naturalistic or observable factors. In making such an assumption, they overstepped the boundaries of science. In the process, they eliminated the possibility that religion might be strongly influenced by that nonobservable "other reality" of which people such as Arnold Toynbee speak.

The influence that Freud, Marx, and Durkheim have had in leading millions of people to reducing reality to what can be known through the senses has not been a positive legacy. In Berger's words, "The denial of metaphysics may well be identified with the triumph of triviality," a "shrinkage in the scope of human experience" that constitutes a profound impoverishment. "Both in practice and in theoretical thought," says Berger, "human life gains the greatest part of its richness from . . . stepping outside the taken-for-granted reality of everyday life" and having "an openness to the mystery that surrounds us on all sides."[12] The late Robertson Davies was less charitable toward those who close their eyes to the gods. About a year before his death in 1995, he told Doug Todd: "They're like people who've cut off both hands. They've lost touch with the whole universe." Davies was equally impatient with agnostics, maintaining they don't want to be bothered with fully exploring the spiritual possibilities they have rejected, "yet they try to make an intellectual position out of it."[13] Obviously, I side with Berger and Davies in rejecting positivism. To limit reality to what can be known empirically is in itself a faith claim that is both intellectually arrogant and practically precarious.

Groups That Will Survive and Thrive

It seems to me that the answer to the question of which religious bodies will survive in the 21st century and beyond is fairly simple. The surviving groups will be those that have been around a long time and continue to have a solid base of support, if not in Canada then elsewhere. Don't underestimate, for example, the Catholic Church in Quebec. The global resources of this powerful multinational corporation ensure its survival pretty much forever. Also don't worry about the Anglicans, Presbyterians, or Lutherans, given their multinational nature. Even the frequently maligned United Church of Canada has those four thousand franchises, a core of staunch supporters, an enviable pool of affiliates, a rich tradition, and young and upcoming leaders who are determined to see congregations flourish. Denominations that are smaller will have tougher times, but only a handful will actually disappear altogether.

The groups that thrive will be groups that are in touch with the spiritual, personal, and social needs and interests of Canadians. We've seen what people say they want; I would venture to say congregations that currently are flourishing are doing a reasonably good job of ministering to all three areas. If some seem a bit insular — a charge frequently directed at some evangelicals, ethnic churches, and groups likes Mormons — the problem often doesn't lie with their failing to address these three areas. It lies rather with their need to expand their ministries so that they touch the lives of other people in their communities and cities who are crying out for "God, self, and society" to be addressed.

But here, I think, it is very important to differentiate between two kinds of "surviving and thriving churches." The first variety will be largely in-turned, functioning to meet the needs of their own members and their children — the initiated, plus offspring. Their focus will be on ministry to the gathered community. Such churches, of course, are already very common and are found in every religious tradition. They are characterized by a homogeneity that can be seen in characteristics such as theology, lifestyle, ethnicity, and social class. They ebb and flow pretty much in accordance with similar-minded people making residential moves or switching congregations. If their pools of children dry up, these kinds of congregations simply pick up and move to another neighbourhood, where new pools of the initiated and their offspring allow them to begin a new life cycle. Sociologically speaking, they look for all intents and purposes like homogeneous "religious clubs."

Congregations that essentially minister to their own have undoubtedly constituted the majority of churches in North America for quite some time. In some instances, the in-turned focus has been the result of unconscious design. In many instances, it has been the unconscious result of necessity: most churches are very small, with the result that sheer survival and the providing of a minimal number of activities is an accomplishment in itself. As you can see, I think the focus is not typically intentional.

The second variety of "surviving and thriving" churches will be those with both a front door and a back door to ministry — where the focus is on ministering to the gathered community and having that community minister to others. These are the kinds of churches that Don Posterski and Gary Nelson have dubbed "Future Faith churches," characterized by "their pursuit of ministry that champions both a love of God and compassion for people," fusing "soul care and social care."[14] In practice, these congregations can be expected to be few because of both inclination and resources. But they will be there, just as some are there today, experiencing organizational viability because there is a clear need for them. Significant numbers of Canadians who are not among the religiously initiated are and will be receptive to the kinds of creative ministries that such churches can provide. To the extent that some groups can address the pivotal spiritual, personal, and relational needs of people, they will do more than survive. Individuals who make up these kinds of churches will not be content to sit in the safety of their sanctuaries and wait for people to come to them.

Canadian legendary rock star Bruce Cockburn told Doug Todd how he drifted away from his United Church background but began attending St. George's Anglican Church in Ottawa during his teens. The church consisted of a hodgepodge of refugee Catholics, West Indians, and prisoners on parole. "The spirit was alive and very viable in that place," he says, "not every time you went, but enough times to remind you what it was. And I've never found another church like that, although I can't say I've honestly made an exhaustive search." Cockburn then offered a poignant line that should send a message to every church serious about ministering to Canadians who are outside their walls: "I feel if a church wasn't really being offered to me, it probably wasn't necessary. And I feel that way about a lot of stuff."[15]

The New Groups about to Be Born

In light of the Christian monopoly that exists in Canada, partly because people are so reticent about turning to alternatives, it will be extremely difficult for new religious movements to make significant headway. New expressions will continue to get a lot of ink. Things novel and deviant always do. But the media attention will not translate into lasting numerical headway. The monopoly is just too complete, with little sign of an imminent change.

Established world religions such as Hinduism, Judaism, Buddhism, and Islam can be expected to know a measure of numerical success while engaging in their ongoing battles with assimilation and acculturation — defections to Christian groups and secularization, respectively. The "but" here is that they will know success precisely because they are established global religions that carry considerable credibility. They are not "new religions."

Will there be any successful "new" religious groups? The data suggest there will be a place in the "Canadian religious market" for new congregations and even denominations that can connect with the religious identification heritages of people and respond to their spiritual, personal, and relational interests and needs.

Since this will involve —at least initially — new groups having to "market" themselves to people beyond their established "clientele," the most effective of these new entries will, of necessity, sometimes be ones that are "larger in order to be better." In major cities and on the edges of smaller communities, we can expect to see the continuing emergence of large, "big box" mega-churches. They will typically start off as independent operations, but they will be linked to the religious memories of affiliates. They will have "Mainline," "Conservative," or "Catholic" flavours in order to resonate with Canadians. Over time, as new "outlets" are established, they may evolve into denominations. But current developments suggest that many of these "independents" may be more comfortable forming alliances with congregations of similar sizes. In some instances, we can expect such congregations to form fairly loose, cooperative associations with other churches, sharing ideas and resources more generally. Nonetheless, history suggests that some will either evolve into denominations, or in time join existing denominations with which they feel affinity.

While new religions can be expected to make limited headway in Canada, that is not to say that new expressions of Christianity will not shake up the religious establishment and in the process contribute to revitalization. In a provocative article in the February 2002 issue of *The Atlantic Monthly*, Toby Lester, a senior editor, has underlined the possibility that the new century may see vital Christian expressions in Africa, Asia, and Latin America having an impact on Christianity in North America, in the form of immigrant churches and missionaries — and, I would add, expertise. "The present rate of growth of the new Christian movements and their geographical range," writes Lester, "suggest that they will become a major social and political force in the coming century."[16]

Historically, the dominant Catholic and Protestant expressions of religion in Canada have been strengthened and culturally diversified through extensive immigration. There is every reason to believe that such a reality will continue to have a significant impact on Christianity in this country, contributing in no small way to religion's renaissance.[17]

What about the People?

Apart from what all this means to the churches, the obvious — and for many people the more important — question is what will happen to the people? What about the spiritual and other needs of that large majority of Canadians who are not currently active in religious groups?

Here the crystal ball gets blurry. On the safe side, one can predict that the needs of growing numbers of Canadians will be met, to the extent that religious groups experience re-emergence. Our findings show noteworthy numbers of people are receptive to greater involvement if groups can be responsive to their varied interests and needs.

But, as I have been saying to leaders for years now, I'm not sure that all of this is necessarily going to have a happy ending. Some groups may be slow to experience rejuvenation, and rejuvenation of the magnitude required, in time for the many people across the country who need ministry to benefit. And even where there is intense commitment to trying to minister to Canadians, the research points to some very serious hurdles facing religious groups.

- One can talk about the opportunity for churches to address *spiritual interests and needs*. But as we have seen, in many instances about all that Canadians and religious groups have in common when they use the term "spirituality" is the word. People in the very religious family that often claims to place the most explicit emphasis on spirituality — Conservative

Protestants — tend to have views of spirituality that vary the most from people who are not active in religious groups. To the extent that such evangelicals are viewed as "born-again Christians," they also have a problem: 26% of Canadians who are not Conservative Protestants say that if they knew nothing about a person except that he or she was "a born-again Christian," they would feel uneasy around them; among people who have unconventional views of spirituality, the figure is 31%. That's a lot of uneasiness that has to be overcome. What's more, forget for the moment about "outsiders": even people who are active in churches as a whole acknowledge that they are not typically sharing their spirituality with people in their own congregations. Given all this, what are the realistic prospects for churches being able to respond to the spiritual quests of people across the country?

- There's no question that individuals have *personal needs*, many of which are not being met. Yet the research shows that in a very large number of instances, churches have not even been aware of the needs of even their most active members. At least two major issues are involved here: can groups do a better job of understanding what is happening in the lives of their members and, to the extent that they become more aware of such needs, are they in a position to respond?

- And then there's the area of *relational needs*. The same problem of awareness arises here, as does the question of how prepared churches are to deal with the wide array of relational issues that people are confronting. How do groups respond to the problems of loneliness and conflict, divorce and cohabitation, the varied relational wants and needs and problems of children, teenagers, singles, parents, and seniors? Beyond platitudes and ideals, what do the churches *really* have to offer?

For years I have found that the media, in particular, work from the assumption that if religious groups fail to address the needs of Canadians, the only question is who will step in and fill the void. In a similar vein, academics speak of "functional alternatives." The

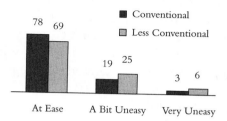

Uneasiness Around Born-Again Christians by Type of Spiritual Need

Conventional
Less Conventional

At Ease	A Bit Uneasy	Very Uneasy
78 69	19 25	3 6

Source: Bibby, Project Canada 2000.

problem with such an assumption is that there is no guarantee the needs people face in these three areas will readily be met by alternatives. United Church theologian Doug Hall recently told Bob Harvey that no adequate substitute for Christianity has been emerging to provide Canadian society with new philosophical underpinnings. Using the example of marriage in Quebec, Hall commented that there is a need to ensure that the growing number of civil marriages become more than just perfunctory events: "Marriage needs some kind of ritual," he says, "the sense of entering something larger than just a covenant between two individuals if it's to get through all the slush that goes into the lives of two people trying to live together."[18] However, it's not at all clear where the ritual will come from if not from religious groups — and from the established ones at that.

We have seen that Canadians are remarkably reluctant to give an audience to religious expressions that are very far removed from the ones they knew growing up. As a result, even the most well meaning and proficient religious alternatives face the problem of literally getting in people's front doors.

- The Mormons, for example, are widely known for the excellent ministry they provide to families; that still doesn't get them beyond the steps of most Anglicans or Baptists or Hindus whose family lives are in disarray.

- The Pentecostals are known for their emphasis on spirituality; a Roman Catholic or Jew with spiritual needs who receives a home-delivered brochure is nonetheless not likely to give the neighbourhood Pentecostal church a try next Sunday.
- The United Church has known success in the areas of counselling and social ministry; that doesn't typically translate into decisions by Roman Catholics or Baptists with personal problems to try out the nearest United congregation.

No, the data we have been gathering now for years suggest a very sobering possibility: if Canadians do not have their needs met by the groups with which they identify, there is a very real chance that they won't have them met at all.

Such a possible void is particularly true in the case of spirituality. Wade Clark Roof sees Americans as being in an "open, questing mood" as they draw on "an expanded spiritual marketplace," maintaining that, in the process, "the boundaries of popular religious communities are being redrawn."[19] Maybe, but if that's the case, they are comparatively cautious. At a time in history when they are raising questions of meaning and death, experiencing and communicating with the gods, and reporting signals of transcendence, Canadians remain extremely wary of new religions and new quasi-religions. They do want answers. As Tom Harpur has put it, people are ultimately spiritual animals and they "will not take stones for bread forever."[20] Still, they want answers from credible sources. Consequently, if the established groups fail, large numbers of people may well go hungry.

Speaking of Harpur, I remember Tom's comment after he read *Anglitrends,* the 1986 summary report I'd prepared for the Toronto Anglican Diocese. He told me I'd gone too easy on the Anglicans. With this warning in mind, let me be emphatic about one thing: *though I have been maintaining that established religious groups have the potential to experience revitalization, this does not for one second mean that revitalization is inevitable.* Rejuvenation from within will be the result of people working very hard and very creatively to turn organizations such as the Anglican, United, Lutheran, and Presbyterian churches around. Likewise, nothing much is going to happen to reverse the fortunes of Roman Catholicism in Quebec without a major infusion of human and financial resources — including possible cooperative ventures with other religious families and parachurch organizations. As far as I know, the gods don't do it on their own.

Any church leader who is foolish enough to mumble about "things going in stages," thinking that revitalization is an inevitable stage in some kind of cyclical process, will find his or her congregation or denomination permanently floundering. All I have been saying is that established groups have a very significant potential competitive advantage over religious newcomers and smaller bodies. They obviously have to do the legwork to capitalize on that advantage . . . Strong enough, Tom?

September 11, 2001: Some Lessons Learned

Only an obscurantist could write a book on religious developments in Canada and not at least reflect on the possible impact on religion of what happened in the United States on September 11, 2001. The devastating event is a dramatic reminder that life is dynamic and fragile and at times startling and shocking. It also serves to remind us that in attempting to understand the role religion plays in the lives of individuals and societies, it's not wise to turn off the camera.

There may be a season for everything. But having understood that in theory, each of us finds it quite another thing to actually experience the fullness of those seasons first hand. As a number of individuals have verbalized throughout this book, when the fragility of one's own life is exposed, it is not uncommon for people — quite unexpectedly — to reach out, almost instinctively, for Something beyond themselves. As millions of people in Canada and around the world watched the events of September 11, 2001, unfold, many found it difficult to experience the massive destruction and deaths even second hand. A lot of reaching out appears to have taken place.

Two months later, in late November 2001, a national poll was conducted for *Maclean's* magazine. The poll revealed some important findings:

- Some 72% of Canadians had become more appreciative of their families, but only 26% said they had less interest in material wealth and possessions. A mere 6% felt less driven to succeed at work.

- On the whole, life had not been seriously disrupted: people who were accustomed to flying were still travelling by air, and only small numbers said they were having more trouble sleeping or were seeking medical or counselling help.

Allan Gregg, the veteran Toronto researcher and social analyst who oversaw the poll, commented, "The approach here is surprisingly rational. It's not hysterical, it's not truculent."[21]

As for the impact of September 11th on spirituality and religion, as mentioned in Chapter 4, there is little doubt that the events caused significant numbers of people in the United States, Canada, and elsewhere to reflect on suffering and death, as well as to give thought to how they themselves were living out life. TSN commentator Rod Smith succinctly expressed things in closing out a sportscast that evening: it was "a day on which sports didn't really matter very much." The same, of course, seemed to be true of just about everything else.

But while the *Maclean's* survey found that, two months later, 72% of Canadians had become more appreciative of their families, just 23% felt a greater need for religious beliefs and only 16% said they felt a greater need to go to a place of worship.[22] The report did not indicate how devout the 23% and 16% were before the attacks; nor did it check to see if the "need to's" had translated into actual change. The proverbial bottom line is that relatively few Canadians appear to have altered their religious beliefs and churchgoing habits much in the aftermath of the disasters in New York and Washington. Writing in mid-December, Ron Graham, for example, noted that "life across North America has begun to feel normal again," and expressed concern that the spiritual lesson not be lost — that death is real, near, and painful, and therefore time and life are to be embraced and cherished.[23]

Esteemed American religious observer Martin Marty of the University of Chicago was among those who saw the potential for limited impact coming, even in the United States. Shortly after September 11th, Marty noted that many Americans appeared to be turning to

"Do You Think the Events of September 11th Have Had an Impact on Religion in Canada?"

Reflections on Life and Mortality . . . but Short-lived

"I believe many turned to prayer after Sept. 11 to seek answers, reassurance, etc. As time passes, I believe things will return to the way they were."
— *An MP from western Canada with no strong religious ties; he is in his early 50s.*

"Our naked vulnerability to such attacks prompted many to reassess their personal exposure to instant terror and death."
— *A 52-year-old commodities manager from Fredericton; he is active in his Baptist church.*

"I think that September 11th had an initial impact on people's religious consciousness, but the memory of North Americans tends to be short-term."
— *A Jewish professor originally from Toronto; she teaches in western Canada.*

"Attendance is up. People appear to be reaching beyond private beliefs and practices for answers that include God."
— *A 49-year-old Mainline Protestant minister who serves a congregation in Newfoundland.*

"There appears to be a coming together of people from varied traditions. We have also shown we have structures that can be mobilized in a time of need."
— *A Roman Catholic sessional lecturer in northwestern Ontario; she is 51.*

"Yes, and I believe it is a positive impact. I hear the word 'spirituality' more in everyday conversation. Whether the renewed awareness of our vulnerability translates into greater levels of attendance is yet to be seen."
— *A prominent Alberta Cabinet minister; he has a United Church background.*

"The dramatic rise in church attendance in the three Sundays after September 11th was unsustainable."
— *A Montreal religious leader in his late 40s who also teaches at McGill.*

"I don't believe we learned anything we didn't already know about human nature. In that sense it was just a blip rather than the setting of a new direction."
— *A Unitarian minister with a congregation on the west coast.*

"We had an amplified sense of uncertainty of life. But we will move on and in many respects already have."
— *A 37-year-old Presbyterian university administrator from Manitoba.*

Greater Awareness of Islam

"Christians need an increased understanding of the diversity of Islam. Sunni, Shiite, Sufi, folk, and militant Islam are all parts of the mosaic of Islam."
— *A 62-year-old professor at an evangelical college in Ontario.*

"Osama bin Laden is exulting because people are suddenly looking for books on Islam. But most are just wondering how he can justify what took place."
— *A Presbyterian minister, 30, with a congregation in the rural Maritimes.*

"Spiritual sensitivity skyrocketed but I doubt it will translate into higher levels of commitment in the long term. The biggest impact is likely to be an increase in knowledge about Islam and awareness of Muslims in Canada."
— *A prominent 46-year-old Christian journalist; he lives in Winnipeg.*

Source: Project Canada Quota Sample, Winter, 2001–02.

churches for comfort and answers. "This will not, however, last indefinitely," he said. Marty felt the possibility of a more lasting impact rested in the ability of churches to respond effectively to what had happened. The opportunity included a chance to minister well to younger people who were among those seeking answers — providing "evidence that the young share the terrors, experience the grief, and need to find resolution and hope as much as their elders." They, Marty pointed out, "have to live longest with terrorism. They have the most to hope for in healing."[24]

In Canada, a professor from the University of Toronto, who describes himself as "Jewish by ethnicity but a secularist in practice," summed up the sentiments of many of the people my research team and I spoke with:

> Yes, I believe the events of September 11th did have an impact on religion in Canada. It seems to me that whenever people confront death, the great majority of them are driven in a more religious direction. Religion helps most people cope with the terrifying fact that we must die, and it offers comfort to them when they are faced with the death of others to whom they are emotionally attached. I do not, however, believe that the events of September 11th will have a profound and lasting impact on most people. In the majority of cases, most of its impact will, I think, be ephemeral, lasting weeks or perhaps a few months.[25]

Similarly, a leading Roman Catholic educator told me in January of 2002 that she did not think the events of September 11th *per se* had had a pronounced effect on religion in this country. But she, like Martin Marty, noted that "the magnitude of participation of people in religious services connected to the occasion illustrates again that our society — though not regularly participating in organized religion — still seeks it out to help them make sense and mark times where they need to remember and reconnect." She also drew attention to a second feature of reaching out: "Such times seem to be occasions for ecumenical liaison and solidarity." While she expressed doubts about how long the two inclinations would last, she pointed out that "religious bodies need to be very attentive to such times of openness to the key questions about life, human nature, religion, and God, which events like September 11th awaken in us."[26]

A third Canadian I spoke with in early 2002 also emphasized the intergroup consequences of what had happened in New York and Washington. Aziz Khaki, a prominent Muslim leader in Vancouver, who is also President of the Pacific Interfaith Citizenship Association, told me that the attacks brought with them both negative and positive consequences for Muslims, including himself personally. The negative took the form of some people being quick to associate terrorism with Islam as a whole, a link that Khaki found deplorable. "As far as I am concerned, the things they did — taking innocent lives and committing suicide — were unbelievable and unacceptable, absolutely in violation of the essentials of Islam. The terrorists were not true Muslims. We condemn what they did in no uncertain terms." The positive, he says, is that "from the beginning, I was contacted by people from a variety of groups, including those who were Roman Catholic, United, and Anglican, who said they wanted to meet with me, that they stood in solidarity. They recognized how unfair it was for people to stereotype and generalize." Says Khaki, "I am very grateful for that." What also surfaced, he reported, was the desire to learn more about Islam. "We have tried to convey the essentials of what Islam stands for — peace, harmony, love, justice, and forgiveness. September 11th has had the effect, not so much of making Muslims more devout, as strengthening our resolve to relate to other people."[27]

Don Posterski, the Vice-President of National Programs for World Vision Canada, offered a fourth Canadian voice. He maintained that "a sense of spiritual disruption increased church attendance for a few weeks in Canada, but only for a few weeks. Compared to our American neighbours, the impact on religion in Canada," he said, "has been minimal. Americans were violated and the pain of war came home for Americans, whereas Canadians were empathetic spectators." Posterski cautioned against unreflective retribution: "The Canadian spirit still desires peace in America and elsewhere. The hope for long-term positive impact will only result if Canadian Christians distance themselves from the unreflective and unchristian nationalism that justifies the unjustified destruction of a distant part of God's creation."[28]

The Impact of September 11th on Religion in Canada: Some Further Thoughts

Increased Reflection on Life and Family

"It has caused people in general to value life and people more."
— *A 43-year-old Pentecostal who lives in Toronto; he is self-employed.*

"The September events have had a big impact on our sense of security in Quebec with New York next door to us. People were prompted to ask the big questions about life and family. All in all, it was a pretty secular reaction."
— *An RC professor in her early 40s who teaches at Laval University in Quebec City.*

"The biggest impact of September 11 will be on Islam itself. A whole new era of self-evaluation and reflection will be a great opportunity for Christians humbly to hold out the Word of Life to disaffected and searching Muslims."
— *A Toronto manager, 61, who is active in an interdenominational Christian church.*

Whose Side Is God On?

"I think many Canadians find the 'God Bless America' jingoism coming up from the United States rather revolting. Canadians learned not to equate God and Country through bitter experience in the First World War, and have been very reluctant to do so ever since."
— *A 54-year-old professor in Saskatchewan who is active in his Anglican parish.*

"Changes in attitudes in the post-9/11 world have made it even more difficult to be a non-believer in what is supposed to be a free society. We are pressured to 'declare' ourselves either on God's side (the West) or Satan's (the enemy). I hear echoes of Joe McCarthy and his Communist witch hunt."
— *A prominent western Canadian newspaper columnist who describes herself as a "lapsed Roman Catholic."*

A Higher Profile for Religion, Positive and Otherwise

"Because of these events it is socially acceptable to speak of God openly in public."
— *A registrar at a private Christian college in Ontario; he is 30.*

"The events have raised the profile of religion. Muslims have realized the need to educate the public on Islam. Christian and Jewish communities have responded positively and inter-faith activities are at an all-time high."
— *A University of Victoria professor with United Church ties.*

"In America, citizens flocked to worship places. In Canada, the events have confirmed our suspicion of people who REALLY believe what they believe."
— *A 29-year-old evangelical "church planter" in rural Ontario.*

"There's a lot more talk about God today, especially in the media — a place where God was formerly quite absent."
— *A Mennonite from Winnipeg who works in international development; he is 44.*

"The gulf has been widened between sceptics and believers. Sceptics will trash all religion as the cause of world turmoil."
— *A 43-year-old church leader who lives in Hamilton.*

Source: Project Canada Quota Sample, Winter, 2001–02.

What the *Maclean's* data, Martin Marty, and these four Canadian voices all attest to is that the events of September 11th did not in and of themselves have an impact on spirituality and religion. Rather, developments as dramatic as these resulted in people reaching out to family, the Heavens, the churches, and each other in response to what they were experiencing. To the extent that people young and older reached out to religious groups, those congregations had a fleeting window of opportunity to demonstrate their worth. As seen in the outlook of these three religious leaders, Canadians who were reaching out to the churches and wandered through a doorway to worship and reflect may have found these respective emphases on meaning, solidarity, and justice. Maybe it would have been enough.

September 11th serves as a reminder that life-jarring events that shake up nations and individuals, leading them to reach out to others and the heavens, at best provide religious groups with an opportunity to respond. In the jargon of the philosopher, such events are necessary but not sufficient causes of involvement and commitment. Religious groups still have to be there, and they have to have something to say. Otherwise, such moments of tragedy are both opportunities lost and responsibilities lost. Churches that are looking to historical and personal events to put people in their pews are missing the point. Even an event as dramatic as September 11, 2001, will at best give churches a chance to show what they are about. The event only produces the need; the churches have to be able to deliver.

In the United States, church attendance during the two weeks following the terrorist attacks rose nationally from 42% to 47%. By early November, attendance had fallen back to its usual 42% level. Commenting on these findings, George Barna said that many Americans who turned to the churches were seeking something that would restore stability and meaning. He added the poignant observation that, unfortunately, few of them experienced anything significant enough to keep them there.[29]

In the face of such widespread expressions of human inadequacy and the need of so many to find Something More, these are not times for churches to fail. The national president of the Catholic Women's League, Vivian Bosch, conveyed things this way to me: "The irony of this event seems to be that, while the thread woven by

God is increasingly being pulled away from the fabric of our society, there is a deep inner cry from many people simply saying, 'Show us God!'"[30]

. . .

There you have it. To look at Canada in the first decade of the new millennium is to see a country characterized by religious restlessness. It's a restlessness magnified considerably by the worldwide attention given religion by the sight of a Pope and millions of young people from around the world descending on Toronto for an 11-day "World Youth Day." As our theistic colour commentator leaves our telecast booth, he shakes his head. "The gods seem to be everywhere," he says, "in the churches, outside the churches, confronting people directly, giving them an array of hints, forcing them to reflect on life and death and purpose in the course of their experiencing the good and the bad of everyday living. What more could they do?" The commentator might be right.

The churches are restless. Canadians are restless. It may well be because, "in the beginning" of this new century, the "Spirit of God which moved upon the face of the waters" back then is moving across the country. What remains to be seen is what will be created . . . this time around.

Methodology: The Project Canada National Surveys

T*he Project Canada Research Program* has been carried out from the University of Lethbridge under the direction of Reginald W. Bibby. National surveys of adults 18 and over have been conducted in 1975, 1980, 1985, 1990, 1995, and 2000, along with complementary surveys of youth in 1984, 1992, and 2000.

THE ADULT SURVEYS

Data Collection. All six of the adult surveys have made use of self-administered questionnaires and have been conducted by mail over approximately a four-month period. Questionnaires have ranged from 11 to 20 pages in length, and have included 300 to 400 variables. The goal has been to generate extensive information on life in Canada, with specific attention given to social issues, intergroup relations, and religion. With minor variations, the procedures have involved (1) mailing the questionnaire with a front-page cover letter, (2) sending a follow-up postcard, and (3) mailing a second questionnaire. Surveys typically have been carried out over a four-month period.

Sampling. A representative sample of about 1,000 cases is sufficient to claim a confidence level of 95% and a confidence interval of four percentage points when generalizing to the Canadian adult population. *Size and representativeness* are the two key criteria in being able to generalize with accuracy from a sample to a population. Considerable care has therefore been taken to ensure that both standards have been met.

Concerning size, an interest in provincial comparisons resulted in 1,917 cases being gathered in 1975, 1,482 in 1980, 1,630 in 1985, 1,472 in 1990, 1,765 in 1995, and 1,729 in 2000. With respect to representativeness, the nation has been stratified by province and community size (>100,000, 99,000–10,000, <10,000), with the samples drawn proportionate to the populations involved. As resources have improved, the number of communities chosen has increased from 30 in 1975 to 43 in 1980, 104 in 1985, 145 in 1990, 228 in 1995, and 304 in 2000. Participants have been randomly selected using telephone directories. Discrepancies between the sample and population characteristics have been corrected by weighting for provincial and community size, along with gender and age. Each of the six samples has been weighted down to about 1,200 cases in order to minimize the use of large weight factors (i.e., three or more).

All the samples are highly representative of the Canadian population. Samples of this size and composition, as noted, should be accurate within about four percentage points on most questionnaire items, 19 times in 20 similar surveys. Comparisons with similar Gallup poll items, for example, have consistently found this to be the case.

The Panels. A major interest of the ongoing national surveys has been to monitor social change and stability. Each survey sample since 1980 has consisted of (a) a core of people who participated in the previous survey and (b) new participants, who are used to create a full national sample of about 1,500 cases. For example, while the first 1975 survey was a typical cross-sectional survey with 1,917 participants, the *Project Can80* sample of 1,482 people included 1,056 who had also been involved in 1975. Each successive sample through 2000 consists of people from each of the previous surveys, along with new additions, filled out to a representative national sample. Various panels can be constructed from the surveys according to the five-year interval desired (e.g., 1975–85, 1980–90, 1975–2000). In 2000, new search possibilities made available through the Internet allowed us to pursue participants who had been lost over the years, strengthening the sample sizes of panels through 2000.

While no claim is being made that these panels are representative of all Canadians, they do provide intriguing and novel data on the attitudes, outlooks, and behaviour of a core of Canadians for a variety of time-spans within the last quarter of the 20th century.

Return Rates. For national surveys, the *Project Canada* return rates have been relatively high — 52% in 1975, 65% in 1980, and about 60% in 1985, 1990, 1995, and 2000. We tend to hear from some 65% of the people who have participated previously and just over 50% of those being contacted for the first time — comparing favourably to the seldom-reported cooperation rates of (at best) around 65% obtained with face-to-face and telephone interviews.

Funding. The 1975 survey was carried out for a cost of about $14,000 and had four major sources: the United Church of Canada ($2,000), the CBC ($3,000), the Solicitor General of Canada ($5,000), and the University of Lethbridge ($4,000). In 1980, the panel portion of the survey was made possible by grants from the Social Sciences and Humanities Research Council of Canada ($10,000) and the United Church of Canada ($2,000). The second phase of *Project Can80*, which involved filling the core out into a full national sample, cost approximately $8,000 and was funded primarily by the University of Lethbridge. *Project Can85* was funded completely by the Social Sciences and Humanities Research Council of Canada ($45,000).

Project Canada 2000 Sample Sizes

RELIGIOUS FAMILY		SURVEY YEAR		REGION	
RCOQ	252	2000	1,240	B.C.	165
RCQ	223	1995	1,239	Prairies	210
MLPROT	354	1990	1,251	Ontario	469
CPROT	73	1985	1,231	Quebec	296
Other Faiths	43	1980	1,300	Atlantic	88
None	172	1975	1,200		
SERVICE ATTENDANCE		AGE		GENDER	
Weekly	257	18–34	361	Female	627
Monthly	99	35–54	505	Male	601
Yearly	579	55+	341		
Never	265				

Project Can90, Project Can95, and *Project Canada 2000* were all funded by the Lilly Endowment (about $65,000 each).

Sample Numbers. In the interest of trying to simplify the reading of tables, I have not typically included sample sizes, except when size was potentially an issue, in which case attention was drawn to the numbers involved. For the information of readers, *Project Canada 2000* sample sizes are provided for some of the key variables used in the book.

THE YOUTH SURVEYS

National "Project Teen Canada" youth surveys of 15-to-19-year-olds have also been conducted as part of *The Project Canada Research Program.* These surveys have generated extensive data on Canadian youth and have served to complement the national adult surveys. Three surveys have been completed, in 1984, 1992, and 2000, and have carried the titles of *Project Teen Canada 84, Project Teen Canada 92,* and *Project Teen Canada 2000.*

The Questionnaires. Each of the questionnaires has been about 15 pages in length and has included some 250 variables; they appear to have taken about 30 to 45 minutes to complete. Since a major objective of the youth surveys was to produce data making intergenerational comparisons possible, the youth surveys have contained many of the same items that appeared in the *Project Canada* adult questionnaires. The topics addressed have been fairly comprehensive and, like the adult surveys, the questionnaires have included themes such as sources of enjoyment, leisure activities, values, beliefs, personal concerns, family life, relationships, views of Canada, views of Canadians, perception of major issues, and hopes and expectations.

Sampling and Data Collection. Each of the three youth samples consists of approximately 3,600 teenagers, a figure which, if representatively selected, makes it possible to generalize to the overall adolescent population with a high level of accuracy. A sample of that size also increases the accuracy of analyses within categories such as region, community size, gender, and race. The students have been drawn from high schools across Canada and CEGEPs in Quebec using multistage stratified and cluster sampling procedures. Guidance counsellors or an appropriate substitute at each school have administered the questionnaires.

The Response and Representativeness. The return rates for the three surveys have been 76%, 85%, and 80%, respectively; the total number of useable questionnaires totalled 3,530 in 1984, 3,891 in 1992, and 3,501 in 2000.

The samples have been variously weighted for region and community size, gender, and school type. In their final, weighted form, the samples are highly representative of Canadian high school students, 15 to 19, permitting generalizations to the population with a very high level of accuracy. On most items in the questionnaires, the national results should come within about three percentage points of the results of other surveys probing the teenage population, 19 times in 20.

Complete methodological details for the youth surveys are found in Reginald W. Bibby, *Canada's Teens* (Toronto: Stoddart, 2001: 327–32). In addition, codebooks summarizing the findings of each of the six adult and three teen surveys and providing the details of each questionnaire, complete with variable names facilitating SPSS analyses, are available through the author.

THE PROJECT CANADA QUOTA SAMPLE

In an effort to obtain qualitative clarification on a number of topics, a quota sample of 200 people across Canada was pursued between mid-October 2001 and mid-January 2002. Individuals known to the author and his research team were initially contacted and invited to respond to one question out of a number given to them. They were also invited to distribute the questions to others — in effect engaging in what is known as geometric or "snowball" sampling. Seven questions were circulated:

1. "Do you think the events of September 11th have had an impact on religion in Canada?"
2. "What do you think is the purpose of life?"
3. "Why is there suffering in the world?"
4. "Do you ever pray privately? If so, why?"
5. "Do you believe in God? If so, what do you have in mind when you speak of God?"

6. "Do you think you have ever experienced the presence of God? If so, can you tell us about it, for example, where/what it was like?"

7. "What do you think will happen to you when you die?"

People were asked to keep their responses to a maximum of three sentences; they also were asked to provide some basic biographical data regarding their gender, age, location, occupation, and religion.

An effort was made to hear from a broad cross-section of people, including opinion leaders in the media, universities, religious groups, and government. The primary means of communication was e-mail. The response was enthusiastic; people seemed anxious to talk about these matters. As a result, the quota goal of 200 respondents was fairly easily attained. This is strictly a quota sample, not a random sample, aimed at providing illustrative observations about some deeply personal and seldom articulated issues from a variety of Canadians. The range of the people who participated can be seen in the biographical notes associated with their comments. Readers are encouraged to address the seven questions themselves, as a way of carrying out a personal check on the representativeness of our participants.

Notes

Preface

1 Acts 17: 24, 25, 27. New Revised Standard Version.

Introduction

1 Cox, 1995: xv–xvi.

2 Berger, 1999: 2.

3 Ibid.: 7–9.

4 Ibid.: 9–11.

5 Rawlyk, 1996: 224.

6 Spong, 1998: 147.

7 Egerton, 1995: 24–25.

8 Berger, 1969: x–xi.

9 Toynbee's preface to Cogley, 1968: v.

10 Genesis 1: 1–2. King James Version.

Chapter One *The Old Story about What's Happening in the Churches*

1 Peter Berger (1961) and Thomas Luckmann (1967), for example, were among those who argued that American religion was experiencing "secularization from within." Participation levels may have remained steady, but the nature of religious organizations and their influence pointed to their having become largely secular in nature.

2 Berger, 1968. Cited in Stark and Finke, 2000: 58.

3 See, for example, Durkheim, 1965 (originally published in 1895) and Wilson, 1966, 1982. An excellent summation of the three dominant facets of the secularization argument is provided by Dobbelaere, 1981.

4 Grant, 1988: 224.

5 Fraser, 2000.

6 Bibby, 2001b: 249.

7 See William Hordern, 1966.

8 Beyer, 1997: 276–77.

9 Grant, 1988: 160.

10 CBC, 1973.

11 Grant, 1988: 161.

12 Bibby, 1987: 12–14.

13 Bibby, 1987: 14–16.

14 Grant, 1988: 204.

15 Garnsworthy, 1984.

16 Bibby, 1987: 1–3.

17 Ibid.: 24–45.

18 Ibid.: 148.

19 Much of the following is described in greater detail in Bibby, 1987: 19–21.

20 Godbout, 2001.

21 Chrétien, 1985. Cited in Bibby, 1987: 143–44.

22 Rouleau, 1977: 9.

23 CBC, 1973.

24 Graham, 1990: 120.

25 Godbout, 2001.

26 Bibby, 1987: 21.

27 Graham, 1990: 136.

28 See, for example, Kelley, 1972.

29 See, for example, Bibby and Brinkerhoff, 1973 and 1983.

30 See, for example, Bill Calderwood, *United Church Observer*, September, 1986: 33.

31 See Bibby, 1993: 187–200.

32 Yearbooks of Canadian and American Churches.

33 Ibid.

34 See Bibby, 1997b and 2000.

35 For details, see Bibby, 1999a and 2000.

36 Bibby, 1993: 109–11.

37 Cited in Bibby, 2001b: 75.

38 For details, see Bibby, 1993: 27–46.

39 Bibby, 1995a: 77.

40 Bibby, 2001b: 196.

41 For details, see Bibby, 1993: 103–5 and 2000.

42 Bibby, 1993: 115.

43 Posterski and Bibby, 1988: 48.

44 Stark and Finke, 2000: 36.

45 Stark and Bainbridge, 1985; Finke and Stark, 1992; Stark and Finke, 2000.

46 Stark and Bainbridge, 1985: 7.

47 Ibid.: 2.

48 Ibid.: 529–30.

49 Finke and Stark, 1992: 238, 250.

50 Ibid.: 252–55.

Chapter Two *Some Very Good News via Some Very Bad Myths*

1 Bibby, 1997a.

2 Project Canada Quota Sample, Winter, 2001–02.

3 For documentation, see Bibby, 1993: 29ff.

4 For a discussion of this failure, see Beyer, 1997: 284ff.

5 Much of the following material dealing with Myths No. 1 and No. 2 is based on Bibby, 1999b.

6 See, for example, Schaller, 1987; Wuthnow, 1988; Mead, 1991; Posterski and Barker, 1993; Hoge, Johnson, and Luidens, 1994.

7 See, for example, Barna, 1991; Anderson, 1992; Easum, 1993; Schaller, 1995; Woods, 1996; Bandy, 1997.

8 Americans such as Robert Bellah (1985) and his associates have written that accelerated individualism has been severely threatening group life at all levels, while Allan Bloom (1985) similarly claimed that the individualistic and relativistic legacies of the 1960s have been devastating for relationships and disastrous for institutions. In Canada, Peter C. Newman (1994) maintains that nothing short of a revolution took place between the mid-1980s and 90s, characterized by Canadians moving from a mood of "deference to defiance" in virtually every area of life. I myself (1990) have similarly noted that individualism and relativism have functioned to severely fragment Canadian society, creating unity problems well beyond the threat of Quebec separation.

9 See, for example, Waxman, 2001: 116–1188.

10 Bibby, 1993: 32, 36–37. According to observers such as Demerath and Yang (1997:5), the situation is similar in the United States as well.

11 Graham, 1990: 123.

12 Hoge, Johnson, and Luidens, 1994: 120.

13 Hadaway and Marler, 1993: 97.

14 Roof and McKinney 1987: 167; Posterski and Barker 1993: 51.

15 Hadaway and Marler, 1993: 102.

16 "Carter Cuts Ties with Church over 'Rigidity,'" Associated Press, Atlanta, 20 October 2000.

17 Wills, 2000; "Book Accuses Catholic Church of Lying," Canadian Press, Toronto, 7 July 2000.

18 For details, see Bibby, 1993: 157–59.

19 Hadaway, 1990: 46.

20 The adult survey response options were "Yes," "Perhaps," and "No"; receptivity levels combine "Yes" and "Perhaps." In the youth survey, the options were "Strongly Agree," "Agree," "Disagree," and "Strongly Disagree," with receptivity levels being a combination of "Strongly Agree" and "Agree."

21 Project Canada 2000.

22 Bibby, 2001b: 118, 197.

Chapter Three *The New Story about What's Happening in the Churches*

1 Todd, 1996: 107–8.

2 Harpur, 1986: 3.

3 See, for example, the *Globe and Mail* stories of 5 June 2000 ("How Do the Churches Atone?") and of 17 June 2000 ("Ottawa Should Pay for School Abuse, Alliance Says.")

4 "Anglicans' Waterloo," *National Post* editorial, 11 July 2001.

5 See, for example, Magnus Linklater, "Vatican Goes Back to Basics," *London Times.* Reprinted in the *Montreal Gazette*, 8 September 2000. Also, "Rabbis Boycott Vatican Meeting" (Associated Press, Vatican City, 22 September 2000).

6 Mann, 1962.

7 Stark and Finke, 2000: 78.

8 See, for example, Stark and Bainbridge, 1985; Finke and Stark, 1992.

9 Stark and Bainbridge, 1985: 7.

10 Stark and Finke, 2000: 36.

11 See Finke and Stark, 1992: 255–74.

12 Finke and Stark, 1992: 17.

13 Ibid.: 1.

14 Bainbridge and Stark, 1982; article summarized in Stark and Bainbridge, 1985: 457–74.

15 Bibby and Weaver, 1985.

16 Nock, 1987.

17 Stark and Finke, 2000: 251.

18 Ibid.: 41.

19 Stark and Finke, 2000: 79. Berger also noted in 1999 that "secularization on the society level is not necessarily linked to secularization on the level of individual consciousness," that religious institutions can lose power and influence "but both old and new religious beliefs and practices can continue in the lives of individuals." He added, "Conversely, religiously identified institutions can play social or political roles even when very few people believe or practice the religion that the institutions represent." (1999: 3).

20 Bibby, 1987: 61.

21 Statistics Canada, 1993: 16–17.

22 Church Planting Canada brochure, 2001: 2.

23 See, for example, Bibby, 1993: 148–51, 157–59.

24 The following material is drawn from Bibby, 1987: 56–61 and 217–19.

25 Clemons, 1998:86.

26 Haroon Siddiqui, "Mixing Religion and Politics," *Toronto Star*, 13 July 2000.

27 Berton, 1982: 58.

28 Finke, 2001: 1.

29 Stark and Finke, 2000: 259–74.

30 McKinney and Finke, 2001.

31 Bibby, 1993: 282.

32 Wuthnow, 1988: 5.

33 I myself have used the metaphor extensively in *Fragmented Gods* (1987); Finke and Stark (1992: 253) are among those who speak of "free-loading customers."

34 Bruce, 2001.

35 Source: A & W website, a-wrootbeer.com, 1 October 2001.

36 McKinney and Finke, 2001: 18–19.

37 An interesting brief overview of Willow Creek's seeker-sensitive orientation is found in the Fall 1999 issue of WorldVision's *Envision* publication. A good summary of the Alpha program courses being introduced to Canadian churches is found in Meed Ward, 2001: 18–23; a case example of Alpha's

effectiveness is offered by Start, 2002. For an exposition of the Anglican Essentials movement, see, for example, Egerton, 1995. An example of Catholic charismatic activity is Father Peter B. Coughlin's work, including 2000.

38 For details, see Bibby, 1993: 40–46 and 1997.

39 Meed Ward, 2001: 22.

40 See, for example, Hall, 1989. See also Bob Harvey's interview with Hall in Harvey, 2001: 51–59.

41 For example, Bibby, 1993: 102.

42 See Bibby, 1997b and 2000.

43 The sample sizes for young people who identify with Other Faiths are relatively small and therefore need to be treated with caution. They certainly require verification through the use of larger samples.

44 Cited in Grant, 1988: 244–45.

Chapter Four *Ongoing Questions Only the Gods Can Answer*

1 In Fred Simpson, "Talking to God," *The Era-Banner*, Newmarket, 15 February 1998: 15.

2 Todd, 1996: 2.

3 Freud, 1957: 102.

4 Stark and Bainbridge, 1985: 528.

5 Thielecke, 1960: 3.

6 Frankl, 1984: 15.

7 Project Canada Quota Sample, Winter, 2001–02.

8 Project Canada 2000.

9 Project Canada Quota Sample, Winter, 2001–02.

10 Some 94% of those people who think they have found the answer to life's meaning agree that "Life has meaning beyond what we ourselves give to it"; among those who are uncertain, the figure is 91%.

11 Project Canada Quota Sample, Winter, 2001–02.

12 Todd, 1996: 53–54.

13 Cited by Allport in the preface to Frankl, 1984: 12.

14 Ecclesiastes 6: 12. This and subsequent references are taken from the New Revised Standard Version.

15 Ecclesiastes 2: 24–26.

16 Ecclesiastes 3: 1, 4.

17 Ecclesiastes 9: 11–12.

18 Stiller, 1999: 1.

19 *Maclean's* (2001–2002): 39.

20 Bibby, 2001b: 50.

21 Project Canada 2000.

22 Project Can95 comment; she also participated in Project Canada 2000.

23 Allport, in the preface to Frankl, 1984: 12.

24 Project Canada Quota Sample, Winter, 2001–02.

25 Ibid.

26 Project Can95.

27 Todd, 1996: 43.

28 Harvey, 2001: 113.

29 Project Canada Quota Sample, Winter, 2001–02.

30 Todd, 1996: 150–51; 190–91.

31 Stiller, 1999: 86.

32 Project Canada Quota Sample, Winter, 2001–02.

33 Cited in Todd, 1996: 41.

34 Project Canada 2000.

35 Trudeau, 1993: 30.

36 Clarkson and McCall, 1990: 34.

37 Bibby, 1993: 118.

38 Ecclesiastes 3: 2.

39 Project Canada Quota Sample, Winter, 2001–02.

40 Project Canada 2000.

41 Cited in Bibby, 1993: 123.

42 Clemons, 1998: 213–14.

43 Gallup polls, 12 May 1945 and #280, January 1960.

44 Project Canada Quota Sample, Winter, 2001–02.

45 Ibid.

46 Ibid.

47 Project Canada Quota Sample, Winter, 2001–02.

48 Ibid.

49 Ibid.

50 "Trudeau Was Ready for Death, Says Former PM's Ex-Wife," Canadian Press, Almonte, Ontario, 18 November 2000.

51 Project Can75.

52 Project Canada Quota Sample, Winter, 2001–02.

53 Project Canada 2000.

54 Project Canada Quota Sample, Winter, 2001–02.

55 Ibid.

56 Harpur, 1983: 240–41. See also Harpur, 1991.

57 Stiller, 2001: 141, 108, 152.

Chapter Five *Relentless Gods*

1 Hick, 1963: 90.

2 Project Can75.

3 Project Canada Quota Sample, Winter, 2001–02.

4 Ibid.

5 Ibid.

6 Project Canada Quota Sample, Winter, 2001–02.

7 Project Canada Quota Sample, Winter, 2001–02. Belief in the Divinity of Jesus has slipped slightly in recent years: 1985 = 79%, 1990 = 74%, 1995 = 72%, 2000 = 72%.

8 Project Canada Quota Sample, Winter, 2001–02.

9 Ibid.

10 Ibid.

11 Project Canada Quota Sample, Winter, 2001–02.

12 Ibid.

13 Ibid.

14 The correlation coefficient (r) here is .793.

15 Project Canada Quota Sample, Winter, 2001–02.

16 Ibid.

17 Canadian Institute of Public Opinion, Gallup Poll of Canada release, 9 April 1955.

18 Project Canada Quota Sample, Winter, 2001–02.

19 Ibid.

20 Ibid.

21 Todd, 1996: 114.

22 Project Canada Quota Sample, Winter, 2001–02.

23 Ibid.

24 Ibid.

25 Project Canada Quota Sample, Winter, 2001–02.

26 Durkheim, 1965.

27 Glock and Stark, 1965.

28 See, for example, Neitz and Spickard, 1990, Yamane and Polzer, 1994, and Yamane 1998.

29 See, for example, Poloma, 1989, 1995, and 1997.

30 See Bibby, 2001a.

31 See Glock and Stark, 1965 and Stark and Glock, 1968.

32 Stark and Glock 1968: 125.

33 Ibid.: 130–31.

34 Cox, 1995; Wuthnow, 1998; Roof, 1999.

35 The material in this section is based on Bibby, 2001b: 283–84.

36 Born between 1955 and 1964, Young Boomers ranged in age from 36 to 45 as of 2000.

37 Bibby, 2001b: 282.

38 Milton, 2000: 160.

39 Webster's, 1992: 299.

40 Harpur, 1998: 38.

41 Project Canada Quota Sample, Winter, 2001–02.

42 Ibid.

43 Ibid.

44 Project Canada Quota Sample, Winter, 2001–02.

45 Additional analyses not shown here reveal that the proportion of males who never pray is higher than females in all three age cohorts (18–34: 42% vs. 30%; 35–54: 29% vs. 21%; 55+: 26% vs. 11%).

Chapter Six *Rumours and Revelation*

1 Berger, 1969: ix–xi.

2 Ibid.: 120.

3 See, for example, Altizer, 1966.

4 Berger, 1969: 2.

5 Cox, 1965; Robinson, 1963.

6 Berger, 1969: 2.

7 Ibid.: 9–10.

8 Ibid.: 30.

9 Berger, 1969: 65–66.

10 Ibid.: 119.

11 Ibid.: 81.

12 Berger, 1969: 81.

13 Ibid.: 84.

14 Rabbi Marc Gellman, NBC, 12 September 2001.

15 Berger, 1969: 84.

16 Carried by most major networks, including CNN, 23 September 2001.

17 As reported by Mike Oliveira, "Churches Packed for Special Masses," Canadian Press, 16 September 2001.

18 Stiller, 1999: 20.

19 Frankl, 1984: 95.

20 I Corinthians 15: 55

21 Berger, 1969: 78.

22 Freud, 1962.

23 Cited in Todd, 1996: 32.

24 Berger, 1969: 80.

25 Ibid.: 67.

26 Berger, 1969: 71.

27 Berger, 1963: 164.

28 Cited in Todd, 1996: 29.

29 "Friends, Fans Mourn George Harrison," Associated Press, London, 30 November 2001.

30 Todd, 1996: 42–43.

31 Frankl, 1984: 64.

32 Berger, 1969: 72.

33 Ibid.: 32.

34 Ibid.: 67.

35 Bibby, 2001b: 120.

Chapter Seven *What People Want from the Churches*

1 Conversation in Calgary, 13 November 2001.

2 Obviously, some religions do not have a God-like reference, including Unitarianism, Buddhism, and Confucianism.

3 See, for example, Bibby, 1993: 57–159 and 2001: 274–76.

4 Bibby, 2001b: 121–22. Some of the material in this section originally appeared in Bibby, 1995c.

5 Redfield, 1994; Moore, 1992; Eadie, 1993.

6 Roof, 1993 and 1999; Wuthnow, 1992 and 1998.

7 Graham, 1990.

8 *Maclean's*, 10 October 1994.

9 Todd, 1996: 1.

10 Much of the material in this section is drawn from Bibby, 1996.

11 Project Canada 2000.

12 Ibid.

13 Nettler, 1976: 10.

14 Bibby, 2001b: 24, 235.

15 Peck, 1978: 15.

16 The data on teens that follows can be found in Bibby, 2001b, particularly 54ff.

17 Bibby, 2001b: 62.

18 Bibby, 2001c.

19 Bibby, 1994b.

20 This section draws heavily on Bibby, 2001b: 248–49 and 316–17.

21 Jenefer Curtis, "The Business of Ethics," *Globe and Mail*, 21 August 1999.

22 Interview in Gruending, 1996.

23 Gallup, 1992.

24 An explicit methodology for such a response to affiliates is found in my book *There's Got to Be More! Connecting Churches and Canadians* (Winfield, B.C: Wood Lake Books, 1995). The authors of a major new study of Catholicism in the United States have further suggested that religious lines of affinity should be supplemented with social lines of affinity. They write that "the best way to establish contact with Catholics who are low in commitment is though people who share their age, marital status, and race or ethnicity, but who remain committed to the Church," noting these variables represent "natural lines of social interaction." See D'Antonio, Davidson, Hoge, and Meyer, 2001: 148–49.

25 Mark 4: 23.

Conclusion

1 For a concise summary of the concepts of "postmodernity" and "postmodernism," see, for example, Bibby, 2001b: 161–67, or Swenson, 1999: 368–83. For examples of the application of postmodern thought to an understanding of contemporary religious developments, see Grenz, 1996, and Lyon, 2001.

2 Stark and Bainbridge, 1985: 1.

3 Freud, 1962.

4 See Marx, 1970; Marx and Engels, 1964.

5 Durkheim, 1965.

6 Ibid.: 431.

7 Ibid.: 477–79.

8 Berger, 1969: 32.

9 Harvey, 2001: 30. Originally appeared in the *Ottawa Citizen*, 18 December 1999.

10 Durkheim, 1965: 475–76.

11 Peers in Egerton, 1995: 8.

12 Berger, 1969: 94.

13 Todd, 1996: 133–34.

14 Posterski and Nelson, 1997: 226–27.

15 Todd, 1996: 96–97.

16 Lester, 2002: 45.

17 For an example of the potential for rejuvenation through the arrival of evangelical immigrants in Ottawa, see Harvey, 2002.

18 Harvey, 2001: 58–59. Originally appeared in the *Ottawa Citizen*, 27 December 1999.

19 Roof, 1999: 9–10.

20 Harpur, 1983: 246.

21 *Maclean's* (2001–2002): 34–39.

22 Ibid.: 39.

23 Graham, 2001: 15–16.

24 Woodruff, 2001; Marty, 2001.

25 Project Canada Quota Sample, Winter, 2001–02.

26 Ibid.

27 Ibid.

28 Project Canada Quota Sample, Winter, 2001–02.

29 *Christian Week*, 8 January 2002: 7.

30 Project Canada Quota Sample, Winter, 2002–02.

References

Altizer, Thomas.
  1966   *The Gospel of Christian Atheism*. Philadelphia: Westminster Press.

Anderson, Leith.
  1992   *A Church for the 21st Century*. Minneapolis: Bethany House.

Bainbridge, William Sims, and Rodney Stark.
  1982   "Church and Cult in Canada." *Canadian Journal of Sociology* 7: 351–66.

Bandy, Thomas G.
  1997   *Kicking Habits: Welcome Relief for Addicted Churches*. Nashville: Abingdon.

Barna, George.
  1991   *User Friendly Churches*. Ventura, CA: Regal Books.

Bellah, Robert, Richard Madsen, William Sullivan, Ann Swidler, and Steven Tipton.
  1985   *Habits of the Heart*. New York: Harper and Row.

Berger, Peter L.
  1961   *Noise of Solemn Assemblies*. Garden City, NY: Doubleday.
  1963   *Invitation to Sociology*. Garden City, NY: Doubleday.
  1967   *The Sacred Canopy*. Garden City, NY: Doubleday.
  1968   "A Bleak Outlook Is Seen for Religion." *New York Times*, 25 April, p. 3.
  1969   *A Rumor of Angels*. Garden City, NY: Doubleday.

Berger, Peter L. (ed.)
  1999   *The Desecularization of the World: Resurgent Religion and World Politics*.
       Washington: Ethics and Public Policy Center/Grand Rapids, MI:
       William B. Eerdmans.

Berton, Pierre.
    1982   *Why We Act Like Canadians*. Toronto: McClelland and Stewart.

Beyer, Peter
    1997   "Religious Vitality in Canada." *Journal for the Scientific Study of Religion* 36: 272–88.

Bibby, Reginald W.
    1986   *Anglitrends*. Toronto: Anglican Diocese of Toronto.
    1987   *Fragmented Gods: The Poverty and Potential of Religion in Canada.* Toronto: Stoddart.
    1990   *Mosaic Madness: Pluralism without a Cause.* Toronto: Stoddart.
    1993   *Unknown Gods: The Ongoing Story of Religion in Canada.* Toronto: Stoddart.
    1994a *Unitrends*. Toronto: Department of Stewardship, United Church of Canada.
    1994b "Who Will Teach Our Children Shared Values?" *Globe and Mail,* 3 February.
    1995a *There's Got to Be More!* Winfield, B.C.: Wood Lake Books.
    1995b *The Bibby Report: Social Trends Canadian Style.* Toronto: Stoddart.
    1995c "Beyond Headlines, Hype and Hope: Shedding Some Light on Spirituality." Presented at the annual meeting of The Society for the Scientific Study of Religion, St. Louis, MO, October.
    1995d *EvangelTrends*. Markham, ON: Evangelical Fellowship of Canada.
    1997a "Going, Going, Gone: The Impact of Geographical Mobility on Religious Involvement." *Review of Religious Research* 38: 289–307.
    1997b "The Persistence of Christian Religious Identification in Canada." *Canadian Social Trends* (Spring): 24–28.
    1999a "Multiculturalism in Canada: A Methodologically Inadequate Political Virtue." *DISKUS* 5: 44, 1–6. On-line journal. Special issue on Multiculturalism and the Recognition of Religion.
    1999b "On Boundaries, Gates, and Circulating Saints: A Longitudinal Look at Loyalty and Loss." *Review of Religious Research* 40: 149–64.
    2000   "Canada's Mythical Religious Mosaic: Some Census Findings." *Journal for the Scientific Study of Religion* 39: 235–39.
    2001a "Restless Gods: The Renaissance of Religious Experience in Canada." Presented at the annual meeting of the Pacific Sociological Association, San Francisco, April.
    2001b *Canada's Teens: Today, Yesterday, and Tomorrow.* Toronto: Stoddart.
    2001c "Canada's Teens: A National Reading on Family Life." *Transition* (Autumn): 3–7.

Bibby, Reginald W., and Merlin B. Brinkerhoff.

1973 "The Circulation of the Saints." *Journal for the Scientific Study of Religion* 12: 273–83.

1983 "Circulation of the Saints Revisited." *Journal for the Scientific Study of Religion* 22: 253–62.

1994 "Circulation of the Saints, 1966–1990: New Data, New Reflections." *Journal for the Scientific Study of Religion* 33: 273–80.

Bibby, Reginald W., and Donald C. Posterski.

1985 *The Emerging Generation: An Inside Look at Canada's Teenagers.* Toronto: Irwin.

1992 *Teen Trends: A Nation in Motion.* Toronto: Stoddart.

Bibby, Reginald W., and Harold R. Weaver.

1985 "Cult Consumption in Canada: A Further Critique of Stark and Bainbridge." *Sociological Analysis* 46: 445–60.

Bloom, Allan.

1987 *The Closing of the American Mind.* New York: Simon and Schuster.

Bruce, Steve.

2001 "A Review of Rodney Stark and Roger Finke, *Acts of Faith: Explaining the Human Side of Religion*." *First Things* (February): 35–37.

Calderwood, Bill.

1986 A Comment. *United Church Observer* (September, 1986): 33.

Canadian Broadcasting Corporation.

1973 "The Quieter Revolution." Television documentary. Toronto: CBC.

Chrétien, Jean.

1985 *Straight from the Heart.* Toronto: Key Porter Books.

Christiano, Kevin J.

1994 *Pierre Elliott Trudeau: Reason before Passion.* Toronto: ECW Press.

Clarkson, Stephen, and Christina McCall.

1990 *Trudeau and Our Times.* Volume 1. Toronto: McClelland and Stewart.

Clemons, Michael Pinball.

1998 *All Heart: My Story.* Toronto: HarperCollins.

Cogley, John.

1968 *Religion in a Secular Age.* New York: New American Library.

Coughlin, Peter B. (ed.).

2000 *He's Alive! Personal Stories of Faith, Conversion and Renewal.* Hamilton: C.C.S.O. Bread of Life Renewal Centre.

Cox, Harvey.

    1965   *The Secular City*. New York: Macmillan.

    1994   *Fire from Heaven: The Rise of Pentecostal Spirituality and the Reshaping of Religion in the Twenty-First Century*. Reading, MA: Perseus Books.

D'Antonio, William V., James D. Davidson, Dean R. Hoge, and Katherine Meyer.

    2001   *American Catholics: Gender, Generation, and Commitment*. Walnut Creek, CA: Alta Mira Press.

Demerath, N.J. III, and Yonghe Yang.

    1997   "A Religious Change and Changing Religions: Who's Switching Where and Why?" Paper presented at the annual meeting of the SSSR, San Diego, November.

Dobbelaere, Karel.

    1981   "Secularization: A Multi-Dimensional Concept." *Current Sociology* 29: 201–16.

Durkheim, Emile.

    1965   *The Elementary Forms of the Religious Life*. New York: The Free Press. Originally published in 1912.

Eadie, Betty.

    1993   *Embraced by the Light*. New York: Ballantine.

Easum, Bill.

    1993   *Dancing with Dinosaurs*. Nashville: Abingdon.

Egerton, George (ed.).

    1995   *Anglican Essentials: Reclaiming Faith within the Anglican Church of Canada*. Toronto: Anglican Book Centre.

Finke, Roger L.

    2001   "Innovative Returns to Tradition: Using Core Beliefs as the Foundation for Innovative Accommodation." Paper presented at the annual meeting of the Society for the Scientific Study of Religion, Columbus, Ohio, October, 2001.

Finke, Roger L., and Rodney Stark.

    1992   *The Churching of America, 1776–1990*. New Brunswick, NJ: Rutgers University Press.

Frankl, Victor E.

    1984   *Man's Search for Meaning*. New York: Washington Square Press. First published in 1946.

Freud, Sigmund.

    1957   *The Future of an Illusion*. Garden City, NY: Doubleday. First published in 1927.

Gallup, George, Jr.
  1992   "The Six Spiritual Needs of Americans." *Yearbook of American and Canadian Churches*: 12–13. New York: National Council of Churches.

Garnsworthy, Lewis S.
  1984   *The Archbishop's Charge to the 132nd Synod*. Toronto: Anglican Diocese.

Glock, Charles Y., and Rodney Stark.
  1965   *Religion and Society in Tension*. Chicago: Rand-McNally.

Godbout, Jacques.
  2001   "Quebec Culture: A Deep Skepticism of Tradition." *The New York Times*, 16 September. Web edition.

Graham, Ron.
  1990   "God's Dominion: A Sceptic's Quest." Toronto: McClelland and Stewart.
  2001   "Death's Gift to Life." *Maclean's*, 17 December: 15–16.

Grant, John Webster.
  1988   *The Church in the Canadian Era* (2nd edition). Burlington: Welch.

Greeley, Andrew, and Michael Hout.
  1986   "Musical Chairs: Patterns of Denominational Change." *Sociology and Social Research* 72: 75–86.

Grenz, Stanley J.
  1996   *A Primer to Postmodernism*. Grand Rapids, MI: William B. Eerdmans.

Gruending, Dennis.
  1996   *Revival: Canada's Christian Churches*. Video. Ottawa: Carleton University.

Hadaway, C. Kirk.
  1990   *What Can We Do about Church Dropouts?* Nashville: Abingdon.

Hadaway, C. Kirk, and Penny Long Marker.
  1993   "All in the Family: Religious Mobility in America." *Review of Religious Research* 35: 97–116.

Hall, Douglas John.
  1989   *The Future of the Church*. Toronto: United Church Publishing House.

Harpur, Tom.
  1983   *Harpur's Heaven and Hell*. Toronto: Oxford University Press.
  1986   *For Christ's Sake*. Toronto: Oxford University Press.
  1991   *Life after Death*. Toronto: McClelland and Stewart.
  1998   *Prayer: The Hidden Fire*. Kelowna: Northstone Publishing.

Harvey, Bob.
    2000   *The Future of Religion*. Toronto: Novalis.
    2002   "Changing the Face of God: New Immigrants' Zealous Christianity is Rejuvenating the Faith in Canada." *Ottawa Citizen*, 27 January, p. A1.

Hick, John.
    1963   *Philosophy of Religion*. Englewood Cliffs, NJ: Prentice-Hall.

Hoge, Dean R., Benton Johnson, and Donald A Luidens.
    1994   *Vanishing Boundaries*. Louisville: Westminster/John Knox Press.

Hordern, William.
    1966   *New Directions in Theology Today*. Volume 1, Introduction. Philadelphia: Westminster Press.

Iannoccone, Laurence R.
    1995   "Voodoo Economics? Reviewing the Rational Choice Approach to Religion." *Journal for the Scientific Study of Religion* 34: 76–89.

Kelley, Dean.
    1972   *Why Conservative Churches Are Growing*. New York: Harper and Row.

Lester, Toby
    2002   "Oh Gods!" *The Atlantic Monthly* (February): 37–45.

Luckmann, Thomas.
    1967   *Invisible Religion*. New York: Macmillan.

Lyon, David.
    2000   *Jesus in Disneyland: Religion in Postmodern Times*. Cambridge, UK: Polity Press, 2000.

Mann, W.E.
    1962   *Sect, Cult, and Church in Alberta*. Toronto: University of Toronto Press.

Marler, Penny Long, and C. Kirk Hadaway.
    1993   "Toward a Typology of Marginal Members." *Review of Religious Research* 35: 34–51.

Marty, Martin.
    2001   "The Voices of Our Young." *Sightings*, 9 October.

Marx, Karl.
    1970   *Critique of Hegel's Philosophy of Right*. Trans. Annette Jollin and Joseph O'Malley. Cambridge: Harvard University Press. Originally published in 1843.

Marx, Karl, and Friederich Engels.
    1964   *On Religion*. New York: Schocken Books.

McKinney, Jennifer, and Roger L. Finke.
2001 "Reviving the Mainline: An Overview of Clergy Support for Evangelical Movements." Unpublished paper.

Mead, Loren B.
1991 *The Once and Future Church*. Washington, D.C.: The Alban Institute.

Meed Ward, Marianne
2002 "The Alpha-tization of Canada." *Faith Today* (September–October): 18–23.

Milton, Ralph.
2000 *This United Church of Ours* (3rd edition). Kelowna, B.C.: Wood Lake Books.

Moore, Thomas.
1992 *Care of the Soul*. New York: HarperCollins.

Neitz, Mary Jo, and James Spickard.
1990 "Steps toward a Sociology of Religious Experience." *Sociological Analysis* 51: 15–33.

Nettler, Gwynn.
1976 *Social Concerns*. Toronto: McGraw-Hill.

Newman, Peter C.
1995 *The Canadian Revolution: From Deference to Defiance*. Toronto: Viking.

Nock, David.
1987 "Cult, Sect and Church in Canada: A Re-examination of Stark and Bainbridge." *Canadian Review of Sociology and Anthropology* 24: 514–25.

Peck, M. Scott.
1978 *The Road Less Travelled*. New York: Simon and Schuster.

Peers, Michael G.
1995 "Speaking the Truth in Love." Preface to George Egerton (ed.). *Anglican Essentials*. Toronto: Anglican Book Centre.

Poloma, Margaret.
1989 "Religious Experiences, Evangelism, and Institutional Growth within the Assemblies of God." *Journal for the Scientific Study of Religion* 285: 415–31.
1995 "The Sociological Context of Religious Experience." In Ralph W. Hood (ed.). *Handbook of Religious Experience*: 161–82. Birmingham, AL: Religious Education Press.
1997 "The 'Toronto Blessing': Charisma, Institutionalization, and Revival." *Journal for the Scientific Study of Religion* 36: 257–71.

Posterski, Donald C., and Irwin Barker.
    1993   *Where's a Good Church?* Winfield, B.C.: Wood Lake Books.

Posterski, Donald C., and Reginald W. Bibby.
    1988   *Canada's Youth: Ready for Today.* Ottawa: Canadian Youth Foundation.

Posterski, Don, and Gary Nelson.
    1997   *Future Faith Churches.* Winfield, B.C.: Wood Lake Books.

Rawlyk, G. A.
    1996   *Is Jesus Your Personal Saviour? In Search of Canadian Evangelicalism in the 1990s.* Montreal/Kingston: McGill–Queen's University Press.

Redfield, James.
    1994   *The Celestine Prophecy.* New York: Warner Books.

Robinson, John T.
    1963   *Honest to God.* Philadelphia: Westminster.

Roof, Wade Clark.
    1993   *A Generation of Seekers.* San Francisco: Harper.
    1999   *Spiritual Marketplace: Baby Boomers and the Remaking of American Religion.* Princeton, NJ: Princeton University Press

Roof, Wade Clark, and William McKinney.
    1987   *American Mainline Religion.* New Brunswick, NJ: Rutgers University Press.

Rouleau, Jean-Paul.
    1977   "Religion in Quebec: Present and Future." *Pro Mundi Vita: Dossiers* (Nov–Dec), no. 3.

Schaller, Lyle E.
    1987   *It's a Different World: The Challenge for Today's Pastor.* Nashville: Abingdon.
    1995   *The New Reformation: Tomorrow Arrived Yesterday.* Nashville: Abingdon.
    1999   *Discontinuity and Hope: Radical Change and the Path to the Future.* Nashville: Abingdon.

Spong, John Shelby.
    1998   *Why Christianity Must Change or Die.* San Francisco: Harper San Francisco.

Stark, Rodney, and William Sims Bainbridge.
    1985   *The Future of Religion.* Berkeley: University of California Press.

Stark, Rodney, and Roger Finke.
    2000   *Acts of Faith: Explaining the Human Side of Religion.* Berkeley: University of California Press.

Stark, Rodney, and Charles Y. Glock.
  1968   *American Piety*. Berkeley: University of California Press.

Start, Sally
  2002   "West Van Businessman Lets Christ Close the Deal." *BC Christian News* (January): 3.

Statistics Canada
  1993   *Religions in Canada*. Ottawa: Industry, Science and Technology Canada. 1991 Census of Canada. Catalogue no. 93–319.

Stiller, Brian C.
  1999   *When Life Hurts*. Toronto: HarperCollins.
  2001   *What Happens When I Die? A Promise of the Afterlife*. Toronto: HarperCollins.

Swenson, Donald S.
  1999   *Society, Spirituality, and the Sacred*. Peterborough, ON: Broadview Press.

Thielecke, Helmut.
  1960   *Our Heavenly Father*. Trans. John Doberstein. New York: Harper and Row.

Todd, Douglas.
  1996   *Brave Souls*. Toronto: Stoddart.

Trudeau, Pierre Elliott.
  1993   *Memoirs*. Toronto: McClelland and Stewart.

Yamane, David.
  1998   "Experience." In William H. Swatos, Jr. (ed.). *Encyclopedia of Religion and Society*. Walnut Creek, CA: AltaMira Press, 179–82.

Yamane, David, and Megan Polzer.
  1994   "Ways of Seeing Ecstasy in Modern Society." *Sociology of Religion* 55: 1–25.

Warner, Stephen R.
  1993   "Work in Progress toward a New Paradigm for the Sociological Study of Religion in the United States." *American Journal of Sociology* 98: 1044–93.

Waxman, Chaim I.
  2001   *Jewish Baby Boomers*. Albany, NY: SUNY Press.

Wills, Garry.
  2000   *Papal Sin*. New York: Doubleday.

Wilson, Bryan.
   1966   *Religion in Secular Society*. London: C.A. Watts.
   1982   *Religion in Sociological Perspective*. London: Oxford University Press.

Woodruff, Mike.
   2002   "Ministry in a New Epoch: An Interview with Dr. Martin Marty."
          The Ivy Jungle Report (October).

Woods, C. Jeff.
   1996   *Congregational Megatrends*. Bethseda, MD: The Alban Institute.

Wuthnow, Robert.
   1988   *The Restructuring of American Religion*. Princeton, NJ: Princeton
          University Press.
   1992   *Rediscovering the Sacred*. Grand Rapids, MI: William B. Eerdmans.
   1998   *After Heaven: Spirituality in America since the 1950s*. Berkeley, CA:
          University of California Press.

Index

industrialization, 1, 18
intermarriage, 22, 27, 35, 39–40, 84
InterVarsity, 72
Invitation to Sociology (Berger),
    172–73
Irving, John, 102
Islam, 235–36, 245. *See also* Muslims
    awareness of, 243
    decline in, 22
    upsurge in, 2, 88

Jehovah's Witnesses, 12, 23, 61, 63
Jesus, 56
Jesus in Disneyland (Lyon), 191
Johnson, Ben, 44
Johnston, Lynn, 56, 125
John XXIII, 18
Judaism, 12, 23, 83, 235–36
justice, 112, 176–77, 181–82

Kapica, Jack, 160
Khaki, Aziz, 245
Kinsella, W.P., 132, 173

Latter-Day Saints, Church of Jesus
    Christ of, 239
    in Canada, 23, 63
    expansion of, 21
Lau, Evelyn, 125
lawsuits, 57, 74–75
leaders, 57, 71–72
Léger, Paul-Émile, 11
Lester, Toby, 236–37
life
    after death, 29, 94, 114–33, 171,
        177, 182, 230
    meaning of, 29, 96–102, 104, 172
    origins of, 96
    quality of, 218–19
Love You Forever (Munsch), 173

Luidens, Don, 44
Lutherans, 76. *See also* Mainline
    Protestants
Lyon, David, 191

Maclean's, 105, 191, 241–42
Mainline Protestants, 74–78. *See also*
    Anglican Church; Lutherans;
    Presbyterians; Protestants;
    United Church
    in Alberta, 59
    and beliefs about death, 128
    church attendance by, 20–21, 74–76
    church membership among, 12, 74,
        77–78
    experiences of God among, 152
    and meaning of life, 99–100
    parents' religion and, 41–42
    and prayer, 159
    receptivity of, 223
    and rites of passage, 89
    and role of religion, 187
Mann, W.E., 59
Man's Search for Meaning (Frankl), 95
market model, 31–32, 34, 35–36, 61
    flaws in, 68–69
    and religious organizations, 31–32,
        34, 35–36, 53–54, 61, 64–65, 67–69
Marler, Penny, 44
marriage. *See also* rites of passage
    concerns about, 211, 239
    as source of new members, 38
Martinuk, Susan, 110
Marty, Martin, 242–44
Marx, Karl, 59, 228, 229–30,
    231, 232–33
Mauss, Armand, 175
McCall, Christina, 114
McCartney, Paul, 173
McKinney, Jennifer, 67, 72

teenagers. *See* young people
Teen Trends (Bibby and Posterski), 85
telepathy, 28–29
terrorism. *See* September 11, 2001
theodicies, 109
theosophy, 64
There's Got to Be More! (Bibby), 49, 191
This United Church of Ours (Milton),
    156
Thompson, Mary, 14
Todd, Doug, 56, 93–94, 101, 102, 110,
    147, 173, 191, 233, 235
tolerance, 44
Toronto, Archdiocese of, 18
Toronto Anglican Diocese, 33, 240
"Toronto Blessing," 151–52
Toynbee, Arnold, 5, 233
tradition
    rejection of, 60
    in religious affiliation, 38, 43, 68
    as religious norm, 33–34, 35
transcendence, signals of, 167–68
    in Canadians, 175–82
Trudeau, Pierre, 114–15, 126–27
truth claims, 65–66

uncertainty, 118–19, 121, 140
Unholy Orders (Harris), 57
Unitarians, 23, 63
United Church of Canada, 32, 71, 72,
    233, 240, 251
    church attendance in, 76
    membership in, 11
    policies of, 21
    young people in, 86
United States
    compared to Canada, 66
    effects of secularization in, 7–8
    religious history of, 60
University of Lethbridge, x–xi, 251

Unknown Gods (Bibby), 3, 26, 27–28,
    115, 191, 225, 231

values, 106–7, 108–9, 203–4
    interpersonal, 211–14, 216
    sources of, 211–15, 218–19, 237
Vancouver Grizzlies, 71

war, 111, 112
Ward, Marianne Meed, 73
When Life Hurts (Stiller), 111
Wicca, 64
Willow Creek Association, 72
Wills, Garry, 45–46
Wilson, Bryan, 8
women
    and beliefs about death, 126, 129
    experiences of God among, 150
    and spirituality, 179, 197
World Vision, 72
World War II, 110
worry. *See* concerns
Wuthnow, Robert, 39, 68, 154, 191, 192

young people, 85–89
    attractiveness of church groups to,
        10, 50, 51
    and beliefs about death, 116, 124, 129
    church attendance by, 76–77, 87
    and family life, 210
    and important questions, 133–34,
        244
    and meaning of life, 100
    and morality, 216–18
    and prayer, 159–60
    religious identity of, 76–77, 83–84,
        86–87, 184–86
    religious socialization of, 25
    sources of happiness for, 106
    and spirituality, 192–94